# Food, Science, Policy and Regulation in the Twentieth Century

Food safety and quality have become issues of major political, economic and cultural importance. Recent and continuing scares, most notably over BSE, *E. coli* and genetically modified produce, have kept food in the forefront of media interest and public discussion. This book examines the twentieth-century history of key aspects of this contemporary debate and includes work from American, Dutch and British scholars. The book brings a multi-national and multi-disciplinary approach to four key themes:

- the role of science and scientists in policy-making, including factors promoting or inhibiting the formation of scientific consensus
- the growth and impact of consumer representation, the popularisation of scientific knowledge of food, and the role of the media
- the extent to which new policies have been shaped or constrained by business and other dominant economic interests
- the role and character of government, and the manner in which policy development has been conditioned by inter-departmental rivalries at national, regional and international levels.

*Food, Science, Policy and Regulation in the Twentieth Century* therefore represents essential reading for a wide range of historians and social scientists and everyone with a scholarly interest in food.

**David F. Smith** lectures in the history of medicine at the University of Aberdeen. He has long-standing interests in the history of nutrition, and edited *Nutrition in Britain*. He co-ordinates the Wellcome-Trust-funded project on the Aberdeen typhoid outbreak.

**Jim Phillips** lectures in economic and social history at the University of Glasgow. He has written widely on British labour, economic and social history. His co-authored publications include articles on food adulteration, arsenic poisoning and milk safety, and *Cheated Not Poisoned: Food Regulation in the United Kingdom, 1875–1938*.

# Routledge Studies in the Social History of Medicine
## Edited by Bernard Harris
*Department of Sociology and Social Policy, University of Southampton, UK*

The Society for the Social History of Medicine was founded in 1969, and exists to promote research into all aspects of the field, without regard to limitations of either time or place. In addition to this book series, the Society also organises a regular programme of conferences, and publishes an internationally recognised journal, *Social History of Medicine*. The Society offers a range of benefits, including reduced-price admission to conferences and discounts on SSHM books, to its members. Individuals wishing to learn more about the Society are invited to contact the series editor through the publisher.

The Society took the decision to launch 'Studies in the Social History of Medicine', in association with Routledge, in 1989, in order to provide an outlet for some of the latest research in the field. Since that time, the series has expanded significantly under a number of editors, and now includes both edited collections and monographs. Individuals wishing to submit proposals are invited to contact the series editor in the first instance.

# Food, Science, Policy and Regulation in the Twentieth Century

International and comparative perspectives

**Edited by
David F. Smith and Jim Phillips**

London and New York

First published 2000
by Routledge
11 New Fetter Lane, London EC4P 4EE

Simultaneously published in the USA and Canada
by Routledge
29 West 35th Street, New York, NY 10001

*Routledge is an imprint of the Taylor & Francis Group*

Typeset in Garamond by Deerpark Publishing Services Ltd
Printed and bound in Great Britain by Biddles Ltd, Guildford and
King's lynn

*British Library Cataloguing in Publication Data*
A catalogue record for this book is available from the British Library

*Library of Congress Cataloging in Publication Data*
Food, science, policy and regulation in the twentieth century : international
and comparative perspectives / edited by David F. Smith and Jim Philips.
    p. cm.
  Includes bibliographical references and index.
   1. Nutrition policy. 2. Food. I. Smith, David F. II. Philips, Jim

TX359 .F667 2000
363.8'09'04-dc21                                          00-058257

ISBN 0-415-23532-4

# Contents

# Plates and captions

# Contributors

**Rima D. Apple**, University of Wisconsin. Rima is a professor with a joint position in the School of Human Ecology and Women's Studies Program at the University of Wisconsin, and has published extensively in the history of medicine and the history of science. Among recent publications are: *Vitamania: Vitamins in American Culture* (New Brunswick, NJ, Rutgers University Press, 1996), and *Mothers and Mothering: Readings in American history* (Columbus, OH, Ohio State University Press, 1997). Her current research focuses on mothers' encounters with expert knowledge and popular science.

**Peter J. Atkins**, Department of Geography, University of Durham. Peter has interests in the geography of food, food in development, and food history. His current research projects include a study of infant feeding 1880–1930, and the dairy food system in its relations with human health in the period 1850–1950. He has written several influential articles on the history of milk quality, safety and distribution. His book on *Food in Society*, co-written with Ian Bowler of the University of Leicester, will be published shortly with Edward Arnold.

**David Barling**, Centre for Food Policy, Thames Valley University. David is the course leader for the MA in Food Policy at Thames Valley University. He has published numerous articles on the regulation of GM foods, in journals such as *European Environment*, *European Journal of Public Health*, and *Environmental Politics*. He was lead author of a policy assessment on GM Foods, entitled, 'The social aspects of food biotechnology: a European view', published in *Environmental Toxicology and Pharmacology* in 1999.

**L. Margaret Barnett**, Department of History, The University of Southern Mississippi. Margaret is author of *British Food Policy During the First World War* (Allen & Unwin, London, 1985). She has a long-standing interest in the history of food faddism and especially Horace Fletcher, and has published several papers on this topic. Her most recent research is on Olga Nethersole and the Peoples' League of Health, which forms the basis of her contribution to this volume.

**Virginia Berridge**, London School of Hygiene and Tropical Medicine. Virginia is professor of History at LSHTM and head of the history group there. In its programme of research, she is supervising work on the history of pharmacy, nutrition policy, medical technology, and the role of the media. Virginia's published research includes work on post war smoking policy and AIDS, and her most recent publication is *Health and Society in Britain Since 1939* (Cambridge, Cambridge University Press, 1999).

**Mark W. Bufton**, London School of Hygiene and Tropical Medicine. Mark is currently a Research Fellow in the LSHTM, where he is a member of the history group. He recently gained his PhD from Exeter University on institutions and technological change in post-war Britain. At the LSHTM he is working on post-war nutrition policy as part of the Wellcome-Trust-funded programme on the relationship between science and policy.

**Lesley Diack**, Department of History, University of Aberdeen. Lesley has recently completed a PhD thesis comparing 'Women, Health and Charity in eighteenth-century Scotland and France'. She is currently researching the history of the Aberdeen typhoid outbreak of 1964, funded by the Wellcome Trust. She presented a paper on the outbreak explored through oral history to the 2000 Annual Conference of the Oral History Society and is preparing this paper for publication.

**Mike French**, Department of Economic and Social History, University of Glasgow. Mike is Senior Lecturer in Economic and Social History at the University of Glasgow. He has written widely on US and British business and economic history. His numerous co-authored publications with Jim Phillips include the first detailed analysis of the evolution and operation of modern British food laws for more than 20 years, *Cheated Not Poisoned: Food Regulation in the United Kingdom, 1875–1938* (Manchester, Manchester University Press, 2000)

**Suzanne White Junod**, United States Food and Drug Administration, History Office. Suzanne received her PhD from Emory University in Atlanta, Georgia in 1994 and is currently the historian responsible for food issues at the US Food and Drug Administration. She has a particular interest in women's health issues, the subject of her current research. Recently, she has published articles on the history and regulation of homeopathy in the US, and documented a 1996 epidemic of diethylene glycol poisoning in Haiti.

**Harmke Kamminga**, Department of History and Philosophy of Science, University of Cambridge. Harmke is a Wellcome Trust Senior Fellow in History of Medicine at Cambridge. Her main research interests are in the histories of biochemistry and nutrition science. She is co-editor of *The Science and Culture of Nutrition, 1840–1940* (Amsterdam, Rodopi, 1995) and *Molecularizing Biology and Medicine: New Practices and Alliances, 1910s–1970s* (Amsterdam, Harwood, 1998). She is writing a book on the making of vitamins.

**Peter A. Koolmees**, Department of the Science of Food of Animal Origin, Faculty of Veterinary Medicine, University of Utrecht. Peter lectures in veterinary public health and veterinary history, which are his main research interests. His publications include work on the history of meat inspection and public abattoirs. He is editor of *ARGOS*, a journal on veterinary history, and incoming president from the World Association for the History of Veterinary Medicine.

**T. Hugh Pennington**, Department of Medical Microbiology, University of Aberdeen. Hugh has been professor of bacteriology at Aberdeen since 1979. His current research focuses on the development and application of DNA typing methods to disease causing bacteria in humans, and the history of antiseptic and aseptic surgical techniques. In November 1996 the Secretary of State for Scotland invited him to lead an inquiry into the Lanarkshire *E. coli 0157* food poisoning outbreak. He is a member of the history of the Aberdeen typhoid outbreak project team.

**Jim Phillips**, Department of Economic and Social History, University of Glasgow. Jim is a lecturer in Economic and Social History at the University of Glasgow. He has written widely on British labour and economic and social history, including work on port transport, the Attlee Labour governments and the Cold War. He has been working on food regulation with Michael French since 1995. Their joint publications include articles on adulteration, arsenic poisoning and milk safety, and *Cheated Not Poisoned: Food Regulation in the United Kingdom, 1875–1938* (Manchester, Manchester University Press, 2000).

**Elizabeth Russell**, Department of Public Health, University of Aberdeen. Elizabeth is professor of social medicine at Aberdeen. Her main interests are health services research, current projects covering ethics of ageing and its effect on the NHS, monitoring surgical adverse events, and inequalities in access to health care. She is a member of the history of the Aberdeen typhoid outbreak project team. Recent publications include 'Ethics of attribution: the case of outcomes indicators', *Social Science and Medicine*, 1998, vol. 47 pp. 1161–9.

**Josh Ruxin**, ontheFRONTIER, a Monitor Group Company, Cambridge, Massachusetts, USA. Josh was educated at the Universities of Yale, Columbia and London, and is now a Vice President with ontheFRONTIER, an advisory company dedicated to business development in emerging markets. Josh's contribution here is based on his doctoral research at the Wellcome Institute, London, on the role of international agencies in the post-war period. Other products of his research include 'The History of Oral Rehydration Therapy', published in *Medical History* in 1994.

**David F. Smith**, Department of History, University of Aberdeen. David lectures in the history of medicine to arts and medical students. He has long-standing interests in the history of nutrition and edited *Nutrition in Britain* (London,

Routledge, 1997). He co-ordinates the Wellcome-Trust-funded project on the Aberdeen typhoid outbreak, and recently sponsored Dr Eve Seguin's successful Wellcome Trust fellowship application, for work on the history of the prion protein hypothesis and the BSE crisis. He hopes to further develop this nascent research group at Aberdeen.

**Gerard Trienekens**, Department of History, University of Utrecht. Gerard is a senior lecturer and researcher in Social and Economic History at Utrecht. His contribution to this volume reflects his established specialist interests in agrarian, local and regional history, and the history of daily life.

# Acknowledgements

The editors and publishers would like to thank the following for granting permission to reproduce images in this work:

Ian Butchart, for the *Non-Communicable Disease?* cartoon on page 225
Graham High, for the *E. coli Inquiry* cartoon on page 227
*Drug Topics*, for Figures 9.1–9.3
US Food and Drug Administration, for Figures 11.1–11.13

Every effort has been made to contact copyright holders for their permission to reprint material in this book. The publishers would be grateful to hear from any copyright holder who is not acknowledged and will undertake to rectify any errors or omissions in future editions of the book.

# 1 Food policy and regulation: a multiplicity of actors and experts

*David F. Smith and Jim Phillips*

The world of food policy making and regulation is very complex. It is populated by a very wide range of actors, broadly classifiable into producers, consumers, and intermediaries, many of them playing more than one role. Relationships between actors are sometimes largely economic, as, for example, in the wholesaler – retailer link in the food chain. A wide variety of different dimensions are of greater importance at other points, for instance, in the provision of food by parents for their children. As every parent knows, for a child the rejection of food offered plays an important role in the development of personal autonomy and character: food likes and dislikes play an important role in the construction of personal identities.[1] In every food exchange, however, confidence in, and suspicions about the food in question, may condition the relationship, and in this context, expertise may play a role in negotiations about food quality, and in providing reassurance. This is true at every level, even within the family ('look daddy's eating up his vegetables!'). But experts (including daddies) can only play an effective role when consensus exists among the parties concerned as to the validity and relevance of their expertise. Everyone eats, and numerous actors, including consumers, by virtue of their position, training or experience, lay permanent or strategic claim to expertise. It is often said by food reformers, frustrated by the resistance of the population to their prescriptions, that everyone thinks that they are an expert on their own diet: they know what they like and think they know what is best to eat for their personal well being. But deference to the views of others is also common. Religious, scientific, medical, or other authorities may be cited as justification for the food preferences, habits, rituals, regimes and dietary restrictions that form aspects of human culture everywhere. Within the interactions and negotiations that constitute more formal food policy making and regulation, actors also alternatively claim or deny expertise. At different times food manufacturers, politicians, and administrators may claim expertise or may defer to others, such as scientists or the public. Scientists may sometimes claim or accept the attribution of very broad expertise; at other times they will define their area of expertise very precisely. While the boundaries of the expertise claimed by actors vary over time, conflicts between experts, as this book demonstrates, seems so widespread in food policy making and regulation that they might fairly be described as endemic.

The complexity of food policy making and regulation reflects the complexity of, and the division of labour within, the modern food system. The economic sectors involved include agriculture, transport, food processing, wholesaling, retailing, advertising, and catering. Food-related activity in Western countries is now an important aspect of the leisure, entertainment and publishing industries, with best-seller lists frequently including cookbooks and other food-related titles. For many, food tourism is one of the most important constituents of their annual foreign holiday. Between holidays, millions of modern westerners regularly consume food in exotic or 'ethnic' restaurants. Equal numbers find themselves entertained by the methods, ingredients and menus demonstrated in popular cooking programmes on television. The diversity of the constituents of recipes in media cookery underlines the fact that the food system is now global. But the international food trade is not just a matter of satisfying the sophisticated tastes of Europeans and Americans. Through international markets in food commodities, the viability and survival of the agricultural and food industries in countries and regions can be influenced by innovations and other changes on the opposite side of the world. Such changes can be matters of economic and even actual life and death for some inhabitants of the planet.

## Historical case studies

The rationale for this collection of essays is the premise that understanding the modern food system and the problems surrounding it may be enhanced by a greater appreciation of its historical development. This book contributes to that understanding by exploring the history of aspects of food policy making and regulation, with emphasis upon the role of expertise, both scientific and more generally defined. The food system is so complex that this historical enterprise must be multi-faceted, multi-dimensional and multi-disciplinary. Economics, political science, geography, sociology, media studies and other disciplines all have much to offer in this area. Theoretical ideas derived from such disciplines may provide useful frameworks for organising historical studies.[2] But the kind of empirical historical case studies that comprise the contents of this book also have a special contribution to make, especially at this early stage of the development of studies in the history of food policy making and regulation. The analyses presented in these chapters provide accounts, based on archival and other primary source-based research, of the nature of the activities constituting food policy making and regulation. They provide some of the evidence upon which 'theory' of food policy and regulation may be constructed and against which such theory must be tested. Although most of the case studies in this book do not devote space to explicit discussion of such theory, all contributors have clearly been influenced by developments in the sociology of science over recent decades. None of the authors suppose that the existence of scientific knowledge about food provides a sufficient condition for the construction and implementation of food policy. Most of the analyses are explicitly or implicitly informed by social constructionism: the notion that the production, as well as the application of scientific knowledge of food cannot be understood without reference to the social interests surrounding and permeating the process.[3]

There is one exception to the general lack of any detailed discussion of theory: Chapter 6, by Harmke Kamminga, on popularisation of vitamins prior to the Second World War. She frames her account within a discussion of Ludwik Fleck's theories of the popularisation of science, which were published during the period she considers. Her use of Fleck demonstrates that many of the elements of modern sociology of science were present in this continental theoretical tradition during the 1930s. Kamminga focuses upon the role that vitamins played in the publications of a variety of scientists, science writers, radical intellectuals and activists from Britain, Germany and the United States during the inter-war period. She considers their works aimed at readerships outside the specialised research communities. She points out that as these actors deployed scientific knowledge of nutrition in more popular arenas, the 'facts' of nutrition, which in some cases were still very controversial in the technical journals, were 'hardened'. Kamminga also shows that the popular writings on vitamins performed a variety of functions. The aim of some authors was to help consolidate the field and status of vitamin research within biomedical research. Other authors attempted to deploy knowledge of vitamins in the pursuit of a variety of political agendas. The processes that Kamminga describes are clearly at play in many of the episodes described in this book. These include: the enlistment of a wide range of organisations in support of the bovine tuberculosis campaign of the People's League of Health described by Margaret Barnett in Chapter 5; the deployment of vitamin supplementation in support of America's war effort, discussed by Rima Apple in Chapter 9; and the widespread acceptance of the paramount nutritional importance of the 'protein gap' between developed and less developed countries during the 1950s to the early 1970s, discussed by Josh Ruxin in Chapter 10.

This volume has been developed partly as the result of a conference held at the University of Aberdeen in April 1999. The notion of 'popularisation' was one of the threads that ran through the discussion and the programme included a screening of the documentary film *The World is Rich* (1947) which was introduced by Tim Boon, of the Science Museum. Boon argued that the film, which features the World Food Plan of nutritionist John Boyd Orr, first director of the Food and Agriculture Organisation, should not be seen as an uncomplicated act of popularisation, but as a highly mediated product of prior agreement between its creators, including the director, Paul Rotha, and Orr. Kelly Loughlin, of the London School of Hygiene and Tropical Medicine, in commenting on the film and reflecting upon the uses of scientific knowledge in the advancement of a wide range of interests, suggested, as an alternative to 'popularisation', the notion of active strategic 'mobilisation' of science. Clearly, the theoretical tools that may be brought to bear upon the complex history of food policy making and regulation are many and varied. It is not possible, within the confines of an introductory chapter such as this one, to attempt any new theoretical synthesis. This synthesis would need to draw upon a wide range of literatures including those dealing with broader questions of policy making and other areas of policy making in modern societies.[4] For this reason our remarks will be largely confined to drawing out similarities between and special features of the chapters, in the process highlighting features which must be taken into account in any more theoretical enterprise. This emphasis will also raise aspects of importance to any participant or observer who seeks a practical understanding of the processes of food policy making and regulation today.

## On experts in policy making and their organisation

The qualifications of experts who staff and provide external advice to, and otherwise influence, departments of national governments and international agencies that deal with food issues, are many and varied. This book forms a sequel to *Nutrition in Britain*, edited by David Smith, which was about the 'processes by which scientists, doctors, activists and politicians have sought to generate, modify, and apply nutritional knowledge, policies and practices – processes which have involved the construction, modification, and breaking of alliances between individuals, groups, and institutions'.[5] As well as focusing more on countries other than Britain, and on international issues, the current volume also combines interests in the role of science and scientists in policy making, with the broader interests of the second editor, Jim Phillips. These interests are represented by his recently published volume, co-authored with Michael French, *Cheated Not Poisoned? Food Regulation in the United Kingdom, 1875–1938*, which examines the social, economic and business context of policy development and enforcement.[6] While *Nutrition in Britain* concentrated substantially upon questions of interactions between nutrition experts of various descriptions and others, the current volume gives greater consideration to issues of food composition and safety and covers the provision and regulation of food in a broader sense. This wider approach encompasses a broader definition and range of 'expertise' in the field of policy making than that featured in the previous volume. The 'experts' in the current volume are not only actors with a scientific training, but also include those with practical experience within the food system, along with journalists and other media agents. Food manufacturers and retailers are frequently accorded authority to make 'objective' judgements during policy making exercises, as shown by French and Phillips in Chapter 2, in their study of the proceedings of a British committee of inquiry on food standards during the 1930s, known as the Willis Committee. They show that actors such as industrialists may at times willingly take on the role of experts, while at other times preferring strategically to attribute expertise to others. Industrialists who are resistant to the imposition by government of compositional regulations may credit consumers, and particularly housewives, with the expertise to discriminate between good and bad products. A similar point is made in the concluding discussion of Chapter 14, where Hugh Pennington reflects upon the roles played by expert committees. He suggest that civil servants, who often lay claim to administrative expertise which allows them to identify the impracticalities of particular proposals, at other times may postpone action by deferring to the views of others: external experts must first be consulted before any action can take place.

The range of professional groups who become involved in food policy is wide, and includes chemists and medical personnel. Such experts may work directly for central government departments or international agencies, and may therefore be regarded as insiders in the policy making process, or may work in industry, or for local authorities, research institutes and universities. They may be members of professional groups that engage in occasional or sustained lobbying for changes in food policy and regulation. In the USA, as Suzanne Junod shows in Chapter 11, the Association of Official Agricultural Chemists played an important role in food policy during the early decades of the century.[7] Similarly, French and Phillips show that in Britain, the chemists' organisation, the Society of Public Analysts, lobbied for the introduction of food compositional standards over a prolonged period. The medical profession is represented in Britain by the British Medical Association, but earlier the more specialised Society of Medical Officers of Health played an important role. In Chapter 13 Mark Bufton and Virginia Berridge reflect on the impact of reports produced in many countries by elite organisations of the medical profession in the 1960s and 1970s: these played an important role in the formation of consensus about the relationship between diet and heart disease.

Besides medical personnel, the professional groups involved in food policy making also include veterinarians. The role of the veterinary profession in food policy and regulation has, to date, received little attention, but several chapters in the current volume deal with aspects of their activities. These include Chapter 4 by Peter Koolmees, one of the few authors to have written about the history of veterinary public health.[8] Koolmees discusses the history of the veterinary profession's role in meat inspection in The Netherlands, and compares it with the development of meat inspection in various European countries. He argues that the political economy of each country has played an important role in determining the relative success of the veterinary profession of that country in winning a role in food regulation. The role of veterinarians is also considered in Chapter 13 by Lesley Diack and her colleagues, in their discussion of the implementation of one of the recommendations of the enquiry into the Aberdeen typhoid outbreak of 1964. They show how the marginal position and the ambitions of this professional group in Britain interacted with rivalry between government departments to condition the response to the recommendation in question.

While professional associations participate in food policy making, organisations have also been established to present the corporate views of manufacturers in discussions with the state. Junod highlights the roles of such groups as the National Preservers' Association and the National Canners' Association in the USA before the Second World War. In Britain, as French and Phillips show, during the same period the Food Manufacturers' Federation and the Manufacturing Confectioners' Alliance participated in debates about pricing and made representations to the Willis Committee. Despite their evident and direct material stake in the subject, the industrialists' views were accorded far greater weight by the committee than those of the chemists, represented by the Society of Public Analysts: it was the chemists who were regarded as the people with an 'axe to grind'. This is a reflection of the role often accorded to scientific experts in inter-war Britain, which made them determined to make the best of the opportunities presented by the Second World War.[9] Bufton and Berridge also refer to the involvement of organisations of the food industry, such as the Butter Information Council in the diet–heart disease issue in the 1970s and 1980s. David Barling in Chapter 15 discusses the role of biotechnology companies and their allies in the European Commission in the process of regulating GM foods.

Organisational mobilisation also plays a role in defending or advancing the interests of consumers. Margaret Barnett, in Chapter 5, characterises the People's League of Health as a prime representative of consumers' interests in pre-war Britain. Founded in 1917, the League engaged in educational and campaigning activities around health issues, but was initially dismissed by officials as irrelevant, or merely 'humoured'. During the late 1920s and 1930s, however, the group served as an effective umbrella for a range of individuals and organisations concerned with pure milk and bovine tuberculosis. Organising around a single and powerful campaigning topic, the League adopted a much more sophisticated and disciplined approach to lobbying, assembled an impressive body of scientific, medical and veterinary expertise, and played a role in consensus formation. As a result, the organisation was taken much more seriously by government departments, even if its goals were not realised in the short term. The People's League of Health contrasts interestingly with the food reform movements and food cults of the Edwardian period that Barnett has written about previously. The core groups of supporters of these earlier movements, like the People's League of Health, were small. The Edwardian food reformers did sometimes win the support of a few respectable scientists, but this support was usually transient. But on the issue of bovine tuberculosis taken up by the League, it proved possible to assemble and sustain a much broader range of respectable medical, scientific and veterinary support.[10] Barnett's account of the development of the People's League of Health is also reminiscent of the developments described by Tim Lang in his analysis, in *Nutrition in Britain*, of the activities of 'Non-Governmental Organisations' on food issues in Britain from the 1970s to the 1990s.[11] The process of learning the rules of the policy making 'game' is important for all actors who aim to influence the policy making process. It is also useful to compare Barnett's account of the League's bovine tuberculosis campaign with the pasteurisation controversy in the 1930s, discussed by Peter Atkins in Chapter 3. This involved the mobilisation of anti- as well as pro-pasteurisation consumer-protectionist arguments, and serves as a pertinent reminder that 'consumers', like 'scientific experts' and other groups of actors, cannot be automatically considered to constitute homogenous groups with the same interests and opinions.

Consumers also enter Junod's account of the development of food compositional standards in the United States, where women's groups, along with the American Home Economic Association, played a key role in the campaign for new legislation during the 1930s. It may be the power of these American women's groups, and their interest in food composition, which partly accounts for the differences in the development of food composition issues in the United States as compared to Britain. In other chapters, such as those by Smith, Bufton and Berridge, and Pennington, there are examples of politicians, scientists, and journalists assuming the role of consumers' champions. In Barling's account of the regulation of genetically modified food, it was the relatively spontaneous and unorganised reaction of large numbers of consumers, alerted by the efforts of environmental organisations and the press, that proved decisive in the rejection of genetically modified food products in the European market.

## Governmental and departmental agendas, interdepartmental relations, and the uses of experts

The range and nature of the economic activities surrounding food draws many different departments of national governments into the support and regulation of the food system, and also involves numerous international agencies. Some departments and agencies have been created specifically to help manage the food system. The range of national government departments includes those dealing with agriculture, fisheries, food, trade, health, consumer protection, finance, education, local government, defence and international relations. The international agencies include those associated with the United Nations, as well as regional economic and political formations such as the European Union. The complex and multi-layered nature of food regulation at both national and international levels makes this a rich and rewarding area for historical research, but it must be admitted that a collection of essays such as this volume can only just begin this exploration. In this book the main national government departments considered include the American Food and Drug Administration, discussed by Suzanne Junod. The British health and agricultural departments feature in several chapters, including Chapters 2, 7, 12 and 13, by French and Phillips, Smith, Diack and her colleagues, and Bufton and Berridge respectively. In Chapter 15, Barling compares the recent activities of the regulators of genetically modified foods in the United States and the European Community. Chapter 10, by Josh Ruxin, also discusses international organisations: in this case the main food-related agencies of the United Nations, the Food and Agricultural Organisation (FAO), the World Health Organisation (WHO), and the United Nations Children's Fund (Unicef) during the post Second World War period.[12]

Competition, active conflicts, negotiations, and strategic co-operation, between government departments, or different sections of international organisations, are among the strongest themes that emerge from the chapters of this book which deal with the processes of policy making at these levels. As well as Diack and her colleagues writing on the 1960s, these kinds of interactions are emphasised by French and Phillips, discussing compositional food standards in interwar Britain, Smith considering nutritional policy making in Britain during the second world war, and Ruxin, focusing on nutrition at the international agencies of the UN. Pennington, reflecting on recent food poisoning problems, and Barling, with reference to GM food regulation within the European Community, confirm that such processes continue to characterise food policy making to the present day. These chapters separately indicate that tensions and disputes between government departments often paralleled tensions and disputes between experts. For example, a government department may form an alliance with outside experts, such as scientists from universities or independent research institutes, with a view to applying pressure upon or resisting competing demands being pressed by a second government department which is interested in the same issue. The second department may be allied with other outside experts, and expert staff in both departments may also be involved. Broadly, government departments are inclined to listen to outside scientific advice that reinforces their attitudes and policies. These kinds of situations are discussed in several chapters.

Disputes between experts may also allow governments and departments to delay or avoid action on food policy issues. In the pasteurisation controversy in the 1930s, discussed by Atkins, both the advocates and opponents of the process deployed scientific arguments about the consequences of the process for human health, and the lack of scientific consensus helped to justify a limited response from the British government. Atkins surveys the many and varied social and cultural factors which prevented the introduction of compulsory pasteurisation in Britain until after the Second World War. His analysis of the division between the pro- and anti-pasteurisation lobbies presents the conflict as essentially a clash between discourses with opposing views on the desirability of modernism and its impact on food systems. The anti-pasteurisation alliance consisted of some dairy farmers and small milk retailers, who opposed pasteurisation on cost grounds, along with activists, who opposed technological solutions to food safety problems on philosophical and ethical grounds. Just as an apparent lack of consensus on pasteurisation allowed the British government to postpone concerted action on milk in the 1930s, a lack of consensus among nutritionists on the links between diet and heart disease, outlined by Bufton and Berridge, allowed the British government to avoid any significant action in this area in the 1970s.

A common tactic deployed by government departments, when faced with food problems or active or potential criticism of government policies, is to establish a committee of inquiry of outside experts. In the 1930s the British Ministry of Health hoped that the existence of the Willis Committee would temporarily satisfy calls for action on the issue of food compositional standards, and also expected that this committee's findings would not place excessive demands upon the government. On the other hand, governments and specific government departments are also often wary of the appointment of such committees. The Scientific Food Committee, discussed by Smith, was formed following criticisms that British wartime food policy was not based on science, and consisted of scientists from outside government departments. However, its establishment was strongly resisted by the Ministry of Agriculture. The Protein Advisory Group of the United Nations, discussed by Ruxin, consisted mainly of scientists who were not permanent members of staff of the UN agencies. It was formed in response to the demands of scientists who were pioneering a new conception of malnutrition which emphasised the key significance of protein deficiency. The British Ministry of Health's Committee of Medical Aspects of Food Policy, examined by Bufton and Berridge, also consisted of outside experts and had broad advisory responsibilities in the area of food and nutrition.

As Pennington suggests, the choice of the chair for expert committees is worth reflecting upon. He comments that it is quite unusual for the government to appoint as chair someone such as himself, professor of bacteriology at Aberdeen University, who has direct research experience of the issue under investigation. And yet he was appointed chair of an expert committee of inquiry into a serious outbreak of *E. coli* 0157 poisoning, which took place in Scotland in 1996 (the Pennington Group).[13] As he points out, the chair of an expert committee is frequently a 'wise man', able to 'referee' in controversies among the committee members and also relate to the senior civil servants and politicians with whom he has to deal. There is, no doubt, often much to be said for the chair of committee deliberating on contentious scientific issues to be from outwith the field in question.

An early example is the appointment by the British government in 1900 of scientific statesman Lord Kelvin, the renowned physicist, to chair an inquiry into arsenical contamination of beer and other food ingredients. Sometimes a chair from outside science altogether is chosen. In the 1930s the British Ministry of Health came to the conclusion that such a chair was most suitable for an expert committee on nutrition. In 1935, the Ministry's first Advisory Committee on Nutrition was reconstituted after the resignation of the chair,

Major Greenwood, professor of epidemiology and vital statistics at the London School of Hygiene and Tropical Medicine. Greenwood had proved ineffective in handling disputes between scientists that constituted the membership, and between these members and outside experts. A non-scientist and member of the House of Lords was then appointed as chair of the reconstituted committee.[14] Committees that feature in this book include the short-lived Scientific Food Committee, formed during the Second World War, and chaired by a physicist, president of the Royal Society Sir William Bragg. The Committee on Medical Aspects of Food Policy, which also originated during the war but was active during the post war period, was chaired by the Chief Medical Officer of the Ministry of Health. The committee that investigated the 1964 Aberdeen typhoid outbreak, possibly the most direct antecedent of the Pennington Group, was chaired by a retired non-scientific civil servant. Just as it seems outside lobbyists such as the People's League of Health refined their tactics over time, it seems that government also learnt (and sometime re-learnt) ways to better manage and control outside scientific advisers.

The reasons for Pennington's unusual appointment probably lie, as he indicates, in the political circumstances in which it was made. In 1996, BSE and other food issues had already shaken public confidence in food safety and the conduct of food policy. In addition, a general election was approaching, where devolution of government in Scotland was to be a key issue. In this context the undoubtedly unpopular and arguably enfeebled Conservative administration made an unusual decision in the hope that the Scottish public would be persuaded that Scottish developments in general and food safety in particular were being taken seriously. It is worth comparing these British expert committees with the Protein Advisory Group (PAG) of the United Nations. As Ruxin shows, from the late 1950s until the early 1970s this group of experts achieved considerable influence in setting the agenda for food and nutrition policy in the three main UN agencies with interests in this field. These were young institutions with, at first, a small number of staff members. They lacked the long-standing traditions and procedures of, for example, the British civil service. By the 1970s, however, PAG policies had proved ineffective and there was little expectation of improvement in view of past experience, changing circumstances, and new scientific concepts. The Group was then discharged. In designing a new advisory structure the much expanded and well established bureaucracy of the UN agencies now ensured that their internal experts and in particular their policy makers played a more important role, and that the autonomous role of outside experts was restricted.

## Popularisation of scientific knowledge of food and the role of the media in policy making

The process of 'hardening' of scientific findings in publications which address a wider audience, described by Kamminga, is easily accomplished by the authors of such publications, but it is it is much more difficult in concrete policy-making processes which involve interactions between a range of opinions and interests. Nevertheless, as Rima Apple shows in Chapter 9, which develops the work published in her *Vitamania: Vitamins in American culture*,[15] when powerful commercial interests are involved, partial and contested scientific claims can form the basis for large-scale dietary movements. While the American Medical Association and Food and Drug Administration thought that supplementing diets with vitamin pills was unnecessary, during the Second World War food producers, pharmacists and advertisers persuaded millions of Americans that vitamin consumption was synonymous with patriotism, military efficiency and productive civilian industry. As Apple shows, these uses of vitamins permeated American culture, to the extent that the vitamin habit was even represented in Hollywood films in which, despite widespread use of vitamin products, the vitamin enthusiast was presented as a figure of fun.

The media and the presentation of images of food and food issues play an important role in several other chapters. Junod reproduces a series of photographs of manufactured foods dating from 1933 which formed part of an exhibition illustrating the many ways in which food packaging could deceive the American public. These played an important role in persuading the American legislature of the need for compositional standards. Smith shows that a critical debate in *The Times* in war-time Britain, combined with the fear of further bad publicity, formed an important part in persuading the government that a committee of experts to advise on food policy was needed. Similarly, the desire to avoid critical press coverage conditioned the response of the British government to the 1964 food crisis discussed by Diack and her colleagues. Writing from his recent personal experience, Pennington reflects upon the modern role of the media. Experts such as himself, and other interested parties, feed media stories concerning food problems, but the influence of the media upon policy making comes largely from its ability to shape the attitudes and behaviour, especially the voting behaviour, of consumers. The political difficulties that John Major's Conservative government faced in the forthcoming British general election, and press interest in the *E. coli* problem, encouraged a positive response by the government to the radical recommendations of the expert group that Pennington chaired. Similarly, Bufton and Berridge suggest that the government's response to expert advice on diet and heart disease during the mid 1980s was partly guided by press reporting of the issue. And in the same way that Kamminga suggests that popular writing on vitamins encouraged scientific consensus on vitamins before the Second World War, they suggest that scientific consensus on the diet–heart issue emerged partly as a result of media activity.

## On the consequences of the implementation of food policies

It seems from the above that the factors facilitating and constraining food policy making include media, public and political interest. In addition, unified or conflicting expertise, the attitudes of businesses at all levels, political and economic conditions, and the state of government or agency finances are all likely to be important. Some particularly powerful combinations of interests may occur as, for example, when business interests correspond with government financial orthodoxy or other circumstances. Similarly, the presence of food scares, crises and panics, as well as immense crises such as wars, are all likely to play an important role.

In their edited collection, *The Science and Culture of Nutrition, 1840s–1940s*, Harmke Kamminga and Andrew Cunningham stated that their aim was to begin to 'make a start at integrating the approaches of social, political and economic history of science and medicine, in relation to nutrition'.[16] These authors would agree that much remains to be done, especially if the field is expanded to include the broader issues of food policy and regulation addressed in the current volume. In Britain, by the time this volume is published, the new Food Standards Agency will have been in operation for at least eight months. The Agency has been established following a sequence of panics and crises in the 1980s and 1990s, of which the greatest arguably has been BSE, and it aims to restore public confidence in food, and to deal with both food safety and the improvement of the population's diet along the lines of modern nutritional advice. Plans are already being developed for the establishment of a similar European-wide institution, and, no doubt, in view of the continuing impact of issues such as genetically modified food, the institutional structures of food regulation will undergo change elsewhere in the world, and at an international level. It might be hoped that the kind of studies presented in this volume will help those involved in such developments to understand better the various scientific, political and economic interests which they are likely to encounter when framing and enforcing policies. Several of the contributors to this volume show that they are keenly aware of the context of innovation in food regulation in which they write: Atkins, Smith and Pennington, for example, all make reference to the Food Standards Agency. It may be that the value of historical studies for those involved in and observing the new regulatory machinery, will be enhanced if, in future, they also cover the consequences of policies, as well as the processes of policy development. Such studies would also link to the concerns of a wider range of historicans.

So far, in this introductory essay, nothing has been said about the consequences of the implementation of food policies, and only one chapter, which has not yet been mentioned, gives any sustained attention to this dimension. In contrast to Smith's chapter, which explores the process of policy making in wartime Britain, but gives no attention to its outcome, the argument by Gerard Trienekens, in Chapter 8, largely concerns the impact of the policies implemented in The Netherlands during the same period. In some ways this account has more in common with some earlier conceptions about what the exploration of links between food and history involves, represented by some of the contributions to the publications associated with the 'Historian and Nutritionist Group' of King's College of London University.[17] Trienekens' chapter points the way towards more comprehensive future approaches in this area – research projects which attempt to analyse not only the process of food policy making and regulation, but also its outcome. It also indicates the additional levels of complexity that may be added by this kind of study and the rich and unexpected insights that might be obtained.

Contrary to the expected finding, Trienekens argues that that the available evidence suggests that until the well-known 'Hunger winter' of 1944–5 the dietary conditions of the Dutch population were well-maintained during the Nazi occupation. His chapter makes this argument available to an English-speaking audience for the first time.[18] As Trienekens indicates, this point of view has proved very controversial in The Netherlands, where it has been attacked by many whose memories of the period suggest a much less favourable interpretation of the food situation. And yet, the idea that wartime rationing and full employment in Britain, in spite of difficulties with imports, led to an improvement of some aspects of the diet and health of the population, despite widespread grumbling about the monotony of the diet, is commonplace. The main differences between Britain and The Netherlands are, of course, the occupation of the latter, the diversion of part of industrial and agricultural production towards satisfying the needs of the Germans, and the brutal treatment of the Jewish population and opponents of the regime. Perceptions of food problems are linked with memories of other problems of daily life during the period. It must also be remembered that the data upon which Trienekens relies are average figures for the population, and hide variations, between the town and countryside, for example. The experience of many will not have been as favourable as the average figures suggest. In view of the traumas of the occupation, it is unsurprising that Trienekens' argument is controversial and has prompted some uncomfortable questions about the roles of various actors at the time. As British editors we hope that this chapter will contribute to scholarship concerned with the impacts of the Second World War, and that it will lead to translations of further aspects of the Dutch debate.

We also hope that the inclusion of Trienekens' chapter will encourage other scholars to develop yet more comprehensive historical research on food policy making and regulation, including the study of consequences as well as processes. To some extent this may be taken as a call for attempts to link the concerns of this volume with some of those of anthropometric history.[19] But the 'consequences' are many and varied and besides changes in body size, health and longevity, include changes in food habits, beliefs, and culture. And just as demonstrating links between 'science' and 'food policy' is not straightforward, demonstrating consequences of policies will be equally complex.

## Acknowledgements

The author or authors of all but two of the subsequent chapter gave papers at a conference that took place in April 1999 at Aberdeen University. This event, the spring conference of the Society for the Social History of Medicine, was entitled 'Science, Medicine and Food Policy in the Twentieth Century' and was organised by the editors. The chapters provided by these speakers either focus on different topics from the original conference papers, or have undergone substantial development in the light of interchanges at the event and in the editing process. Chapter 15, by David Barling, on the regulation of genetically modified foods, was specially commissioned to ensure that the book included an area of contemporary history which had assumed growing current importance in the course of 1999 and 2000. The Aberdeen typhoid outbreak, the subject of Chapter 12 by Lesley Diack and her colleagues, was represented at the conference only by an exhibition of press cuttings about the affair, prepared at an early stage of a research project. The chapter is based upon subsequent archival and oral history research.

The editors wish to take this opportunity to thank all those who contributed to the conference and who have been involved in the preparation of this book. Our thanks go to those who have produced chapters, most of whom have also provided helpful comments upon this chapter. We also thank the speakers whose papers could not be included in the book, either to maintain an appropriate focus or because of the lack of space. These are Annemarie de Knecht van Eekelen who also helped to organise the conference by liasing with the Dutch speakers, Flurin Condrau, Vincent Knapp, Timothy Boon, Jo Swabe and Anne Hardy. Thanks are also due to Jenny Cronin, Walter Duncan and Lena Håglin who provided posters, to Richard Perren, Eddy Higgs, Susan Williams, Richard Hankins, Sally Horrocks, Steven Sturdy, Roger Cooter, Andrew Hull, Kelly Loughlin, Elizabeth Dowler, Sally Sheard, Phillip James, Robert Bud, Derek Oddy and Michael Worboys who acted as discussants, to Susan McLaurin, Catherine Geissler, Annie Anderson and Bob Tyson who chaired sessions, and to the Aurora Dancers who provided entertainment. Many of the discussants produced written comments which were of great help to the editors. Thanks are due to the Wellcome Trust and Aberdeen University Faculty of Arts and Divinity for their financial support of the conference, and to the US Food and Drug Administration for a subsidy towards the cost of inclusion of the photographs illustrating Chapter 11. Thanks are due to Valentine Cardinale, editor of *Drug Topics*, and to I. Butchart, the *Sunday Times*, G. High and *The Scotsman*, for permission to reproduce the photographs and cartoons, which illustrate Chapters 9 and 14. The editors wish to acknowledge the excellent advice of two anonymous referees, and Bernard Harris, series editor, and the assistance of the staff of Routledge whose efficiency has facilitated the production of this volume. David Smith wishes to thank his family for their forbearance, especially Lorna, Catherine and Eve, during the conference organisation and editing process.

A few months after the Aberdeen conference the sad and shocking news arrived that Vincent Knapp, of Potsdam College, State University of New York, had died of cancer. No doubt the trip to Aberdeen was tiring for Vincent in the (then unknown) circumstances. Yet many participants will fondly recall his enthusiastic participation in the conference dinner which took the form of an 'out-of-season' Burns supper (although to one of the editors he expressed a degree of scepticism about the composition and merits of the haggis), and how much he enjoyed a trip to Dunnottor Castle. All who witnessed it will certainly remember his spirited defence of his paper. Many thanks to Vincent, and all the others who contributed to the success of the Aberdeen conference and hence to our ability to prepare this volume for publication.

# References

1  C. Driver observes in *The British at Table 1940–1980*, London, Chatto & Windus, 1983, p. 179, that 'At an elemental level, the way a person cooks and eats is a form of auto-biography'.
2  For a discussion of some modern theoretical approaches to the food system which might usefully inform historical analyses, see P. J. Atkins and I. R. Bowler, *Food in Society: Economy, Culture, Geography*, London, Arnold, 2000. Examples of social scientific case studies on food choice in the 1990s, some of which may find fruitful applications in historical interpretations, may be found in A. Murcott (ed.), *The Nation's Diet*, London, Longman, 1998.
3  A useful lead into the literature in this area is provided by L. Jordanova, 'The social construction of medical knowledge', *Social History of Medicine,* 1995, vol. 8, pp. 361–81. For examples of social constructionism applied to (mostly) modern food issues see D. Maurer and J. Sobal (eds), *Food, Eating, and Nutrition as Social Problems: Constructivist Perspectives*, New York, Aldine de Gruyter, 1995, and D. Maurer and J. Sobal (eds), *Weighty Issues*, New York, Aldine de Gruyter, 1999. For a lead into the additional literature which provides a variety of approaches to the science/policy interface, see V. Berridge and J. Stanton, 'Science and policy: historical insights', *Social Science and Medicine*, 1999, vol. 49, pp. 1133–8, and the other articles in the special issue of the journal of which this forms a part.
4  A useful lead into this literature is provided by M. J. Hill, *The Policy Process in the Modern State*, London, Wheatsheaf, 1997. A range of competing perspectives are located in the following: P. Hall, *Governing the Economy: The Politics of State Intervention in Britain and France*, London, Polity, 1986; R. MacLeod (ed.), *Government and Expertise: Specialists, Administrators and Professionals*, Cambridge, Cambridge University Press, 1988; S. Peltzman, 'Toward a more general theory of regulation', reprinted in G. J. Stigler (ed.), *Chicago Studies in Political Economy*, Chicago, University of Chicago Press, 1988; R. A. W. Rhodes, *Understanding Governance: Policy Networks, Governance, Reflexivity and Accountability*, Buckingham, Open University Press, 1997.

5  D. F. Smith (ed.), *Nutrition in Britain: Science, Scientists and Politics in the Twentieth Century*, London, Routledge, 1997, p. 2.

6  M. French and J. Phillips, *Cheated Not Poisoned? Food Regulation in the United Kingdom, 1875–1938*, Manchester, Manchester University Press, 2000.

7  This chapter is based upon a PhD thesis on the subject of food regulation in the USA, and subsequent research. S. R. White [Junod], 'Chemistry and controversy, regulating the use of chemicals in foods, 1883–1959,' unpublished PhD thesis, Emory University, 1994.

8  See, for example, P. A. Koolmees, *Symbolen van Openbare Hygiëne. Gemeentelijke slachthuizen in Nederland 1795–1940*, (Symbols of Public Hygiene. Municipal Slaughter-houses in The Netherlands 1795–1940), Rotterdam, Erasmus, 1997.

9  D. F. Smith, 'Nutrition science and the two world wars' in Smith, 1997, op. cit., 1 pp. 142–65, and Chapter 7 of this volume.

10  L. M. Barnett, 'Fletcherism: the chew chew fad of the Edwardian era', in Smith, 1997, op. cit., pp. 6–28; L. M. Barnett, ' "Every man his own physician": Dietetic Fads, 1890–1914', in H. Kamminga and A. Cunningham (eds), *The Science and Culture of Nutrition, 1840s-1940s*, Amsterdam, Rodopi, pp. 155–78.

11  T. Lang, 'Going public: food campaigns during the 1980s and early 1990s', in Smith, 1997, op. cit., pp. 238–60.

12  Ruxin's chapter is largely based upon the wide ranging archival and oral history research conducted for his PhD thesis: J. Ruxin, 'Hunger, science and politics: FAO, WHO and UNICEF nutrition polities, 1945–1978', unpublished PhD thesis, University of London, 1996.

13  The Pennington Group, *Report on the Circumstances Leading to the 1996 Outbreak of Infection with E. coli 0157 in Central Scotland*, Edinburgh, Stationery Office, 1997.

14  D. F. Smith, 'Nutrition in Britain', unpublished PhD thesis, Edinburgh University, 1987, chapter 3.

15  R. D. Apple, *Vitamania: Vitamins in American Culture*, New Brunswick, NJ, Rutgers University Press, 1996.

16  Kamminga and Cunningham, op. cit., p. 2.

17  D. J. Oddy and D. S. Miller, *The Making of the Modern British Diet*, London, Croom Helm, 1976; D. J. Oddy and D. S. Miller, *Diet and Health in Modern Britain*, London, Croom Helm, 1985; C. Geissler and D. J. Oddy, *Food, Diet and Economic Change Past and Present*, Leicester, Leicester University Press, 1993.

18  Among his publications are G. Trienekens, *Voedsel en Honger in Oorlogstijd 1940–1945. Misleiding, Mythe en Werkelijkheid*, (Food and Hunger in Wartime 1940–1945. Deception, Myth and Reality), Utrecht/Antwerpen, Kosmos-Z&K Uitgeuvers, 1995.

19  For a good lead into the anthropometric history literature, S. Coll and J. Komlos, 'The biological standard of living and economic development: nutrition, health and well-being in historical perspective', in C.-E. Núñez, (ed.), *Debates and Controversies in Economic History*, Madrid, Fundación Ramón Areces, 1998, pp. 219–82; B. Harris, 'Health, height and history: an overview of recent developments in anthropometric history', *Social History of Medicine*, 1993, vol. 7, pp. 277–320; J. Komlos (ed.), *Stature, Living Standards and Economic Development: Essays in Anthropometric History*, Chicago, University of Chicago Press, 1994; J. Komlos and J. Baten (eds), *The Biological Standard of Living in Comparative Perspective*, Stuttgart, Franz Steiner Verlag, 1998; R. Steckel, 'Stature and the standard of living', *Journal of Economic Literature*, 1995, vol. 33, pp. 1903–40; R. Steckel and R. Floud (eds), *Health and Welfare during Industrialisation*, Chicago, University of Chicago Press, 1997. One example of a study which combines some aspects of policy formation, policy implementation and anthropometric history is Bernard Harris' *Health of the School Child*, Buckingham, Open University Press, 1995.

# 2 Compositional food standards in the United Kingdom: the case of the Willis Inquiry, 1929–1934

*Mike French and Jim Phillips*

In the late 1990s, food quality and safety has assumed immense public and political importance. Recent and continuing scares, most notably over BSE, genetically-modified and hormone-treated foods, along with concerns in Britain about *E. coli*, explored by Hugh Pennington in the final chapter of this volume, have kept food in the forefront of media interest and public debate. A central strand of this debate has focused on the regulatory role of the British government, which has been criticised for failing to achieve a balance between the interests of food producers and consumers. Calls have been made for new forms of regulation, including the introduction of a Food Standards Agency, dedicated to promoting or defending the views and interests of food consumers. This body was established in the UK in April 2000, and was immediately faced with competing advice from powerful groups, including the farming lobby, the food industry and consumers' representatives.[1]

This chapter focuses on an episode of history which carries important parallels with these contemporary developments. Public discussion of food quality and regulation in inter-war Britain was to a very large extent dominated by the question of compositional standards, that is, whether all foods should be subject to precise legal definitions. In 1930 the Ministry of Health established a departmental inquiry on the subject, chaired by Sir Frederick Willis, a career civil servant who had served the Local Government Board as a Medical Officer. The Willis Inquiry's work was suspended as a result of the economic and political crisis of 1931, but it resumed in 1933, gathering evidence from numerous business, professional and consumer-protectionist organisations before reporting in 1934. The episode has been examined briefly elsewhere by the present authors, in the context of a study of the evolution of UK food laws from the 1860s to the 1930s.[2] This detailed treatment is intended to develop two key themes which characterise the current debate about food quality and safety, and are highlighted elsewhere in this volume: the discretionary and sometimes opportunistic role of state officials, identified by David Smith; and the problems of labelling and the most appropriate forms of consumer representation, analysed by Suzanne White Junod. Central to the discussion is the role of the Ministry of Health, established in 1919, which shared responsibility for food laws in England and Wales with the Ministry of Agriculture and Fisheries (MAF) and, in Scotland, with the health and agricultural departments of the Scottish Office. MAF's powers were mainly confined to the monitoring of agricultural produce and animal health. The Ministry of Health, on the other hand, had responsibility for the Sale of Food and Drugs Acts (SFDA), providing central guidance to local authorities which undertook the law's routine enforcement. So there was a degree of local autonomy, but the Ministry of Health had substantial influence over the manner in which the SFDA were applied. Established in 1875, and strengthened in 1899, these laws had been based on the notion that consumers were being 'cheated rather than poisoned',[3] and provided two definitions of adulteration – anything which rendered food 'injurious' to health, or which altered, 'to the prejudice of the purchaser', its 'nature, substance and quality'.[4]

These twin definitions of adulteration were important, for in the 1920s and 1930s the Ministry of Health only supported changes to the SFDA which were required on public health grounds. In 1932 the Chief Medical Officer, Sir George Newman, used his annual report to note that the intensification of food processing, with the deployment of chemical preservatives and vitamins, had created 'A New Problem in Food Adulteration'.[5] Yet the Ministry of Health ignored suggestions from consumer-protectionist advocates that these changing manufacturing conditions required changes to the anti-fraudulent aspects of the 1875 and 1899 legislation. In so doing the ministry arguably undermined the original emphasis on outlawing the sale of fraudulent as well as dangerous food. The Victorian laws had been ambiguous about compositional standards, affording legal protection to manufactured items, provided their mixed nature was clearly labelled. This was in response to pressure from manufacturers, including Colman's and Cadbury's, which had found retailers of their mustard and cocoa powder being prosecuted for adulteration. Colman's mustard contained turmeric, chillies and other spices, and some forms of Cadbury's cocoa powder included sago and other starches. Both manufacturers persuaded the committee of MPs which drafted the 1875 SFDA, one of whom was Jeremiah Colman himself, that such labelled mixtures should not be treated as adulterated articles.[6]

Aside from labelled mixtures, under the established SFDA the compositional legitimacy of other foods was essentially determined on a case-by-case basis. As the findings of one magistrate or court were not necessarily binding on another, it was often very difficult for local authorities to approach particular prosecutions with confidence. Given this uncertainty, and the high costs of mounting what could be lengthy prosecutions, many cases were simply dropped. In these circumstances the Society of Public Analysts (SPA), the professional organisation of officials responsible for analysing food that was suspected of being adulterated, became the most prominent and persistent advocate of general standards. The SPA believed that official compositional standards would simplify the process of obtaining convictions and therefore reduce adulteration. These would define upper and lower limits for particular ingredients in particular foods. Samples which did not meet these limits would automatically be defined as 'adulterated'. The SPA also believed that the existing legislation on adulteration had become outdated as the processes of production had changed, with adulteration attaining subtler and more complex guises. These developments accentuated the need for compositional standards. In the 1920s and 1930s the SPA's position came to be supported by a variety of organisations with a common interest in consumer protection: the Society of Medical Officers of Health, local authorities charged with enforcing the SFDA, the People's League of Health and the various wholesalers', retailers' and women's consumer groups which constituted the British working class co-operative movement.[7]

This 'public interest' criticism of the UK food laws resembled the parallel developments in the United States, analysed by Suzanne Junod elsewhere in this book. In the 1920s and 1930s a number of factors came together in the USA which focused attention on the need for reform of the 1906 Pure Food and Drug Act. This was the product of a drawn out campaign by a pro-regulation coalition of state chemists, federal officials, and wider reform movements, notably women's organisations, brought together and directed by Harvey Wiley, chief chemist in the Department of Agriculture.[8] Yet despite Wiley's considerable success in expanding the scale and scope of his Bureau of Chemistry, which evolved eventually into the Food and Drug Administration in 1930, resistance from food manufacturers prevented the introduction of enhanced consumer-protectionist legislation until 1938.[9]

In the UK, as in the USA, there were substantial obstacles to increased consumer protection. But business opposition to compositional standards and increased regulation generally was even more assertive than in the USA, with manufacturers arguing that voluntary standards and market forces rather than state direction were the best guarantee of consumer protection. And while elements in the US Federal government cultivated reform, in the UK central government departments actively resisted it, content to support the mainstream business position. Officials at the Ministries of Health and Agriculture were reluctant to press new restrictions on the activities of producers in the difficult economic and trading conditions of the 1920s and 1930s, especially as the pro-standards lobby was based on consumer-protectionist rather than public health arguments. As one Ministry of Health official was to note in 1920, it was his department's job to protect consumers against poisoning but not to ensure that they received value for money.[10] Indeed the extensions of government intervention in the 1920s and 1930s were more immediately evident in marketing schemes intended to reduce surpluses and improve farm incomes.

## Standards before the Willis Inquiry

These competing arguments and perspectives were most clearly evident between 1929 and 1934, during the establishment and conduct of the Willis Inquiry. Before focusing on this debate about general standards and definitions, it is important to emphasise that a number of standards were adopted for specific products prior to 1929. This distinction between individual and general standards is important, for individual standards were easier to achieve, largely on the basis that they emerged primarily from unified or essentially unchallenged business demands. The introduction of powers to frame general compositional standards, on the other hand, was much less straightforward, involving competing business opinion and often including substantial opposition. Standards duly emerged in a piecemeal fashion for spirits and margarine and for drugs, the latter based on the British Pharmacopoeia. The passage of the 1899 Sale of Food and Drugs Act led to standards for milk (1901) and butter (1902,1906), issued by the Board of Agriculture. The Board of Agriculture's involvement reflected the dairy farmers' lack of confidence in the Local Government Board (LGB), the central government department which had been given primary responsibility for the first SFDA in 1875.[11] The Milk Regulations specified a minimum standard of 3 per cent fat solids and 8.5 per cent of non-fat solids, and the Butter Regulations set an upper limit of 16 per cent water content. Both broadly approximated with the views of public analysts, but were also shaped by business representatives who gave evidence to the House of Commons and Board of Agriculture committees which drafted the 1899 legislation and subsequent regulations.[12] In 1923, following a debate which had developed over the course of two decades, standards were also introduced for condensed and evaporated milk. Again, these were supported by public analysts and medical professionals, but there was also a business case for standards, articulated by representatives of Nestlé, St. Ivel and United Dairies, who claimed that rival American firms had attained an unfair competitive advantage by supplying low-fat and hence cheaper condensed milk. The UK-based manufacturers successfully obtained regulations which established four grades of condensed milk, all based on contents of fat and milk solids which exceeded the American standard. In 1928 Ministry of Health officials rejected the idea of European dairy standards on the grounds, accepted by the SPA, that UK standards were sufficient and superior. Meanwhile officials at the Ministry of Agriculture and Fisheries, as the old Board of Agriculture had been reconstituted in 1919, indicated that British farmers regarded the regulations as valuable 'protective measures'.[13]

Dairy produce apart, there was a long-running campaign by vinegar brewers to secure monopoly rights on the term 'malt vinegar'. Malt brewers wanted less expensive rival products, derived from acetic acid obtained through chemical processes, to be labelled as either 'imitation' or 'artificial' vinegar, and lobbied government from the 1890s onwards.[14] The vehement opposition of the acetic acid producers deterred central government intervention, despite the analysts' support for vinegar standards. Eventually, in 1935, the Malt Vinegar Brewers' Federation reached an agreement with the SPA which recognised the distinct character of the malt article.[15] Co-operation with the SPA on voluntary standards was also embraced as a commercial ploy by jam producers. This provides a further point of contrast between business approaches to standards and regulation in the UK and the USA. Junod notes that some jelly manufacturers were keen to have their product standardised. The industry was intensely competitive, so there were clear advantages in adopting standards and transparent labelling of jar-sizes and relative proportions of sugar, fruit and other ingredients. British jam producers faced similarly competitive conditions, but preferred voluntary grading to statutory standards. This was certainly the position of the Food Manufacturers' Federation, a major employers' organisation with 750 members and a combined workforce in excess of 150,000 in the 1930s. In 1930 the Food Manufacturers' Federation enlisted the SPA's support for an agreement requiring members to grade their jam as 'Lower' or 'Full Fruit Standard'.[16]

While working with specialised producers who sought specific standards to gain a commercial advantage, the SPA's more important long-term aim was a system of general food standards. The SPA had first advocated a national agency to advise government on a range of food definitions in the 1890s, and the idea was supported by the 1894 House of Commons Select Committee on Food Products Adulteration and the 1903 Royal Commission on Arsenical Poisoning.[17] The Local Government Board responded by establishing a separate Foods Section in 1905, which was intended to undertake research and advise local and central government, but not to operate as the source of general standards.[18] This was the government's only practical initiative, although the Foods Section at least drafted legislation outlining powers for the LGB to define foods.[19] This failed to come before Parliament and was abandoned on the outbreak of the First World War.[20] But the war generated developments which led to demands for other kinds of regulation, driven by the shortages which led to the establishment in 1916 of the Ministry of Food. Pressure on basic foods led in the first instance to the new Ministry rationing and fixing the prices of selected items, including sausages and jam, which entailed setting criteria for composition and weight or volume.[21] Continuing shortages were believed by the government to be the root of an upsurge in industrial and social protest in November and December 1917, which blunted the war effort by disrupting munitions production. For the authorities this bore an obvious and uncomfortable resemblance to developments in revolutionary Russia, and in January 1918, to avert further food-related unrest, the government established the Consumers' Council. This was designed to incorporate working class thinking into food policy, drawing representatives from the War Emergency Workers' National Committee, the Trades Union Congress, the co-operative movement and the Women's National Industrial Organisation. Described by Peter Gurney as a 'kind of safety valve for the antagonism of working class consumers', the Council retained influence only for the duration of the war, and was disbanded in 1921.[22]

Although wartime weights and measures schemes were perpetuated in legislation for a few commodities, more general price controls were abandoned after the war,[23] and so the Consumers' Council's main concerns – prices and alleged profiteering – remained politically contentious during the 1920s. This resulted in the establishment of a Royal Commission on Food Prices, which focused mainly on the meat and wheat trades. In 1925 the Royal Commission's work resulted in the establishment of a Food Council, which represented a broader spectrum of opinion than the Consumers' Council, including members from government departments and retail organisations as well as the co-op and union movements.[24] The Food Council concentrated on questions of supplies and prices rather than food quality, though in 1926 it considered the issue of short weight and measures in a report to the Board of Trade.[25] Weights and Measures Acts and their enforcement were a parallel strand of consumer protection against fraud to the Sale of Food and Drugs Acts, with similar forms of local enforcement and general oversight by a government department, in this case the Board of Trade. There was a comparably slow and piecemeal move to extending the range of commodities sold by net weight. Local authorities and professional associations of weights and measures inspectors consistently advocated legislation to set definitive national guidelines, and specific measures were enacted when leading manufacturers in the tea and bread industries supported continuation of wartime measures. But more extensive provisions were resisted, notably by confectionery firms, the Food Manufacturers' Federation and grocers on the grounds that they would handicap trade without benefiting consumers.

The process of developing strengthened forms of consumer protection under the SFDA was equally tortuous. In 1920 the LGB's responsibilities for food laws were assumed by its departmental successor, the Ministry of Health. This new department adopted an even less ambitious approach to food laws than the LGB. In the autumn of 1920 Ministry of Health officials effectively blocked one of the final acts of the war-time Ministry of Food, an attempt to revive the pre-war draft legislation allowing the government to set standards for a range of products.[26] The Ministry of Health's central objection to this was articulated by L. G. Brock, the assistant secretary detailed to consider its desirability. 'Our primary object', he noted, 'must be to protect the public from being starved or poisoned and not merely to secure value for money'. Brock added that the Ministry of Food proposals, which included 'heroic measures' on factory inspections and sampling, were unpopular with food manufacturers.[27] Ministry of Health officials secured a postponement of the Bill and the prospect of any further departmental challenge to their responsibilities under the SFDA was finally removed in 1921, with the dissolution of the Ministry of Food.

## The SPA and the case for general standards

Despite the removal of the government department which had been seeking strengthened forms of consumer protection, the SPA continued to advance the case for general food standards in the 1920s. Pointing to the changing nature of food manufacturing, with the growth of prepared and pre-packaged foods, the SPA argued that the Sale of Food and Drugs Acts had become outdated. Although the original legislation had partially countered overtly hazardous adulteration, it did not give consumers adequate protection against the more 'sophisticated' manufacturing practices of the 1920s. Under the SFDA the prosecution had to demonstrate that a fraudulent article was not of the 'nature, substance and quality demanded'. In the face of conflicting 'expert' evidence proffered by the defence, the absence of definite standards complicated the task of securing legal convictions and in the 1920s the SPA had to content itself with the piecemeal addition of the few standards, some via reputation and others via private agreement, described earlier. The SPA also welcomed the establishment of official guidelines on a limited number of preservatives in 1925, under the Public Health (Preservatives etc in Foods) Regulations.[28] These were introduced after a lengthy official inquiry and in the face of some determined business opposition, most notably from the cream trade, bakers and manufacturers of meat products. The Ministry of Health regarded the public health argument for limited regulations, outlawing the use of formaldehyde, salicylic acid and boric acid, and restricting the use of sulphur dioxide and benzoic acid, as unequivocal. But considerable flexibility was shown in the application of these regulations, delayed until 1927 to allow producers to find alternative methods of preservation, and the degree of business opposition was to influence significantly the Ministry of Health's approach to compositional standards from 1929. The department would take the view, in the words of Sir George Newman, Chief Medical Officer, that in the wake of the preservatives regulations, and given the continuing economic and trading pressures, producers were due 'a rest' from further legislation.[29]

While the preservatives regulations reinforced the Ministry's opposition to standards, they strengthened the SPA's determination to secure further legal compositional definitions. In May 1929, having failed to overcome the Ministry of Health's opposition to standards, the SPA asked the Committee of Civil Research to investigate the issue.[30] This committee was the forerunner of the Cabinet's think tank, the Economic Advisory Council, which was established in 1930.[31] The SPA's initiative prompted an anxious discussion within the Ministry of Health. J. N. Beckett, the official regularly charged with monitoring food regulatory matters, outlined the case for a general inquiry into standards and adulteration. There had been no such inquiry since the 1894–6 Commons Select Committee on Food Products Adulteration, and standards could offer considerable benefits in countering the increasingly sophisticated nature of adulteration. But Beckett was all too aware of the potential hazards of standards, which could lead to higher prices, eliminate from the market 'wholesome but inferior' goods, and allow one business to secure its own commercial formula as the official definition.[32] These objections were broadly accepted by Beckett's senior colleagues, including Newman and Sir Arthur Robinson, Permanent Secretary of the Ministry of Health, who were both reluctant to impose new restrictions on business, and unconvinced of the health grounds for standards. At the same time the SPA's approach to the Committee of Civil Research placed the department in some difficulty, with its authority on food and drugs questions potentially being called into question. Newman was advised by one of his medical officers, J. M. Hamill, that the 'analysts have evidently grown weary of our reluctance to do anything ... and have cast around to find some other body from which more might be hoped'.[33]

Beckett attempted to resolve this dilemma, suggesting that instead of basing the inquiry on the sole and direct issue of standards, it be established as a more general survey of 'composition and description of food' under the SFDA. As the Ministry of Health already bore the general responsibility for the SFDA, the relative interests of other departments in such an inquiry would be slight.[34] The Department of Health in Scotland, which had initially favoured an inquiry by the Committee of Civil Research, accepted this position in November. The inquiry would be chaired by an external figure and take evidence from a range of outside individuals and organisations, but report directly to the Minister of Health and Secretary of State for Scotland, who would be responsible for the government's response.[35] At this point, however, there was a significant delay in proceedings, arising from the Ministry of Health's essential reluctance to undertake the inquiry. Newman was especially cautious, his thoughts dominated by the belief that business opposition to further state intervention would make it impossible to secure standards. A departmental memo prepared in January 1930 gives the flavour of Newman's thinking, noting that producers 'regarded themselves as having been already unduly harassed by the legislation and regulations of recent years'. Given the additional fact that adulteration figures had been falling steadily for around fifty years, the memo concluded that 'there was a case for postponing the question of further legislation'.[36]

Eventually, with the need to preserve the Ministry of Health's undiluted food and drugs responsibilities over-riding the basic opposition to new regulations, the need for a general inquiry of the type favoured by Beckett was accepted by ministry officials in February 1930. But it was October 1930 before the task began of assembling personnel for the inquiry, including representatives of business (unrelated to food manufacturing or retailing), county and metropolitan councils, and consumer interests. In pursuit of the latter, officials invited 'two or three ladies' onto the committee: Jennie Adamson, wife of the Labour government's Scottish Secretary of State, and Mary Cotterell, director of the Co-operative Wholesale Society. Representatives of the Ministries of Health and Agriculture and the Scottish Department of

Health were also included on the fifteen-member committee.[37] Finally, in May 1931, a committee was established to assess whether changes to the law on 'the composition and description' of food were desirable. The committee was chaired by Sir Frederick Willis, a career civil servant who had worked at the pre-1914 Local Government Board.[38]

## The Willis Inquiry

The Willis Committee met just once, on 24 June 1931. It was then suspended in September, following the economic and political crisis that resulted in the resignation of the Labour government and the establishment of the Conservative-dominated 'National' government which immediately sought economies in state expenditure.[39] The Ministry of Health accepted this postponement without complaint, and although the worst effects of the financial crisis had apparently been reversed by the spring of 1932, no attempt was made to revive the Willis Committee. A. B. Maclachlan, a Ministry of Health medical officer, noted on 9 March that the 'cumbersome body' did not need to be reconvened, and if it expired then at a later date a 'smaller and more manageable committee' could be established.[40] On 18 March Sir Arthur Robinson told the National government's Minister of Health, Edward Hilton Young, that the Willis Committee 'can very suitably remain suspended – departmentally we were never keen on it'.[41] This frank admission demonstrates that senior Ministry figures were content to use the political and financial crisis as a pretext for suppressing the investigation which had been thrust upon them by the SPA and the Committee of Civil Research. It is also a particularly sharp illustration of the Ministry's absence of activist ambition relative to that of the US Food and Drug Administration, which by 1933 was lobbying energetically for the reform of the 1906 Pure Food Act.

Having been formed by opportunistic officials, in 1933 the Willis Committee was revived by opportunistic officials. This was to alleviate political pressure on Walter Elliot, the Minister of Agriculture, who was facing persistent calls in parliament for cheese standards from a Cheshire MP, R. J. Russell. Russell claimed that the case for standards enjoyed the 'unanimous support' of Cheshire producers who wanted the term 'Cheshire' to be applicable legally only to cheese produced in the county.[42] The Ministry of Agriculture was embarrassed by a campaign with this type of rural support: while opposing compulsory food standards it was anxious to avoid publicly opposing an influential section of the farming industry. So, in a further twist to the bureaucratic-driven history of the standards inquiry, his officials advised Elliot to ask Young to revive the Willis Committee. This would allow the Ministry of Agriculture to cite the existence of a general inquiry on food standards as an explanation for failing to support particular standards for cheese.[43] Ministry of Health officials agreed to this request, taking the opportunity to narrow the committee's terms of reference from the general question of whether the SFDA required alteration to the particular question of whether definitions or standards were desirable.[44]

Re-appointed on 24 July, the committee began gathering oral evidence on 20 September 1933, before reporting in March 1934. The first witness was Beckett of the Ministry of Health, who outlined his department's ambivalent position: 'We see there are certain abuses, or potential abuses, in the absence of standards and definitions, and we see there are certain difficulties about prescribing standards or definitions'. The committee would, he said, have to 'balance the two sets of difficulties'. Examples of these difficulties came out in discussion. Beckett agreed, for example, that court proceedings often failed because there were no definitions or standards in place. When Jennie Adamson praised the voluntary jam standards which the SPA had established with the Food Manufacturers' Federation, Beckett was cautious about extending the practice to other commodities. Where the standard was fixed too high, 'you will be cutting off from the market the inferior jams which are quite good, quite pure and harmless, and good food and cheaper'. Adamson's colleague on the inquiry team, W. Barratt, a Northampton boot manufacturer, objected that this reasoning was akin to that of Leeds 'jerry-builders' who constructed back-to-back houses deemed 'good enough for a certain section of the public'. In other words, the poor would only receive inferior quality jam. Better this, retorted Beckett, than that they eat no jam at all.[45]

This approach was flatly contradicted by the SPA's representatives, F. W. F. Arnaud, J. T. Dunn and E. Hinks, who used the hearings to restate the case for comprehensive standards based on the advice of a standing committee with wide investigative powers. On the issue raised by Beckett, of standards leading to higher prices and lost trade, Arnaud observed that sales had not fallen with the adoption of jam standards. More forcefully, Hinks stated that, 'we should represent very strongly that you could never admit the excuse that an article of food should not be what it purports to be on account of its price'. They further argued that standards could not be raised through market forces and the exercise of consumer choice based on product labelling. Arnaud believed that consumers themselves would be unable to determine comparative values of fat content in cheese, and hence opposed any attempt to have declaratory labels of contents in lieu of standards. Similarly, he would accept grading of products only where 'apparent by the name' rather than by 'mathematical exercise'. The SPA's perspectives were reinforced by a separate witness, H. E. Monk, public analyst for Salford. Monk was a regular contributor of articles on food laws and safety to *Food Manufacture*, a journal established in 1926, which emphasised the extent to which 'progressive' and 'responsible' producers were committed to improved quality through scientific research and technological innovation.[46] By working with *Food Manufacture* Monk was evidently keen to expand the co-operation between analysts and manufacturers which was already in place with the voluntary jam standards. And his evidence was consistent with the journal's sponsorship of 'responsible' business. The Ministry of Agriculture's representative on the inquiry, A. T. A. Dobson, asked Monk about the possibility that regulations would drive people out of business 'if you only look after the interests of the consumer'. Monk replied that 'the only people you would drive out of business would be the dishonest and the fraudulent'. Dobson then asked about the consequences for 'the small man', the small dairy farmer producing cheese that might not match up to established standards. To Monk this implied notion that goods of limited quality were being produced simply strengthened the argument for minimum guaranteed standards. Dobson responded by raising the issue of how much protection consumers actually required, suggesting that in Monk's scheme of things the average 'housewife' was a 'nincompoop', unable to exercise discretion and choice when shopping. Monk was, he said, giving the 'impression that she (the housewife) cannot go and buy anything without being had by the man selling it to her'. Monk insisted that he was not being ungenerous to the average consumer's intelligence. It was simply impossible, he argued, for the average housewife, or indeed 'somebody far cleverer', in certain cases to tell whether they were obtaining good or bad value for money.

The positive case for standards and enhanced consumer protection was supported by numerous subsequent witnesses at the inquiry. These included members of the Society of Medical Officers of Health and the representative bodies of the local authorities charged with enforcing the SFDA, namely the County Councils' Association and the Municipal Corporations' Association, along with the Co-operative Congress and the People's League of Health. All advanced a public interest case based on informing and protecting consumers. The People's League was represented by Professor Jack Drummond, who appears elsewhere in this volume as an 'insider' (Chapter 7). Drummond said that misleading advertising and labelling undermined consumers' ability to make informed choices, so corrective legislation was needed. Among the reformers there were some differences of opinion, notably about the character of any standing advisory committee. A. V. Alexander, a former and future Labour Cabinet Minister, representing the Co-op, was especially cautious in this respect, believing that the final responsibility for fixing standards should not rest with such a committee or even the minister, but with parliament. 'We are already halfway to Mussolini', he said, emphasising his disapproval of 'the growth of government by regulation', unfettered by parliamentary control.[47]

Business evidence to the inquiry also revealed significant divisions of opinion. Several of the firms and associations who were already seeking regulation to give their products a commercial advantage, notably the Malt Vinegar Brewers' Federation and the Cheshire Cheese Federation, repeated their calls for definitions, although they opposed mandatory standards.[48] The Food Manufacturers' Federation and the Manufacturing Confectioners' Alliance (MCA), along with the Margarine Manufacturers' Association, opposed any extension of the limited existing framework of standards and definitions. The FMF's President, G. P. Shippam, the meat and fish paste manufacturer, insisted that standards were both unnecessary and unenforceable: unnecessary because essentially the industry already delivered a high quality of product to the 'housewife'; and unenforceable because many manufactured articles, most notably sauces and pickles, were too complex for exact analysis. At the same time, however, Shippam conceded that some items, including jams and baby foods, might usefully be standardised on a voluntary basis, and that his organisation would not stand in the way of a central advisory committee, provided it was based on business expertise rather than the SPA. The producers' case against standards was also made by the MCA, which characterised the SPA's emphasis on fraud as an affront to the intelligence of consumers. This was also 'ungallant, because the purchasers are generally women'.[49] In evidence to the Inquiry the MCA's representative, Paul S. Cadbury, claimed that standards would prevent producers from developing products to meet changing consumer taste, inflate prices and so restrict the overall confectionery market. He argued at length that unregulated market forces and branded goods were the best guarantee of quality. Asked whether minimum milk fat standards would enhance consumer confidence in milk chocolate, Cadbury replied, 'the best confidence is that you sell a good quality article and put money into advertising it, and it would be very foolish to do anything which would shake confidence in a proprietary article. I think that is far better than any standards.' Unlike manufacturers of products like condensed milk and malt vinegar, Cadbury was opposed to standards that might, in theory, have given his own goods a competitive advantage over budget rivals. Alleging that standards would force cheaper items off the market, he added, 'I am not speaking with any personal interest in the lower quality articles, but I like to see children develop a taste for chocolate which I hope as they grow up and have more money will be to my personal advantage'.[50]

The Federation of Grocers' Associations was more equivocal than the manufacturing organisations. Its representatives, Arthur E. James and W. Herman Kent, suggested that standards would only benefit consumers if they were not so strenuous as to take the price of goods 'beyond the means of the poorest person'. They added that responsibility for any illegalities should be placed on producers rather than retailers,[51] a traditional grocers' argument founded in the perceived iniquity of the 1875 Sale of Food and Drugs Act which had placed the focus of inspection and prosecution on retailing rather than manufacturing premises.[52]

Towards the end of proceedings Willis took evidence from the Food Group of the Society of the Chemical Industry. Established as recently as 1932, this consisted of chemists employed in the food industry, so to some extent it represented a potential bridge between the worlds of business and chemical analysis. The Food Group was represented at the Inquiry by Dr Leslie H. Lampitt, chief chemist at Lyons, who suggested that standards for tea, coffee, jam, cream and cheese could be established to protect consumers without affecting price. This qualified support for standards, from a source who combined scientific and industrial expertise, lent greater legitimacy to the SPA's claims and prompted apparent consternation within manufacturing circles. A number of processors discussed the situation with their chemists to 'avoid a recurrence of the difficulty', and Lampitt himself continued to speak publicly about standards solely in terms of the difficulties of establishing them beyond a very narrow range of products.[53]

## The Willis Report

This reassertion of the producers' confident anti-standards argument was consolidated by the contents of the Willis report, published on 20 March 1934. The views of the manufacturers were broadly endorsed, Willis finding that 'a large proportion' of food was of high quality and that 'many manufacturers take a pride in the production of good quality articles and exercise great care in their manufacture'. On the central question of whether consumers enjoyed sufficient protection against fraudulent trade, the committee unambiguously sided with producers and dismissed the views of the public analysts. The 'average housewife' was described as being capable of exercising skill and discretion when making her purchases. So Willis and his colleagues concluded that 'the case for the extension of standards and definitions to all articles is not made out', and advised that the law be changed to allow for the establishment of standards and definitions on a limited basis only. In a further recommendation which would disappoint the public analysts, Willis concluded that the responsibility for definitions should reside with the Ministry of Health and the Scottish Health Department alone. On the basis that these departments possessed the necessary resources and expertise to determine any appropriate consumer-protectionist standards, the idea of establishing a new advisory body was definitely ruled out.[54]

These findings essentially confirmed the status quo of minimal standards acceptable to the FMF, and offered reassurance that any future standards would only be introduced after full consultation with the Ministry of Health, which through the conduct of the inquiry had demonstrated a desire to accommodate the needs and views of manufacturers. So the report was acceptable to opponents of further standards, and the journal *Food Manufacture* described the Willis report as a 'very satisfactory document'. The rejection of a standing advisory committee was highlighted, along with the positive emphasis on 'the integrity of the British food manufacturer and the quality of his products'.[55] The SPA had hoped in 1932 that the inquiry would lead to the establishment of a comprehensive system of compositional standards, devised and enforced by a new agency which included public analysts. So the SPA President placed a rather over-optimistic construction on the outcome of the inquiry, seeing the possibility of Ministry of Health-issued piecemeal standards as a concession to 'the main contention of the Society, namely, the necessity for extended statutory powers for establishing definitions and standards for articles of food'.[56]

The moderate recommendations on legal changes removed what little sense of urgency there was in the government machine in terms of realising even limited compositional standards. Ministry of Health and Scottish Health Department officials agreed that immediate legislation was unnecessary,[57] and in fact Willis's recommendations were only finally put into effect under the 1938 Food and Drugs Act. This allowed the Minister of Health to issue regulations 'prohibiting or restricting the addition of any substance to, and regulating generally the composition of, any food'. The delay and the character of the 1938 legislation were in keeping with the Ministry of Health's conduct of the standards debate since the SPA's approach to the Committee of Civil Research in 1929. In 1936 a new element was introduced to the debate, with the ministry inviting a further examination of food legislation, this time by the Local Government and Public Health Consolidation Committee.[58] Set up in 1931, and having completed the bulk of its work with the passage of the 1936 Public Health Act, this body was charged with bringing together statutes and regulations on food issued under the Public Health as well as the Sale of Food and Drugs Acts. The Public Health Consolidation Committee reported in 1937, and the 1938 legislation followed.[59] So the power to regulate for compositional standards eventually arrived, although not so much as a direct result of the Willis Report but rather as part of a wider bureaucratic tidying-up exercise. And crucially it consolidated the Ministry of Health's departmental responsibilities for food regulation. A strong indication that the ministry's consumer-protectionist ambitions were still low came in 1939, when it was approached by the Malt Vinegar Brewers' Federation, seeking a standard under the 1938 Act to distinguish malt from 'imitation' vinegar. A Ministry of Health official observed that the Federation 'apparently supposes, like some other interested parties, that on 1 October next [1939, when the Act took effect] standards and definitions in accordance with their own views will descend like manna from Heaven'.[60] The acerbic tone reflected the ministry's anxiety to give as little encouragement as possible to the idea of a standard for vinegar – or any other product.

## Conclusion

The debate about compositional standards in inter-war Britain, advanced principally through the establishment and operation of the Willis inquiry from 1929 to 1934, highlights two key themes which emerge elsewhere in this volume: the most appropriate forms of consumer representation; and the discretionary and sometimes opportunistic role of state officials. In addition, the episode demonstrated the powerful presence of business opinion and economic imperatives in debates about food supply and regulation.

Food manufacturing had become more complex and 'scientific' in the late nineteenth and early twentieth centuries. Sally Horrocks has highlighted the extensive commitment by a number of UK producers to research and development. Scientists were employed to find safe, legal and cheaper methods of producing articles which, in physical appearance and taste, seemed unchanged. Hence Crosse & Blackwell changed the recipe and method of producing Branston's Pickle, while maintaining consistency of flavour and colour.[61] At the Willis Inquiry producers claimed that the changing nature of production, including increased processing, undermined the case for consumer-protectionist standards. Representing the Food Manufacturers' Federation, George Shippam cited sauces and pickles as examples of processed foods which could not be standardised, given the constant modification of recipes and chemical composition. The Willis report accepted Shippam's argument, paraphrasing it to explain the impossibility of enforcing uniform standards.[62] The gap between Willis and the SPA on this issue is worth emphasising. Willis observed that the very complexity of manufacturing made the possibility of enhanced protection more remote. But the SPA believed that as the process of food manufacturing became more complex, the need for reinforcing consumer protection with compositional standards became greater.

In these circumstances, particularly as scientists were enhancing profitability by changing recipes, it was legitimate for the SPA to question whether consumers were still obtaining value for money. It was also reasonable for the SPA to ask whether consumers were able to make effective choices by consulting the labels of competing mixed articles. In the United States in the 1930s, as Suzanne Junod indicates in chapter eleven, the Federal government responded to consumer-protectionist lobbying by strengthening regulations on standards and product labelling. These changes took place within the New Deal framework of expanding government intervention, and resulted from campaigning by the Department of Agriculture and the Food and Drug Administration. In Britain food labelling was also important in debates over food regulation, seen variously as a vital source of information for consumers and an alternative to greater state intervention, such as standards. But there was no equivalent pressure from within the UK government machinery, and no similar legislative initiatives emerged. Nor were there efforts to link food regulation to controls over patent medicines or attempts to dramatise either food scares or the fraudulent character of misleading food packaging.

Herein lies this chapter's second key theme, the discretionary role of government officials, especially at the Ministry of Health. Here officials opposed the notion that the government's responsibilities on food extended to ensuring that consumers received value for money, operating on the basis that new laws were only justifiable on health grounds. The change of government in 1931, when Labour gave way to a Conservative-dominated 'National' coalition, had a visible impact on developments, with the Willis Committee suspended in pursuit of financial savings. But behind the scenes the Ministry of Health's approach was unchanged, officials exercising decisive influence throughout the establishment and operation of the inquiry between 1929 and 1934. The discretionary and opportunistic behaviour of these officials was evident in three main stages. First, when the SPA approached a rival organ of government, the Committee for Civil Research, asking it to investigate, the Ministry of Health established an inquiry which officials opposed in principle, but accepted as the price for preserving their departmental control over food legislation. Second, officials exploited the financial and political crisis of 1931 to suspend the inquiry. And without lobbying by Cheshire cheese producers in 1933 the suspension would have remained indefinite. This third example of bureaucratic opportunism saw Health officials agree to revive the inquiry in order that the Ministry of Agriculture could be excused from acting on cheese standards.

It is, of course, important to place the Ministry of Health's limited ambitions in the context of the politics and economics of the Depression, when the composition of food was of secondary importance to its volume and price.[63] To some extent the government's priorities in these circumstances resembled those of the First World War, when the practical operation of the Sale of Food and Drugs Acts had been suspended with policy focusing on supply rather than quality.[64] So it was in the late 1920s and early 1930s, when any new measures which may have affected supply and price had to be approached with caution. Ministry officials assessed that compositional standards were unnecessary on public health grounds; if they inflated cost they could actively undermine public health by inhibiting consumption of nutritious products. It is worth adding that working-class organisations, which in other conditions might have assumed a greater commitment to consumer protection, probably viewed standards in the same way. In the era of the General Strike and large-scale unemployment trade unions had more pressing concerns than the contents of food.

Finally, it is important to re-emphasise the significance of the Ministry of Health's reluctance to interfere with dominant commercial interests by instituting a general system of compositional standards. This bureaucratic caution indicates that concerns about the powerful presence of business opinion in debates about food safety and regulation in the 1980s and 1990s have significant antecedents in the 1920s and 1930s. Newman's preoccupation with business anti-regulation sentiment was shaped by forceful and continuing corporate representation on the issue of standards. Before submitting oral testimony to the Willis Inquiry, in common with other witness organisations, the Food Manufacturers' Federation outlined its general views in written form. This was in November 1933, when the financial and economic pressures which forced the inquiry's temporary suspension were in substantial retreat. 'Generally', the Federation noted, 'it may be argued that the present time, when there are signs of trade revival which may so easily be checked, is not opportune for any considerable disturbance of present practice'.[65] Such pressure contributed to the Ministry of Health's opposition to comprehensive powers for general compositional standards. It also figured in the delay in implementing the Willis Committee's limited recommendations until 1938.

# References

1 See the agency's web-site: www.foodstandards.gov.uk.
2 M. French and J. Phillips, *Cheated Not Poisoned: Food Regulation in the United Kingdom*, 1875–1938, Manchester, Manchester University Press, 2000, pp. 144–53.
3 *Report from the Select Committee on Adulteration of Food Act (1872). Proceedings and Minutes of Evidence*, Parliamentary Papers, 1874 (262), VI, 243, pp. iii–viii.
4 Sale of Food and Drugs Act, 1875, *Public General Acts*, 1875, Chapter 63.
5 Ministry of Health, *On the State of the Public Health. Annual Report of the Chief Medical Officer*, London, HMSO, 1932, pp. 135–42.
6 *Select Committee on Adulteration of Food Act*, pp. 54–63, 111–16.
7 French and Phillips, op. cit. pp. 127, 147.
8 J. H. Young, *Pure Food: Securing the Federal Food and Drug Act of 1906*, Princeton, NJ, Princeton University Press, 1989; M. Okun, *Fair Play in the Marketplace: The First Battle for Pure Food and Drugs*, DeHalb, Illinois, Northern Illinois University Press, 1986; C. A. Coppin and J. High, 'Umpires at bat: setting food standards by government regulation', *Business and Economic History*, 1992, vol. 21, pp. 109–118.
9 C. O. Jackson, *Food and Drug Legislation in the New Deal*, Princeton, NJ, Princeton University Press, 1970. For contrasting views on consumer groups in the 1930s see E. Hawley, *The New Deal and the Problem of Monopoly: A Study in Economic Ambivalence*, Princeton, NJ, Princeton University Press, 1969, pp. 75–90, 198–204, and the chapter by Cohen and McGovern in S. Strasser, C. McGovern and M. Judt (eds), *Getting and Spending: European and American Consumer Societies in the Twentieth Century*, Cambridge, Cambridge University Press, 1998.
10 L. G. Brock, Departmental memo, October 1920, MH 6/30, Public Record Office (hereafter PRO).
11 Board of Agriculture (Intelligence Division), *Annual Report*, 1900, pp. 4–6.
12 The Sale of Milk Regulations, 1901, Statutory Rules and Orders, 1901, No. 657; House of Commons, *Report on Food Products Adulteration*, Parliamentary Papers, 1894 (253), pp. 28, 169; The Sale of Butter Regulations, 1902, Statutory Rules and Orders, 1902, No. 355; *Final Report of the Departmental Committee etc. Minutes of Evidence*, Cd. 1750, 1904, pp. 333–40, 434–41.
13 See the file on the Federation Internationale de Laiterie in MAF 101/339, PRO.
14 J. M. Hamill, 'On the preparation and sale of vinegar', Local Government Board Foods Section, Report No. 5, 1906.
15 'Vinegar: definition and standards', 1933–9, MH 56/333, PRO.
16 *Food Manufacture*, May 1931.
17 *Final Report of the Royal Commission to Inquire into Arsenical Poisoning from the Consumption of Beer and other Articles of Food and Drink*, Cd. 1848, November 1903, pp. 44–6.
18 LGB, *Annual Report. Supplement Containing the Report of the Medical Officer*, 1905–6, Cd. 3656.
19 Food and Drugs Bill, 1913, Clause 1(1).
20 *The Grocer*, Vol. CIV, 16 August 1913, p. 399; Food and Drugs Bills of 1913 and 1914, copies in MH 56/12, PRO.
21 L. M. Barnett, *British Food Policy in the First World War*, London, Allen & Unwin, 1985.
22 P. Gurney, *Co-operative Culture and the Politics of Consumption in England, 1870–1930*, Manchester, Manchester University Press, 1996.
23 Barnett, op. cit.
24 Food Council, First Meeting, 31 July 1925, MAF 69/6, PRO.
25 *Report by the Food Council to the President of the Board of Trade on Short Weight and Measure in the Sale of Foodstuffs*, 1926, Cmd 2591.
26 Sale of Food Bill, 1920, Clauses 8 and 10, MH56/30, PRO.

27 Brock to MacFadden (Inspector of Foods, Ministry of Health), 25 October 1920, MH56/30, PRO.

28 *The Analyst*, 1926, vol. 51, p. 125 and 1927, vol. 52, p. 191.

29 Newman to Robinson, 11 December 1929, MH56/1, PRO.

30 Edward Hinks (President, SPA) to A. F. Hemming (Assistant Secretary, Committee of Civil Research), 17 May 1929, MH56/1, PRO.

31 Peter Hennessy, *Whitehall*, London, Harper Collins, 1990, p. 82.

32 Beckett to Newman and Robinson, 8 July 1929, MH 56/1, PRO.

33 Hamill to Newman, 9 July 1929, MH 56/1, PRO.

34 Beckett to Robinson, 2 October 1929, MH 56/1, PRO.

35 Fraser to Beckett, 6 November 1929, MH 56/1, PRO.

36 Unsigned memo, 10 January 1930, MH 56/8, PRO.

37 Two other women came onto the committee as appointees of the Scottish Secretary of State: Elona Beck, a Dunfermline JP, and Jean Roberts, a Glasgow City Councillor. Ten other ordinary members were appointed: W. Barratt, a Northampton boot manufacturer, Beckett and Hamill of the MoH, G. A. Birse of the Scottish Department of Health, H. F. Carlill, of the Board of Trade, Dobson of MAF, H. E. Goodby, a metropolitan Councillor, R. A. Robinson, from Middlesex County Council, H. Shaw, a Newcastle member of the British Chambers of Commerce, and G. Stubbs, a public analyst.

38 *Report of the Departmental Committee on the Composition and Description of Food*, Willis, Cmd. 4564, London, HMSO, April 1934, p. 2.

39 C. L. Mowat, *Britain Between the Wars*, London, Methuen, 1968, pp. 379–93.

40 Maclachlan memo, 9 March 1932, MH56/1, PRO.

41 Robinson to Hilton Young, 18 March 1932, MH56/1.

42 *Parliamentary Debates*, 5th Series, Vol. 274, 822–4, 14 February 1933.

43 Elliot to Hilton Young, 3 May 1933, MH56/12, PRO.

44 Cmd. 4564, p. 3.

45 Willis Committee, 20 September 1933, MH 56/2, PRO. This resembled the argument of nineteenth century planners and builders, justifying the construction of back-to-back housing before the Royal Commission on the Health of Towns in the 1840s; see M. Beresford, 'The back-to-back house in Leeds, 1787–1937', in S. D. Chapman (ed.), *The History of Working Class Housing: a symposium*, Newton Abbot, David and Charles, 1971, p. 112.

46 *Food Manufacture*, December 1927, p. 201.

47 Willis Committee, 10 October 1933, 1 November 1993, 9 January 1934, 20 February 1934; MH56/2–4, PRO.

48 Willis Committee, 11 and 31 October 1933; MH56/2, PRO.

49 Food Manufacturers' Federation Bulletin, November 1933, pp. 244–6.

50 Willis Committee, 27–28 November 1933 and 9 January 1934, MH56/3–4, PRO.

51 Willis Committee, 14 November 1933, MH56/3, PRO.

52 Willis Committee, 20 September and 14 November 1933, MH56/2–3, PRO.

53 FMF Bulletin, 20 February 1934.

54 Cmd. 4564, para. 16–18, 32–34.

55 *Food Manufacture*, June 1934.

56 *The Analyst*, 1932, vol. 57, p. 216 and 1936, vol. 61, p. 229.

57 Vallance to the Secretary of State, 5 June 1934, HH 64/4, Scottish Record Office (SRO).

58 *Local Government and Public Health Consolidation Committee. Third Interim Report*, Addington, Cmd. 5628, London, HMSO December 1937.

59 *Local Government and Public Health Consolidation Committee. Draft of a Food and Drugs Bill*, Cmd. 5629, London, HSMO December 1937.

60 Unsigned Departmental minute, 29 June 1939, MH 56/333, PRO.

61 S. M. Horrocks, 'Quality control and research: the role of scientists in the British food industry, 1870–1939', in J. Burnett and D. J. Oddy (eds), *The Origins and Development of*

*Food Policies in Europe*, Leicester, Leicester University Press, 1994, pp. 131–3; and 'Nutrition science and the food industry in Britain, 1920–1990', in A. P. den Hartog (ed.), *European Diet in the Twentieth Century*, East Linton, Tuckwell Press, 1995, pp. 7–18.
62 Cmd. 4564, para. 14.
63 An exception was agricultural policy where MAF promoted various marketing schemes intended to increase prices and farm incomes. As in the First World War in the conduct of these schemes a degree of consumer representation was used to provide legitimacy.
64 Ministry of Health, *First Annual Report*, 1919–1920, Cmd. 923, London, HMSO, 1920, p. 55.
65 FMF Memorandum to Willis Committee, 21 November 1933, MH 56/5, PRO.

# 3 The pasteurisation of England: the science, culture and health implications of milk processing, 1900–1950

*Peter J. Atkins*

The risk theorist, Ulrich Beck, is reported to have called the carnivorous part of the British diet 'an experiment inflicted upon us by the beef industry'.[1] He was referring to the scare connecting Mad Cow Disease (Bovine Spongiform Encephalopathy) to new-variant CJD (Creutzfeldt–Jacob Disease), a debilitating and fatal human brain disease. He might equally well have been thinking of *E. coli* 0157, Brucellosis, Crohn's Disease, or any of the other health hazards that have been associated with animal products recently.

This chapter seeks to build upon the recent heightened interest in our food environment, by demonstrating that one of the most controversial present day issues about food standards, whether milk should or should not be compulsorily pasteurised, had a prehistory before the Second World War. This was part of a debate about the role of the state in food systems, when central and local government was becoming actively involved in regulating food production and sale, and in setting standards of hygiene, composition and purity. The state's activity at that time was uneven and depended upon the foodstuff concerned and the pressure exerted by interest groups. As Anthony Giddens has noted, assessing and coping with risk is a highly political activity, due to the assignment of values and prioritisation of responses, and the history of food regulation in the twentieth century provides many examples of this.[2]

Our focus will be upon the milk industry, particularly on the struggle to eliminate bacterial danger using the heat treatment technology known as pasteurisation. There was a passionate public debate about pasteurisation from about 1900 to 1945, which we will examine through an account of the views of the two camps, the pro- and the anti-pasteurisation lobbies. It will be argued that this was essentially a clash between discourses that were opposed in their views on the desirability of the modernisation of food systems.

Our point of departure will be the contention that throughout the century it was mainly the relationship between science and the state that constituted the shape of food regulation. A naive model might assume that the discovery of 'facts' about food hygiene provided the raw material for policy action, and such a history would be a simple matter of matching laboratory research results with legislation. In reality, neither the science, nor the policy-making was straightforward. Almost every aspect of the scientific knowledge was contested, with some issues the subject of angry controversy. As regards the need for pasteurisation and the best technology for achieving it, the confusion afforded space on the battlefield to two main anti-pasteurisation groups. The first consisted of dairy farmers and small milk retailers, for whom the *status quo* was the cheapest and most profitable option. The second was a group of activists who for philosophical and ethical reasons opposed modern techno-logical solutions to problems of disease in the food system.

## The solidification of science and technology

The year 1901 was a turning point for the role of science in the milk food system. As described by Peter Koolmees in Chapter 4, this was when Robert Koch publicly challenged the view that tuberculosis could spread from animals to humans. In doing so Koch created a reactive wave of research by scientists who wished to prove him wrong.[3] But the Sale of Milk Regula-tions were also made in 1901, and for the first time the state legally defined and enforced a minimum level of fat in milk. The aim was to control adulteration, previously a common fraud,[4] but the effect was far reaching, because here was a government becoming embroiled in a debate about what should be considered 'natural'. The proportions of fat, solids-non-fat, and water in a cow's milk varied with many factors, such as feed, stage of lacta-tion, and breed, but now there would be penalties if minimum standards of composition were not met. Farmers were to be presumed dishonest if the level of water in their milk was too high.[5]

Such state surveillance was facilitated by the use of scientific instruments for measuring the specific gravity of milk and the initiation of advanced biochemical investigations. These, along with new bacteriological methods, made it possible from the turn of the century for local authority laboratories to pass judgement upon the integrity and hygienic quality of milk.

One of the infectious diseases discovered to be common in the milk of the day was bovine tuberculosis.[6] Despite Koch's views, most public health and medical professionals continued to believe it was a significant threat to human health and solutions were sought. The one arousing greatest enthu-siasm was pasteurisation, a method of heating milk until most pathogens are killed. But there was also much opposition. As noted in *A Dictionary of Dairying*, published in 1950: 'Probably no subject outside religion and poli-tics has been the cause of more prolonged and bitter controversies than the proposal compulsorily to pasteurize all milk'.[7] Much of the fuel for this controversy was uncertainty concerning the science and technology of both bovine tuberculosis and pasteurisation.[8] Successive generations of politicians cited this as a reason for inaction, and until 1950 they also ruled out, on the grounds of cost, the only effective alternative intervention to pasteurisation, which was the area-based slaughter of the 40 per cent of the dairy herd infected.

The first issue to be clarified was the aetiology and epidemiology of bovine tuberculosis. Koch's speech at the 1901 International Congress on Tuberculosis in London led to the establishment of a Royal Commission on Tuberculosis. This was unusual in being research-based and the reports issued in 1907 and 1911 assumed an aura of scientific confidence in identifying infected milk as the main cause of non-pulmonary human tuberculosis. Nevertheless, Koch's allies mounted a rearguard action that lasted for decades, and many members of the milk trade and most of the public continued to believe that the danger of catching tuberculosis from milk was insignificant.

The adoption of pasteurisation was slow at first. The first commercial equipment was manufactured in Germany in 1880, and by 1885 milk was regularly pasteurised in Copenhagen and Stockholm, but little happened in Britain for a further twenty years.[9] Only 1.5 per cent of Britain's supply was pasteurised in 1926.[10] The majority of retail milk was still raw in 1939 and this remained true in many small towns and rural areas well into the 1950s. One reason was that the early machinery was unreliable. In the so-called 'flash' process, for instance, milk was heated quickly to a high temperature in batches and then cooled, but the technology was primitive and was incapable of ensuring that the milk was treated evenly. The method was banned by the Milk (Special Designations) Order (1923), but continued in use unofficially for a time for milk that was not declared heat-treated. It was superseded, for the next two decades, by low temperature machines (63–71°C for 30 minutes) which heated the milk as it passed through a succession of large vessels. Finally HTST (High Temperature Short Time) methods were introduced in Britain in the 1940s, involving heating for 12–20 seconds at 75–6°C, giving a more effective result.[11]

In 1923 the technology then in use was considered to be 'from the consumers' point of view, absolutely useless'.[12] This was because heated milk, if not fully pasteurised, was a dangerous medium for the growth of bacteria. Table

*Table 3.1* Proportion of pasteurised milk failing the phosphatase test[13]

| *Where the pasteurised milk was sold* | *Percentage of samples failing to pass the phosphatase test* | |
|---|---|---|
| | *1935 survey* | *1937 survey* |
| To public in London | 44 | 32 |
| To public in towns over 20,000 population | 34 | 17 |
| To school children in London | 46 | 14 |
| To school children outside London | 58 | 22 |
| Total percentage | 47 | 22 |

3.1 suggests that matters were still unsatisfactory a decade later. The data are based on the phosphatase test, an indicator of whether pasteurisation had been carried out properly, developed by Graham (later Sir Graham) Selby Wilson, professor of bacteriology at the London School of Hygiene and Tropical Medicine. Surveys in 1935 and 1937 showed that many samples still contained viable mycobacteria. It is hardly surprising, therefore, that the public remained sceptical until the general adoption of the perfected technology after the Second World War.

## The public health debate about pasteurisation

In the light of the technological and theoretical uncertainties, how was it that a network of pro-pasteurisation lobbyists came into existence? The answer lies in the respective strength and political mobilisation of the two sides, for and against pasteurisation. From 1900 to about 1930 the anti-pasteurisation campaigners held the field. Under a broad banner opposing state intervention in dairy farming or the dairy trade, they were able to forestall or dilute the legislation that came forward. This was achieved by skilful parliamentary manoeuvring and by a fortuitous combination of events that saw Westminster's attention focused on a series of other major issues.

By 1930, it was obvious that the limited measures which had been introduced (the Milk and Dairies Act which came into operation in 1925, followed by the Milk and Dairies Order, 1926), were not having much impact. The pro-pasteurisation activists therefore began to regroup.

First, a highly motivated group of eminent doctors and scientists became involved in calling for pasteurisation. Wilson and Viscount Dawson of Penn, the King's physician, seem to have been the co-ordinators. They wrote letters to *The Lancet*, the *British Medical Journal* and *The Times* that were widely quoted.[14] By 1933 the government's own medical advisers were willing to state that 'it is clear that the only way of ensuring a safe general milk supply is pasteurisation'.[15] Wilson's book *The Pasteurization of Milk* (1942) was also a major landmark, and appeared in the same year as a Medical Research Council report warning of the increase of tuberculosis during the War.[16] Second, the British Medical Association (BMA) and other societies attempted an institutional route for expressing their concerns about milk. The BMA sponsored several delegations to the government but received most publicity for its 1938 poster and advertisement campaign warning of the dangers of unpasteurised milk. This caused controversy to such an extent that several newspapers refused BMA copy, presumably fearing the response of the milk trade.[17] Third, several weighty reports were published, giving statistical data on bovine tuberculosis and arguing for legislation on pasteurisation, which would at least allow individual local authorities to adopt schemes. The reports from the People's League of Health (1932), discussed by Margaret Barnett in Chapter 5, and a committee appointed by the Economic Advisory Council (1932), were especially pertinent. The more limited pronouncements of the Milk Reorganisation Commissions of 1933 and 1935 had gravitas, and, more importantly, gained the imprimatur of government for certain policy shifts.[18]

It is worth noting that the public health politics of the 1930s and 1940s were not overwhelmingly pro-pasteurisation. Even within the medical profession there were many opponents and one can detect the exasperation this caused in editorials in the medical press:

> Pasteurisation is one of those subjects that tend to generate more heat than light. It is a great pity that medical men who oppose pasteurisation support their case by misstatements of fact, or by ignoring those facts which are available to anyone who will take the trouble to spend an hour or two in a medical library. It is a pity, because their misstatements and ill-informed views are given much prominence in a press often enough, unfortunately, more anxious to please certain interests than to get at the truth of the matter.[19]

The opposition, although in a small minority by 1930, provided policy makers with a loophole. Thus Earl de la Warr, parliamentary secretary to the Ministry of Agriculture, in 1931 issued a call for unanimity before the state could be expected to intervene:

> The medical profession ... would also help the government if they would make up their minds as to what they really felt about milk. Before the medical profession come down on the farming industry for not taking certain steps about milk, they should really make up their minds what they wanted the farmers to do.[20]

## Capitalism and germs

From the turn of the century heat treatment of milk started in Britain in a small way.[21] It was introduced in London by Wiltshire United Dairies, Express Dairies and other large companies as a means of delaying souring and increasing shelf-life.[22] There was no initial concern about disease *per se* and retailers did not declare the intervention to their customers, who would then have realised that freshness was not always guaranteed. The cynical interpretation of one writer in the *British Medical Journal* was not far from the truth:

> If it had not been essential for the dairy trade of today (a series of large combines collecting milk of various ages over a wide area) to find some system whereby they could ensure delivery to the consumer in a sweet condition, it would appear doubtful that general pasteurisation of milk would ever have come to the fore.[23]

Producer-retailers, however, were responsible for about 20 per cent of milk sold and they opposed pasteurisation.[24] They offered 'milk from the cow' and, since many could not afford their own pasteurising and bottling plant, compulsory pasteurisation would have meant taking their own milk to a depot and receiving an anonymous product in return.[25] The direct link with the land, upon which their goodwill depended, would be destroyed. They opposed the move towards compulsory pasteurisation implicit in the Milk Industry Bill of 1938 and, partly because of MPs representing their interests, it did not reach the statute book.[26] The large dairy companies, ever anxious to eliminate smaller competitors, were in favour of compulsory pasteurisation and supported war-time efforts to rationalise delivery rounds, to the detriment of the producer-retailers.

## Resistance from neo-romanticism and anti-modernism

In considering perceptions of the pros and cons of pasteurisation, it is worth investigating the intellectual roots of the ideas deployed. Starting with the environmentalism of the early twentieth century, we can trace its origins to the dirt and disease-obsessed hygienist discourse of the Victorian era. But it also had a new element of what Frank Trentmann calls 'neo-romanticism', a bourgeois cultural movement that had offshoots in various countries.[27] The fresh air, hiking and healthy body ideas of the popular German youth movements of the 1920s and 1930s had their parallels in Britain and inspired broad-spectrum responses across the class and political divides. The Boy Scouts, Girl Guides, Ramblers' Association, Youth Hostel Association and Kibbo Kift Kin all represented a muscular interpretation of leisure in the open countryside, and a new and institutionalised experience of nature.

Complementary to such action-based and lifestyle philosophies was the flood of writing about rural England that peaked in 1930–45.[28] H. J. Massingham is an example of one author who helped create an interpretation of the countryside as a repository of precious traditional values. Together these ideas and the fresh air activities forged what for David Matless is 'a particular landscaped version of English citizenship', a new set of identities which were mediated through the relationship between humans and nature.[29] Several strands of the critique of modernism and other neo-romanticist expressions were related to the anti-pasteurisation position.

The first cluster of criticisms arose out of ideas concerning organic farming and clean milk. There was much scepticism about modern farming methods such as the use of fertilisers and other chemicals, and also about mechanised cultivation and machine milking. On the one hand these techniques were seen as displacing jobs in the countryside and encouraging migration to urban areas. On the other, modern farming was accused of degrading soil fertility and leading to soil erosion.[30]

In response, figures such as Lady Eve Balfour attempted to popularise organic farming, drawing inspiration from techniques of recycling organic matter that had been developed in colonial India.[31] A common aim was the re-establishment of mixed farming, considered to be the optimum type of enterprise for English ecological conditions. It comprised a holistic system in which waste products were swapped between the arable and livestock sides, reducing the need for artificial inputs. The greatest possible self-sufficiency also had the merit of minimising the risk of introducing disease with new stock.

Pasteurisation was criticised by organic farmers as proof of the failure of modern farming. It treated the symptoms and not the cause of the problem, the over-intensification of production in conditions of dirt and disease, coupled with a disregard for traditional principles of good husbandry. Lady Balfour was especially critical of pasteurised milk. In her view, it was in the interests only of dirty producers and large dairy companies. Pasteurisation allowed the former to 'get away with' dirty milk that would otherwise go sour, while the latter were enabled 'to sell milk several days old without the customer being aware of the fact'. For Lady Balfour,

> … pasteurisation can never be a good thing in itself. It should be regarded even by its advocates as the lesser of two evils. The necessity for it, where it exists, is a confession of failure. The aim should be to abandon the practice just as soon as the need for it – unhealthy cows and dirty methods – can be eliminated.[32]

This version of the argument saw pasteurisation as both unnecessary and counter-productive. What was needed was a revolution in farm hygiene that would guarantee a dirt- and germ-free product. In order to begin the task of changing attitudes, Wilfred Buckley and Waldorf Astor founded a National Clean Milk Society in 1916.[33] Their campaign lasted for over a decade and involved a wide range of activities. They sponsored National Milk Conferences in the 1920s, at which the issues were formally debated, but their most important contribution was the encouragement of research on the best methods of clean milk production.[34] This was undertaken from 1920 onwards at the Research Institute in Dairying at Reading (later the National Institute for Research in Dairying), and was inspired by the leadership of Robert Stenhouse Williams.[35]

A second major strand of anti-modernist thinking was concerned with the effect of the perceived unwholesomeness of food on the long-term future of the 'British race'. The origins of the depressed tone of much of the literature lay in the turn of the century 'physical deterioration' debate that erupted after many army recruits were found unfit to fight the Boers.[36] Such fears were rekindled by inter-war reports using rather a different rhetoric and methods of data collection, such as John Boyd Orr's *Food, Health and Income* (1936), which claimed that half of the population was undernourished.[37] Although many politicians played down such statistics, others argued that the modernisation of British society had been a failure in terms of the living standards and health of the majority of the people. Viscount Lymington, for example, commented:

> For all our medical work in reducing certain contagious diseases and prolonging the expectation of life, a man full of vigorous health is almost a museum piece in this country. Subnormality in health and degenerative disease in mild or acute form are the average in this country, so much so that we take it for granted.[38]

One explanation adduced was that these weak and unhealthy bodies were the result of poor childhood nutrition and the debilitating effects of urban living, but worries were also expressed about the effect of poor quality food upon the population generally. By the 1930s a link was asserted between declining fertility of the soil and the health of the race, with interesting echoes of the blood and soil rhetoric that was to take hold in Germany. Viscount Lymington, a Conservative MP 1929–34 (later the Earl of Portsmouth), was one advocate of this view of deterioration.[39] For him whole foods, including milk, unmodified by processing, were an essential part of national salvation.

It was the lot of milk to bear much ideological baggage, including notions about racial health and vigour. Those concerned with such issues, including some eugenicists whose usual focus was upon hereditary factors, claimed that the strength and fertility of the nation would be threatened by making milk unnatural by pasteurisation. One correspondent to the *British Medical Journal*, for example, claimed in 1938 that as a result of pasteurisation, 'the shadow of depopulation and national decline is looming in the near future'.[40]

Concerns about poor diets and their consequences had encouraged activists to demand a government-sponsored system of school milk provision, in the hope that well-nourished children would contribute to renewed national virility. The first feeding trials, financed by the National Milk Publicity Council, were started in Birmingham in 1922–3.[41] By 1930, 35,000 children received free milk, subsidised by Local Education Authorities and a further 48,000 paid for a daily supply. The National Milk Publicity Council reached an additional 500,000 with their own scheme of school milk provided in one-third pint bottles for 1d.[42] In 1934 this activity was replaced when the government's own nation-wide milk-in-schools scheme was introduced, which reduced the price to 1/2d. The main objective of this, however, was to help a beleaguered dairy industry find a new outlet. Most of the milk supplied to schools was not pasteurised and, ironically, more children than ever were exposed to the dangers of raw milk.[43]

One final point should be mentioned on the theme of the health of the race. Another argument against pasteurisation was the suggestion that milk infected with bovine tuberculosis could help build immunity in the population against the human form of the disease. The principle of inoculation was well understood in the early century but, despite experiments and false dawns, no reliable anti-tuberculosis vaccine was developed. The BCG vaccine was not commonly used in Britain until the 1950s. In this light, the consumption of raw milk was proposed by some as the only practical mechanism of mass-inoculation. In truth, there is evidence that long term exposure to bovine tuberculosis does indeed reduce morbidity and mortality from the human form. However, the dose of bacteria administered by contaminated milk was uncontrollable and estimates indicate that over 200,000 deaths were caused by transmission of tuberculosis from animals to humans in England and Wales during 1900–50.[44]

A third, important group of anti-modernist themes was coupled with right wing opposition to state intervention. Lymington, for instance, asserted that successive governments were to blame for the inter-war agricultural depression because of their 'interference' in farming. He thought the Milk and Dairies Order (1926) had 'made cowshed costs fantastic at the instance of theorists in the Ministry of Health'. He deplored, as 'state socialism', the establishment by the National Government of the Milk Marketing Boards in 1933 and resigned from parliament soon afterwards.[45] He argued that pasteurisation lessened the incentive to produce clean milk and guaranteed only the consumption of 'bulked cemeteries of cooked germs'. He thought compulsory pasteurisation a 'supreme folly'.[46]

Lymington had early sympathies with fascism: he visited Hitler and Mussolini and he narrowly avoided internment in 1939.[47] He was also drawn into William Sanderson's 'English Mistery', a society stressing the need for a revival of pre-industrial traditions and Anglo-Saxon identity. Membership included Reginald Dorman-Smith, who became Minister of Agriculture (1939–40) and Rolf Gardiner, an organic farmer and opponent of processed foods. Gardiner had been a member of the Social Credit movement as an undergraduate and built strong links with the German youth movements in the 1920s.[48] When he took up farming in Wiltshire he formed the 'Springhead Ring' of enthusiasts in youth work, folk dance, forestry and farming, and his estate became a meeting place for German visitors and British Germanophiles. Gardiner wrote about his desire for closer links across the North Sea and this crystallised after 1933 into an admiration for Nazism.[49] He later claimed that National Socialism had betrayed the principles of blood and soil, and called for the replacement of centralised planning by local, organic reconstruction according to traditional yeoman values. His vision was always hierarchical, however, with landowners such as himself providing the lead socially and economically.[50]

Lymington, Gardiner, and other prominent conservative thinkers were critical of the power of capital in modern society. They regretted its role in industrialisation and urbanisation, and the associated social problems. The separation of consumers from farmers by corporate intermediaries such as food companies or marketing boards was another negative consequence that encouraged processing and preservation of perishable foodstuffs. They were nostalgic for the roots of English civilisation, and proposed a modified version of rural society that would be yeoman-dominated and centred on small-scale communities.

This was not new. There had been a widespread call for a movement 'back to the land' in the first two decades of the century. Lloyd George had been captivated by the idea and had devoted much energy to this and other rural matters, such as land tenure reform. The neo-romantics had an idealised vision of hardy, self-reliant farmers, and organisations such as the Rural Reconstruction Association (founded 1925) and the Kinship of Husbandry took up these ideas.[51] The latter was established by Lymington and included Gardiner, writers Massingham and Edmund Blunden, and historian Arthur Bryant. They were in close touch with German 'green' ideas.

A fourth strand of environmental neo-romanticism was its spiritual dimension, or what David Matless calls nature-mysticism.[52] This entailed a reverence for the sublimity and wholeness of nature which extended from the transcendental contemplation of landscape, through what nowadays would be called 'deep ecology', to a desire for 'whole' and 'natural' foods. D. H. Lawrence was an inspiration to many with his self-confident Nietzschian individualism, and a strong bio-mysticism derived from Haeckel and Emerson.[53] Lawrence's philosophy was vitalistic and based upon a belief in the restless energy of the universe. His novels stand for the preference of many of his contemporaries for the life force of the organic over the cold calculation of a mechanistic modern civilisation.[54] He is reported to have written to Gardiner supporting the latter's connections with the German youth movement and commenting: 'the Germans take their shirts off and work in the hay: they are still physical: the English are so woefully disembodied'.[55]

Further ideological input came from the theosophical teaching of Rudolf Steiner (1861–1925) on biodynamic farming. The immediate source for this was Ehrenfried Pfeiffer, a disciple of Steiner, whose farm in Holland became a place of pilgrimage for the British ecological élite in the 1930s.[56] Steiner's lectures on agriculture, delivered in 1924, stressed the spiritual cosmic features of the environment rather than the materialist interpretation of chemists.[57] The Kinship of Husbandry was well aware of Steiner's work and it is no surprise that the writings of Lymington and Gardiner have vitalistic overtones. Much anti-pasteurisation rhetoric absorbed the notion of hidden energies and unknown qualities. Such ideas also derived momentum from the mythic appeal of mother's milk.[58] As breast-feeding declined amongst certain groups of women, some of this respect was transferred to the obvious substitute, cow's milk.

Our fifth and final element of anti-modernism drew strength from the new scientific knowledge of nutrition, which was embraced by some who might otherwise have based their anti-pasteurisation arguments on vitalism. Immediately after the First World War, just when pasteurisation was becoming common in large cities such as London and Glasgow, new scientific findings appeared to confirm the idea that milk (and other foods) might contain important but unknown substances which were threatened by pasteurisation and other forms of processing. This was the so-called 'newer knowledge of nutrition' which demonstrated the presence in milk and other foods of micronutrients that became known as 'accessory food factors' or 'vitamines' (later 'vitamins'). F. G. Hopkins had worked on this topic from 1906 to 1912 but it was the further research of others that established the detailed implications.[59] By 1920 vitamins were more widely known and after this, milk drinkers became gradually aware of the micronutrients they were consuming.[60] Concerns were raised about the effect of pasteurisation upon the vitamin content of milk and questions were even asked in the House of Commons about the matter.[61]

Arguments about the alleged effects of pasteurisation upon the vitamin content of milk were related to those based on vitalism and anti-modernist sentiments. During the 1930s the research of E. C. V. Mattick and J. Golding showed that rats fed on a diet of sterilised milk were unable to reproduce, and that those fed solely on pasteurised milk suffered from vitamin B deficiencies.[62] These findings formed part of the basis of the arguments about racial vigour mentioned earlier. Another example, linking anti-modernism, notions of 'dead' milk and the 'newer knowledge of nutrition' is provided in a contribution by L. J. Picton, Hon. Secretary of the Cheshire Medical Committees, to the *British Medical Journal* in 1938:

> Much of modern food is processed, preserved, refined, sterilised, dead ... Contrast the insipid pasteurised fluid of today to the milk of our forefathers ... We are constantly told there is 'no significant difference' between the processed milk and the fresh, as if the loss of ascorbic acid (vitamin C) and the insolubility of lime and phosphorus caused by heating were of no account.[63]

## Post-war debates

At the end of the Second World War, Ben Davies, a spokesman for the milk trade, confidently asserted that 'the old debates on pasteurisation were over'.[64] The official historian of the food system during World War Two saw wartime government control as a turning point. The balance of power had shifted decisively in the favour of those who advocated pasteurisation and 'the "milk enthusiasts" had entered into their kingdom at long last'.[65] Gradually, pasteurisation spread in the 1950s from the large cities to smaller towns and rural areas. Tuberculosis was becoming less of a threat and the Tuberculin Tested grade of milk was finally abolished in 1964 as no longer necessary.

The anti-pasteurisation movement may have hoped to be left in peace as a niche market among consenting consumers aware of the risks, but they came under periodic attack during the last twenty years of the century. Pasteurisation was made compulsory in Scotland in 1983 and there were moves to extend this to England and Wales in 1989 and again in 1997–98 as a result of the international regulatory drive of the Codex Alimentarius Commission of the United Nations. The latest debate gained much publicity, mainly due to lobby groups such as the Campaign for Real Milk and the Association of Unpasteurized Milk Producers and Consumers, founded in 1989 and headed by Sir Julian Rose. These groups deploy several arguments but the most powerful one concerns freedom of choice.[66] The quality press was supportive of this and was particularly scathing about the efforts of the 'health police' and the 'nanny state' in attempting to impose pasteurisation.[67]

After a lengthy consultation process about the possible compulsory enforcement of pasteurisation in England and Wales, the Ministry of Agriculture in January 1999 renewed its approval of 'green top' milk but at the same time increased the stringency of the hygiene tests it has to pass. This will squeeze

22 H. A. Macewan, *The Public Milk Supply*, London, Blackie, 1910, p. 80; W. V. Shaw, 'Report on the pasteurization of milk in England', in *Departmental Committee of Production and Distribution of Milk*, (Chairman, W. Astor), Third Interim Report, *Parliamentary Papers*, 1919, vol. xxv (Cmd. 315), pp. 634–41.

23 N. MacFadyen, 'Pasteurisation of milk', *British Medical Journal*, 1938, vol. 1, pp. 148–9, 259.

24 R. J. Hammond, *Food. Volume 2: studies in administration and control*, London, HMSO and Longmans, Green, 1956, pp. 252–3.

25 W. G. Savage, 'Pasteurisation in relation to milk distribution', *The Lancet*, 1931, vol. 1, pp. 543–6.

26 J. L. Davies, 'The production, marketing and supply of milk', *Proceedings of the Nutrition Society*, 1944, vol. 2, pp. 123–37, at 132.

27 F. Trentmann, 'Civilization and its discontents: English neo-romanticism and the transformation of anti-modernism in twentieth century western culture', *Journal of Contemporary History*, 1994, vol. 29, pp. 583–625.

28 For instance the output of the Batsford publishing house. See M. Chase, 'This is no claptrap: this is our heritage', in C. Shaw, and M. Chase (eds), *The Imagined Past: History and Nostalgia*, Manchester, Manchester University Press, 1989, pp. 128–46.

29 D. Matless, 'The art of right living: landscape and citizenship, 1918–39', in S. Pile and N. J. Thrift (eds), *Mapping the Subject: Geographies of Cultural Transformation*, London, Routledge, 1995, pp. 93–122.

30 Viscount Lymington, *Famine in England*, London, Witherby, 1938.

31 E. B. Balfour, *The Living Soil: Evidence of the Importance to Human Health of Soil Vitality, with Special Reference to Post-War Planning*, London, Faber & Faber, 1948 (eighth edition).

32 Ibid. pp. 210–11.

33 W. Buckley, 'Limits of pasteurisation: better milk means more business', *The Milk Industry*, 1922, vol. 2, no. 8, pp. 79–81.

34 The 1923 conference attracted delegates from seventy-five County Councils and Local Authorities, forty-five from companies and universities, and fifteen from overseas. Anon., 'National Milk Conference', *The Dairyman, The Cowkeeper and Dairyman's Journal*, December, 1923, pp. 184–207.

35 K. Vernon, 'Science for the farmer? Agricultural research in England 1909–36', *Twentieth Century British History*, 1997, vol. 8, pp. 310–33.

36 F. L. Dodd, *The Problem of the Milk Supply*, London, Baillière, Tindall & Cox, 1904, chap. 1; B. B. Gilbert, 'Health and politics: the British Physical Deterioration Report of 1904', *Bulletin of the History of Medicine*, 1965, vol. 39, pp. 143–53.

37 J. B. Orr, *Food, Health and Income*, London, Macmillan, 1936.

38 Viscount Lymington, 'The policy of husbandry', in H. J. Massingham (ed.), *England and the Farmer: A Symposium*, London, Faber, 1941, pp. 12–31, at p. 13.

39 Viscount Lymington, 1938, 1941, op. cit.

40 H. Sutherland, 'Pasteurisation of milk', *British Medical Journal*, 1938, vol. 1, p. 704.

41 A. Jenkins, *Drinka Pinta: The Story of Milk and the Industry that Serves it*, London, Heinemann, 1970.

42 Sir C. Trevelyan, President of the Board of Education, written answer, *Parliamentary Debates (Commons)*, 1930, vol. 244, cols 1863–64.

43 J. Francis, *Tuberculosis in Animals and Man*, London, Cassell, 1958, pp. 91–2. For more details and further references to the start up of the milk-in-schools scheme, see B. Harris, *The Health of the School Child*, Buckingham, Open University Press, 1995, pp. 124–5.

44 P. J. Atkins and N. J. Cox, 'Consumptive bodies and risk: the comparative pathology of bovine tuberculosis in Britain, 1850–1950', unpublished ms, 2000.

45 Viscount Lymington, 1938, op. cit.; Earl of Portsmouth, *Alternative to Death: The Relationship Between Soil, Family and Community*, London, Faber, 1943, p. 85.

46 Viscount Lymington, 1938, op. cit., pp. 255–7.

47 Earl of Portsmouth, *A Knot of Roots: An Autobiography*, London, Bles, 1965.

48 See Chapter 6 for some background to Social Credit.

49 R. Griffiths, *Fellow Travellers of the Right: British Enthusiasts for Nazi Germany 1933–9*, London, Constable, 1980, pp. 144–5.

50 R. Gardiner, 'Rural reconstruction', in H. J. Massingham, op. cit., pp. 91–107.

51 M. Fordham, *The Land and Life: A Survey of Problems of the Land in Relation to the Future Rural Life of Britain, with a Policy for Agriculture after the War*, London, Routledge, 1942.

52 D. Matless, 'Nature, the modern and the mystic: tales from early twentieth century geography', *Transactions of the Institute of British Geographers*, 1991, new series, vol. 16, pp. 272–86.

53 A. Bramwell, *Ecology in the 20th Century: A History*, New Haven, Yale University Press, 1989, p. 113.

54 R. Ebbatson, *Lawrence and the Nature Tradition: a Theme in English Fiction 1859–1914*, Brighton, Harvester, 1980, pp. 28–66.

55 R. Griffiths, op. cit., p. 144.

56 E. Pfeiffer, *Bio-Dynamic Farming and Gardening: Soil Fertility, Renewal and Preservation*, New York, Anthroposophic Press, 1940 (second edition).

57 R. Steiner, *Agriculture*, London, Biodynamic Agricultural Association, 1958, pp. 9–10.

58 F. McKee, 'The popularization of milk as a beverage during the 1930s', in D. F. Smith (ed.), *Nutrition in Britain: Science, Scientists and Politics in the Twentieth Century*, London, Routledge, 1997, pp. 123–41, at 123.

59 E. V. McCollum, *A History of Nutrition: The Sequence of Ideas in Nutrition Investigations*, Boston, Houghton Mifflin, 1957, pp. 201–424.

60 V. G. Plimmer and R. H. A. Plimmer, *Vitamins and the Choice of Food*, London: Longmans, Green, 1922; R. H. A. Plimmer and V. G. Plimmer, *Food, Health and Vitamins*, London, Longmans, Green, 1925.

61 Major Boyd-Carpenter, Minister of Labour representing the Ministry of Health, written answer, *Parliamentary Debates (Commons)*, 1922, vol. 159, col. 2030.

62 E. C. V. Mattick and J. Golding, 'Relative value of raw and heated milk in nutrition', *The Lancet*, 1931, vol. 1, pp. 662–7; E. C. V. Mattick and J. Golding, 'Relative value of raw and heated milk in nutrition', *The Lancet*, 1936, vol. 1, pp. 1132–4; vol. 2, pp. 702–6.

63 L. J. Picton, 'Pasteurisation of milk', *British Medical Journal*, 1938, vol. 1, p. 812; L. J. Picton, 'Diet and farming' in H. J. Massingham op. cit., pp. 108–30, at 112.

64 Anon., 'Veterinary and medical control of milk supply', *British Medical Journal*, 1945, vol. 1, 340–1.

65 R.J. Hammond, op. cit., pp. 271–2.

66 B. M. Pickard, *The Case for Untreated Milk*, Haughley, Stowmarket, Soil Association, 1984; Soil Association, *Government Consultation on the Proposed Ban on Raw Cow's Drinking Milk: Draft Submission*, Bristol, Soil Association, 1998.

67 For instance J. Blythman, 'Raw deal', *The Guardian*, 28 June 1997, p. 41, and 6 December 1997, p. 55.

68 M. Pyke, *Food and Society*, London, Murray, 1968, pp. 77–80.

# 4   Veterinary inspection and food hygiene in the twentieth century

*Peter A. Koolmees*

During the past few decades, scholars from a wide range of disciplines in Europe and North America, including historians, sociologists and physicians, have investigated aspects of public health in the past.[1] Within this well-established research area, attention to issues of veterinary public health has been limited, in spite of the considerable overlap between the public health care provided by physicians and veterinarians. This is particularly true with respect to the quality control of food of animal origin and zoonoses (infectious diseases communicable from animals to humans). Much attention has been paid to the role of physicians and chemists in safeguarding food quality and in improving public health.[2] However, the contribution made by veterinarians to food quality control is often underestimated.[3]

Veterinary public health may be defined as all the interactions between animals and animal products on the one side and human health on the other. The history of this field has been recorded predominantly by veterinarians, who have described developments from antiquity, and especially scientific and technical progress throughout the twentieth century.[4] These studies mainly deal with the recognition of animal disease problems as they have affected public health, and with the establishment of national and international organisations. They pay little attention to the development of food hygiene and related social and economic factors.

To obtain deeper insights into the development of veterinary inspection and food hygiene in The Netherlands, this chapter will focus on two issues. Firstly, it will explore the role of the veterinary profession in the quality control of food of animal origin. Secondly, it will examine the scientific development of meat hygiene, particularly the long-continued preoccupation of veterinary inspectors with bovine tuberculosis. Finally, some parallels will be drawn between the pressures and controversies in the first decades of the twentieth century and the role of the veterinary profession in the present day context of integrated quality control.

## Extension of veterinary services

*Hominum animaliumque saluti* (to the benefit of man and animal alike) is a motto often used by Dutch veterinarians to indicate their role in maintaining animal resources and protecting animal and human health. However, the task of protecting human health only became part of the domain of the veterinarian at a relatively late stage. Veterinary medicine gradually developed from an applied science supporting agriculture and the military to its present role in the medical sciences. Today, a well-developed veterinary infrastructure exists in the western world, within which the production and supply of safe foods of animal origin is one of the main tasks. This infrastructure is usually taken for granted and only becomes the focus of attention when food poisoning scandals occur. Nevertheless, the ready availability of safe foods such as dairy products and meat, has only been established through a slow and laborious process. Before responsibilities involving food hygiene and zoonoses control were entrusted to veterinarians around 1900, the professionalisation and scientific progress of veterinary medicine were necessary.[5]

The rise of veterinary medicine in The Netherlands in the second half of the nineteenth century coincided with the strong development of intensive livestock farming and meat and dairy production. Cattle breeding expanded from 1870 as a result of a rising demand for meat domestically. There were also increasing opportunities for exporting meat and meat products to industrialised countries like Great Britain, France and Germany, where the living standards and disposable income of the working class were improving. The increase in production was realised by intensive farming based on fertilisers, increased animal feed production, innovations in cattle breeding, and the organised struggle against animal diseases. More and more veterinarians were needed. Akin to more industrialised neighbouring countries, a quantitative and qualitative improvement in diet occurred in The Netherlands due to industrialisation, economic growth, and a gradual rise in the standard of living. Between 1850 and 1930, the annual *per capita* meat consumption in The Netherlands increased from 27 to 50 kg.[6]

During the nineteenth century, knowledge of the chemical composition of food and nutrients requirements increased. Many physiologists, chemists and physicians stressed the importance of a high protein intake. Most authorities considered that about 90 kg of meat per year was required as the minimum quantity for optimum nutrition. They stated that a population deprived of protein of animal origin would become weak and produce only moderate labourers and soldiers.[7] In England, the level of meat consumption remained high throughout the nineteenth century, which was noticed with envy by other European countries. Economists attributed the seemingly effortless manner in which Britain created its Indian Empire to the high meat consumption of the British and the vegetarianism of the Indians.[8] Further, technologists argued that European nations with the highest meat consumption not only generated the most successful colonists, but also produced the most technological innovations. The British veterinarian Stewart Stockman believed that the future belonged to 'the flesh-eating nations'.[9]

Such notions provide an explanation as to why not only many scientists, physicians and veterinarians, but also politicians, economists and military leaders and strategists attached great importance to high meat consumption. Consequently, a broad consensus existed that more meat in the diet was desirable, prerequisites for which were improvements in the quantity and the quality of supplies. The growth of meat consumption and concern about its quality provide the immediate context of the entry of the veterinary profession into food hygiene.

## Veterinarians and meat hygiene

A review of the meat supply around 1900 reveals that the cheap meat consumed by the working class left much to be desired. In the Dutch countryside home slaughtering was common. In most cities, butchers slaughtered animals in small, privately owned butcheries. From around 1870, population growth and urbanisation went hand in hand with an expanded network of butcheries, where slaughtering often took place under unhygienic conditions. The city of Utrecht, for instance, with a population of about 100,000 in 1890, had 114 registered private butcheries, 378 'shops' where meat was sold, and a market for cheap meat and sausages. Meat from knackers' yards was marketed or processed into pies and sausages and sold to the poor. Often this involved meat from slaughtered animals infected with bacteriological diseases such as anthrax and tuberculosis, with the parasitic nematode worm trichinella, or with tapeworms, as well as meat from animals that had died from disease or other causes. A mere four inspectors monitored all these enterprises.[10]

Under these circumstances consumers were left almost unprotected against fraud and adulteration. For instance, old, worn out and even dead horses were collected and processed by knackers, after which the meat was sold as 'smoked beef'. Almost inevitably, calamities followed. This was even more the case as the chain between producers and consumers became longer and more complicated in view of the development of a large-scale international meat trade.[11] Poor conditions characterised meat and sausage processing due to lack of awareness of hygiene. The increasing number of butcheries represented a nuisance for the population. The transport and slaughtering of animals, and the storage and transport of offal within the cities, damaged the environment. Numerous outbreaks of trichinosis and meat poisonings occurred, infecting hundreds and killing dozens of people.[12] Consequently, local and national authorities were confronted with complaints about the filth and nuisance of butcheries, and the poor quality of the meat offered.[13] The outbreaks of meat-borne diseases alarmed the authorities and demonstrated the need for meat hygiene control. Improvement of the urban environment, the meat trade, and meat inspection regulations, became regular issues in local and national politics towards the turn of the century. Radical measures were needed.

A programme was available which contained the two essential factors for effective meat inspection: mandatory inspection by veterinarians and centralised slaughtering in public abattoirs on the outskirts of towns. Such a programme was drawn up by French and German hygienists at the end of the eighteenth century. Local and national health boards advocated these measures, but active intervention by a centralised state bureaucracy was needed for progress to be made.[14] Following the French example, health boards were established in most larger towns in The Netherlands in the second half of the nineteenth century. Within these boards, the 'hygienists', a group of progressive physicians, engineers, physicists, chemists, lawyers, veterinarians and civil servants, played a predominant role. They tried to realise public health programmes by means of a scientific approach and professionalisation, but their great accomplishment was to turn public health into a political issue.[15] Due to the veterinarians' knowledge of food hygiene, they participated in these health boards from the outset.

Despite the programme of the French and German hygienists, in the first half of the nineteenth century there was essentially no scientifically based meat inspection in Western Europe and hardly any veterinarians involved in meat inspection. Untrained inspectors were appointed in larger towns, but from 1860 veterinarians involved in the health boards began to advise on all matters concerning veterinary public health. They were able to deploy their training in the recognition of diseased animals and their knowledge of zoonoses. The veterinarians focussed on a scientific and legally based form of meat inspection, research on meat poisonings, humane slaughtering, and regulations for the collection and destruction of butchery and slaughterhouse waste. However, physicians played a predominant role in the health boards. In their view, veterinarians lacked scientific knowledge and were responsible for livestock only. In the physicians' view, public health, including meat inspection, should remain in their own competent hands. Initially, mainly physicians wrote about meat hygiene. Nevertheless, in various countries, veterinarians started to publish on the subject, claiming this new field for themselves. In their books and articles, these authors stressed the importance of veterinary medicine for society as a whole. They argued that it was essential for a prosperous livestock industry and for safeguarding the quality of foods of animal origin, and therefore for preserving the health and working capacity of the labouring classes.[16]

The efforts of veterinarians to establish veterinary public health were strongly supported by national veterinary associations. These associations recognised the potential job opportunities in meat inspection services and slaughterhouses and a possible broadening of the legal basis of the profession.[17] Because of the contributions of veterinarians to municipal and national health boards, the authorities reinforced or updated their regulations on meat inspection. A large number of towns made plans to establish abattoirs, often initiated by veterinarians. Besides local activities, some veterinarians were involved in formulating national meat inspection legislation.

## Public abattoirs

As for slaughterhouses, Napoleonic France was the European leader; until well into the nineteenth century, the Parisian abattoirs (built 1810–14) were regarded as exemplary. The French example was followed in some European countries, especially in Belgium, but from around 1880, Germany, Switzerland and Austria–Hungary took the lead. England, Spain, The Netherlands, and the Scandinavian countries lagged behind.[18]

In general, there was strong opposition to public slaughterhouses from butchers in all West European countries. Having played an essential role in the municipal meat supply for centuries, they feared the public slaughterhouses would undermine their profession. They would be forced to slaughter cattle at the public abattoir under supervision. The competency of municipal authorities to establish a public slaughterhouse and to prohibit private slaughtering, the so-called 'slaughter-warrant', became a politically contentious issue around 1900. In a number of countries, this matter was settled by a National Nuisance Act. Most local authorities hesitated in establishing slaughterhouses due to the large financial expenditure required, possible increases in meat prices, and questions of profitability. Competition for local financing came from other expensive sanitary reform projects. In lengthy debates between supporters and opponents of municipal slaughterhouses, two factions could be distinguished. Hygienists, with demands for adequate meat inspection, allied with animal protectionists and citizens with nuisance complaints, were opposed by a coalition of butchers and meat traders whose independence was threatened. At first, economic interests and the objections of butchers outweighed the public health arguments. By the turn of the century, however, the stimulus of socialist ideas, and the increasing acceptability of interference by local and national authorities in commercial life, tipped the balance in favour of public slaughterhouses. Ultimately, though, the decision to establish a public slaughterhouse depended mostly on the financial position of the municipality and hence upon general economic fluctuations.[19]

The enactment of the Dutch meat inspection law in 1919 stimulated the building of public slaughterhouses indirectly, since it involved hygienic requirements concerning private abattoirs and butchers' shops, and obliged local authorities to establish a meat inspection service. Many private butcheries could not meet the new requirements, leading many cities to build public slaughterhouses in order to institute an adequate meat inspection service. Between 1883 and 1940, a network of eighty-six municipal slaughterhouses developed in The Netherlands. Apart from the positive influence of the Meat Inspection Act, it was mainly the favourable financial position of the cities from 1922–9 that contributed to this rapid growth.[20]

## Meat inspection legislation

When we compare the period in which state control of the quality and supply of meat was instituted in various countries, considerable differences can be identified. The timing of implementation of centralised slaughtering in public abattoirs and mandatory meat inspection under veterinary supervision depended on the different political and economic situations in each nation. Until the 1920s, The Netherlands lagged behind compared to other countries due to the liberal doctrines of free trade and the restriction of state interference that prevailed. Attempts by hygienists to introduce regular meat inspection failed due to the authorities' belief that consumers were their own best food inspectors. As with aid to the poor and other aspects of public health, meat inspection was considered best left to the private sector. Meat inspection was unattractive for another, more practical reason: it would hinder exports and free trade in meat and meat products. In the absence of strong direction from central government, progress towards full veterinary inspection of slaughterhouses was a gradual process in The Netherlands and England.[21]

By the turn of the century, the lack of effective meat inspection was felt badly because serious outbreaks of meat-borne disease still occurred regularly. In addition, foreign markets demanded veterinary surveillance to guarantee quality standards of meat imported from The Netherlands. Several reports, including a comprehensive one from the Netherlands Veterinary Association,[22] clearly documented the deplorable situation of meat inspection and lack of public abattoirs. Due to the increased political influence of socialist organisations and politicians, central government began to take more responsibility for social legislation, as part of the process of modernising society. The socialists had fifteen of the 100 seats in Parliament by 1913, and twenty-two by 1918. The government became more willing to spend public money on social provisions, as part of the gradual transition from the state as 'night-watchman' to modern welfare. In 1892, 6 per cent of the national budget was spent on education, social care and housing; by 1913 this had increased to 25 per cent.[23] As part of these general trends, the government was urged to enact meat hygiene legislation.

The slaughter-warrant was instituted by the Nuisance Acts of 1875 and 1901. As a result of complaints about the quality of exported meat, a law regulating the inspection of meat for export was passed in 1902. However, this act was only permissive: companies could still export meat without inspection. Following the example of Denmark, the inspection of meat for export became mandatory in 1907. In 1914, a bill on domestic meat inspection was prepared but its passage was delayed by the First World War. During the war, the government was forced to intervene more and more in economic matters, in order to safeguard food supply and distribution. Measures included the control of food quality, because of the increasing frequency of adulteration. Immediately after the war, the government pressed on with legislation. The 1914 domestic meat inspection bill became law in 1919. This was part of a programme of social legislation quickly enacted after a failed attempt, in November 1918, by social-democratic leader P. J. Troelstra (1860–1930) to launch a socialist revolution in The Netherlands. Both the Food and Drugs and Meat Inspection Acts became effective in 1922.[24]

In England, the situation was similar. In 1932, veterinary officer T. Dunlop Young compared meat inspection regulations in England with other countries. He quoted German veterinarian Robert von Ostertag (1864–1940), founder of scientific meat inspection, as stating in 1905: 'England, which is otherwise so well organised with regard to public sanitation and called the cradle of hygiene, is entirely without a regulated system of meat inspection'. Regarding the adoption of public abattoirs Young described England as 'one of the most dilatory' countries.[25] In 1924, the Public Health (Meat) Regulations were adopted in England but adequate veterinary inspection was not achieved until 1966 when local authorities were finally given powers to control hours of slaughter in private slaughterhouses.[26] In Scotland, progress was made much earlier. In 1892 local authorities acquired powers to establish public abattoirs and prohibit private slaughterhouses where such abattoirs existed. The Public Health (Scotland) Act 1897 provided for the appointment of veterinarians as meat inspectors. Modern abattoirs were established in Edinburgh and Glasgow by the late 1900s and by the 1930s very few private slaughterhouses existed in Scotland. In 1908 about 125 public abattoirs were operative in Scotland; in England and Wales this figure was approximately one hundred.[27]

In general, in countries with a strong tradition of centralisation, state intervention in agriculture and public health was more common, and in such countries, the slaughter-warrant was instituted much earlier. Meat inspection acts became operative at an early stage in Belgium and Norway (1891), Luxembourg (1892), Germany (1903), France and Spain (1905), Austria–Hungary (1908), Switzerland (1909), and Denmark (1911).[28] In these countries, national governments were more willing to spend public money on the creation of a social infrastructure, including food quality control.[29] Apart from improvements in meat hygiene regulation and centralised slaughtering in municipal abattoirs, however, an effective meat inspection also required a solid scientific basis.

## Scientific development of meat hygiene

The establishment of veterinary schools stimulated the development of veterinary science. Schools founded at Lyon in 1762 and Alfort near Paris three years later provided the first formal training. Their graduates often staffed further schools set up in Austria, Italy and Germany, and, by the end of the eighteenth century, in most of the rest of Western and Eastern Europe. In these institutions, research was conducted on the transmission of animal diseases by the consumption of meat from infected animals. The standing

*Table 4.1.* Stages in meat hygiene research

| | |
|---|---|
| Before 1850 | Lack of epidemiological knowledge about pathogens: are enteric infections sometimes meat-borne? |
| 1850–1880 | The identification of trichinosis and other food-transmitted helminthic diseases. |
| 1880–1950 | The establishment of the aetiology of bacterial diseases and the identification of several meat-borne pathogens. |
| 1950–1975 | The identification of new microbiological and chemical risks. The development of the concept of intervention rather than inspection only. |
| 1975–1985 | The implementation of strict codes of hygienic practices in meat production. Intervention: irradiation and lactic acid decontamination suggested. |
| 1985–present | New concepts of inspection: Integrated Quality Control (IQC), Hazard Analysis and Critical Control Points (HACCP), predictive modelling, risk assessment. |

of meat inspection as a veterinary discipline increased when the scientific backgrounds of several diseases related to meat consumption were discovered (Table 4.1). Firstly, there were findings in parasitology. The tapeworm cycle was discovered in the 1860s and meat inspectors were then able to conduct preventive control. Systematic examination of each slaughter animal involving the incision of certain organs and tissues revealed the presence of tapeworms (*Taeniae*) or bladderworms (*Cysticerci*). A microscopical examination of muscle tissue from the diaphragm made the detection of *Trichinella spiralis* possible. The occurrence of parasites declined, especially where trichinella control was instituted.

From 1880, meat hygiene research obtained a more scientific character and bacteriological meat research in slaughterhouse laboratories ensued. The pioneering studies of Louis Pasteur, Robert Koch and others, such as the veterinarians Auguste Chauveau (1827–1917), Andreas Gerlach (1811–78), John McFadyean (1853–1941) and Daniel Salmon (1850–1914), were decisive for the further developments. Their discoveries in bacteriology included the aetiology of meat poisonings.

Between 1880 and 1950, a number of meat-borne pathogens were isolated.[30] The veterinary and medical debate over the 'germ-theory', and the precise aetiology of diseases that were a threat to both human and animal health, lasted for decades.[31] New questions arose as concern shifted from one disease to another. Much of the action for meat inspection and slaughterhouses regulation in Europe, was fought over the question of whether enzootics were transmissible to man. The major subject of this debate was bovine tuberculosis. Its aetiology was a matter of scientific controversy until the 1910s, and it was left to local authorities and their sometimes-untrained inspectors to decide whether a carcass was unfit for human consumption.

This resulted in frequent disputes with the meat (and milk) trades over tuberculous cattle.

Koch's work on tuberculosis influenced meat inspection greatly. After his discovery of the tubercle bacillus (*Mycobacterium tuberculosis*) in 1882, it was generally accepted by the medical and veterinary professions that tuberculosis in humans and cattle was identical. The two professions advocated measures to prevent the transmission of tuberculosis through milk and meat at national and international congresses in the 1880s and 1890s. Initially, there was a tendency to declare all meat from tuberculous cattle unsound. At the international veterinary congress at Baden-Baden in 1899, scientists agreed on the decisions to be made when tuberculous cattle were encountered in slaughterhouses. It was accepted that meat from animals with general tuberculosis (i.e. lesions in muscles and several organs) should all be condemned. Likewise, the infected organs should be removed from animals with small local lesions, after which the meat could be consumed, provided it was properly sterilised. This agreement lasted until 1901, when Koch retracted his statement about the identity of human and bovine tuberculosis at the international congress on tuberculosis in London. Based on his research he stated that the bovine tubercle bacillus was not pathogenic for humans and that consequently no special control measures or legislation were needed.[32]

During this congress, several researchers disagreed with Koch's dictum. However, the views of the famous scientist had a great impact and public discussion was stimulated by the press. Consequently, regulations and guidelines were disregarded in some European cities and meat and milk from tuberculous cattle entered the food chain. The public concern was reflected in the appointment of research commissions in several countries and a stream of reports followed. The confusion regarding inspection of tuberculous cattle waned from around 1910 when it was established that there were three distinct species of tubercle bacilli (human, bovine, and avian) and that the bovine type could indeed infect human beings, especially children. Legislation was reinforced and updated and uniform inspection measures were agreed at the international veterinary congress of Rome in 1912. Inspection of dairies and mandatory pasteurisation of milk was introduced in most West-European countries and the USA in the 1920s.[33]

As it became clear that tuberculosis caused serious human illness as well as a loss of animal production, attempts were made to eradicate this zoonosis. This was even more the case when slaughterhouse data and tuberculin tests revealed that 20–60 per cent of livestock in some countries was infected. In several countries campaigns against bovine tuberculosis were started, but failed because measures were only taken against clinical cases. Governments were reluctant to accept the high costs associated with compensating farmers for infected animals that had to be slaughtered. Successful campaigns against animal diseases like bovine tuberculosis and brucellosis were not realised before the 1950s and 1960s. In The Netherlands bovine tuberculosis was eradicated after a five-year campaign (1951–6), financed by the Marshall plan for European reconstruction, and by farmers through a levy on milk. By 1963, tuberculosis had been eradicated from cattle in Denmark, Finland, and The Netherlands, and almost eradicated in Britain, the USA, Norway, Sweden, Canada, Luxembourg and Switzerland.[34]

At around the time of the near elimination of bovine tuberculosis, the problem of drug residues in meat acquired increasing importance. There is a long tradition of giving animals substances to obtain therapeutic, prophylactic or growth-promoting effects. Apart from treatments such as injections, the majority of drugs are administered as additives to feed or drinking water. Therefore, residues of these substances may be present in milk, meat, and meat products, and will be consumed by humans. The potential danger of veterinary drugs was recognised in the nineteenth century when some scientists warned against the excessive use of mercury and arsenic compounds in veterinary practice. Research on applied dose, toxicity level, and withdrawal periods before slaughter was conducted from around 1890. Legislation to control the release of new veterinary drugs became effective by the turn of the century. During the 1960s, analysis of drug residues in meat was incorporated into meat inspection guidelines, when the application of antibiotics and growth promoters in animal production increased.[35]

During 1950–75, it became clear that conventional meat inspection could not guarantee the absolute hygienic reliability of 'approved' meat. It was not effective against salmonellosis, the detection of drug residues, and problems involving abattoir effluent. Macroscopic inspection became less significant and the importance of laboratory research increased. It became apparent that more and more foods of animal origin played a role in the epidemiology of zoonoses. Much emphasis was laid on the introduction of strict codes of hygiene in meat production. However, infections and intoxications transmitted by meat continued to occur in the 1970s and 1980s. New strategies for monitoring meat production lines and an extension of surveillance to earlier stages of production were called for. One possible solution was the introduction of a decontamination step in the slaughtering process. Procedures such as irradiation and lactic acid treatment were discussed in detail in the 1980s, but have not yet been permitted in the European Union. In the 1980s it became clear that the demands for safe and high quality products could only be met via a longitudinally integrated quality control system, in which the primary responsibility for quality lay with producers. In the framework of the HACCP (Hazard Analysis and Critical Control Points) and IQC (Integrated Quality Control) concepts, much research was conducted on hygienic slaughter equipment and techniques, while critical control points in the pork, cattle and poultry slaughterlines were mapped. Recent research has focused on risk assessment, risk perception and predictive modelling. The latter involves the development of computer models for microbiological risk analysis under a variety of conditions and product formulations, and the detection of critical parts of the production and distribution processes.[36]

## Changes in traditional meat inspection

Around 1900, empirical meat inspection was transformed into an applied veterinary science. During the early decades of the twentieth century new research was published, and theoretical and practical meat inspection became part of the veterinary curriculum. The entry of veterinarians into public health was gradually accepted by the medical profession and by society. Veterinarians provided an answer to concerns about the public health aspects of the meat trade and the extension of their professional activities was laid down in meat hygiene legislation.

National and international associations for professional veterinary food inspectors were founded and meat hygiene became an important issue for international congresses. Meat hygiene was also important for the Office International d'Hygiène Publique and the Office International des Epizooties, established in Paris in 1907 and 1924. The same holds, more recently, for the Animal Production and Animal Health Divisions of the Food and Agricultural Organisation in Rome, the Veterinary Public Health Division of the World Health Organisation in Geneva,[37] and the Standing Veterinary Committee of the European Union in Brussels. All these factors contributed to the development of a professional meat inspection corps.

Traditional meat inspection is based on ante- and post-mortem inspection of each animal by a qualified veterinarian, involving pathological anatomical examination and bacteriological tests in certain cases. Meat is stamped and declared sound, conditionally sound, or unfit for human consumption. Regulations and guidelines were based on the handbook by Von Ostertag (1892)[38] for more than half a century. This was reprinted many times and translated into English and Russian. The traditional concept of meat inspection was quite successful until the 1960s, becoming more effective within centralised slaughtering under professional supervision and as home slaughtering decreased. By the 1960s diseases like tuberculosis and brucellosis were almost eliminated and the incidence of parasitic diseases was minimal.

From the 1960s, however, fundamental transformations in animal production, food technology, the supply chain, meat consumption, human–animal relations and society, have precipitated changes in the science, ideology and practice of veterinary public health. These particularly concern surveillance strategies and state intervention. Larger production units became operative, and the speed of slaughtering lines increased, resulting in less time for inspection. The effectiveness of post-mortem inspection based on incision, palpation and visual inspection has been under discussion since the 1980s. Key phrases were scaling-up, more uniformity in inspection methods, lower inspection expenses, and rational employment of personnel.[39]

Among the problems that inspectors faced were *salmonella* and *campylobacter* infections, which do not necessarily produce clinical illness or pathological lesions. For these diseases a system based on risk assessment of critical points at all stages of production is required. Modern inspection requires transfer of data on the health status of animals from veterinary practitioners responsible for their care, to their colleagues in the abattoir or meat plant. Safety is the outcome of continuous evaluation of risks. Clear European Union and national legislation should provide criteria about acceptable or unacceptable health risks. In such a new system, producers remain fully responsible for the safety and quality of their products. The authorities only demand certain safety levels and verify whether producers comply.[40]

In the face of increased competition and new inspection charges and regulations, there have been major structural changes. The Fresh Meat (Hygiene and Inspection) Regulations based on European Community Directive 91/497 have been influential. Many small slaughterhouses could not comply and lost their 'EC approved' status and their licence to export their meat. For example, more than 200 of the 780 slaughterhouses in England and Wales closed during 1992.[41] This holds for the majority of public abattoirs built in France and The Netherlands in the early twentieth century. These could no longer compete with large-scale private slaughter-houses which proved more cost-effective and quicker to incorporate new technology. As a result of this process in The Netherlands, more than one hundred job opportunities for veterinarians as directors and deputy directors of public abattoirs have been lost to the profession.[42]

## Conclusions

The growth of meat consumption and the meat trade was associated with great concern over the quality of the product and its impact on human health. As outlined above, the veterinary profession acquired responsibility for and even a monopoly on meat inspection. Their expertise gave them responsibilities in zoonoses control, hygiene of foods of animal origin, and animal welfare. However, past achievements have conditioned the profession to a specific role in public health, which has made it somewhat conservative in responding to new needs and demands.

Despite recent efforts to improve meat inspection, the public image of producers and veterinarians involved in meat production is now somewhat negative due to recent scandals. Debates about meat safety in the light of the BSE crisis, culminating in the recent French–British 'Beef war' and fraud in animal feed production in France and the low countries, continue to affect public opinion.[43] As with tuberculosis around 1900, the authorities are forced to take public action, but knowledge of health risks is often limited. As long as consensus among scientists and objective information from research is lacking, policy making is difficult. Consequently, public concern regarding food safety is nourished; a concern that is frequently exploited by the media and anti-meat lobbyists.

Both the livestock industries and veterinary profession are faced by challenges of concerned consumers, animal rights activists, and environmental lobbyists. Veterinarians are seen as having been active in increasing animal production but passive over the negative effects of intensive farming and animal welfare. Critics argue that the limits to mass production in the live-stock industry have been reached.[44] Today, animal health and welfare, consumer and environmental protection, all have to be considered, as well as economic factors. However, there are signs that the veterinary profession has begun re-appraising its role.[45] Regular reviews of the profession's contribution to food hygiene and zoonoses control will be necessary if it wishes to retain an important role in public health. The environmental reservoir of zoonotic enteric pathogens will continue to impose pressure on human health through animals and animal products. Similarly, society will continue to need a well-developed and adequate veterinary infrastructure as one of the main keys to safeguarding human health.

# References

1  See, for example, J. Goudsblom, 'Public health and the civilising process', *Milbank Quarterly*, 1986, vol. 64, pp. 161–88; A. de Swaan, *In Care of the State. Health Care, Education and Welfare in Europe and the USA in the Modern Era*, Cambridge, Polity, 1988; H. J. Teuteberg, 'Food patterns in the European past', *Annals of Nutrition and Metabolism: European Journal of Nutrition, Metabolic Diseases and Dietetics*, 1991, vol. 35, pp. 181–90; A. Labisch, 'History of public health – history in public health. Looking back and looking forward', *Social History of Medicine*, 1998, vol. 11, pp. 1–13; D. Porter (ed.), *The History of Public Health and the Modern State*, Amsterdam, Rodopi, 1994.
2  E. Hanssen and W. Wendt, 'Geschichte der Lebensmittelwissenschaft', in J. Schormüller (ed.), *Handbuch der Lebensmittelchemie* (vol. 1), Berlin, Springer Verlag, 1965, pp. 1–75; P. B. Hutt and P. B. Hutt II, 'A history of government regulation of adulteration and misbranding of food', *Food, Drug and Cosmetic Law Journal*, 1984, vol. 39, pp. 2–73; J. M. Jones, *Food Safety*, St. Paul, Minnesota, Eagan, 1992.
3  W. W. Rosser, 'Corollary development of the professions of veterinary medicine and human medicine in the United States', *Veterinary Heritage*, 1991, vol. 14, pp. 3–29.
4  J. H. Steele, 'Veterinary public health: early history and recent world developments', *Journal of the American Veterinary Medical Association*, 1978, vol. 173, pp. 1497–1504; C. W. Schwabe, *Veterinary Medicine and Public Health*, Baltimore, Williams and Wilkins, 1984, (third edition); D. Grossklaus, E. Weise, H. Kolb, P. Teufel, J. Wegener, D. Protz, W. Mieldy and W. Scharmann, 'Notes on technical progress in veterinary public health', *Revue Scientifique et Technique / Office International des Epizooties*, 1991, vol. 10, pp. 995–1018; W. Schönherr, 'History of veterinary public health in Europe in the 19th century', *Revue Scientifique et Technique / Office International des Epizooties*, 1991, vol. 10, pp. 985–94; G. Reuter, 'Veterinärmedizin und Gesundheitsvorsorge', *Berliner und Münchener Tierärztliche Wochenschrift*, 1997, vol. 110, pp. 431–5.
5  J. R. Fisher, 'Of plagues and veterinarians: BSE in historical perspective', *Argos*, 1997, vol. 16, pp. 225–35; P. A. Koolmees, J. R. Fisher and R. Perren, 'The traditional responsibility of veterinarians in meat production and meat inspection', in F. J. M. Smulders (ed.), *Veterinary Aspects of Meat Production, Processing and Inspection. An Update of Recent Developments in Europe*, Utrecht, ECCEAMST, 1999, pp. 7–31; J. Swabe, *Animals, Disease and Human Society: Human–Animal Relations and the Rise of Veterinary Medicine*, Routledge, London, 1999, pp. 113–7, pp. 12–14, 152.
6  Koolmees, Fisher and Perren, op. cit.; M. Knibbe, *Agriculture in the Netherlands 1851–1950. Production and Institutional Change*, Amsterdam, NEHA, 1993, pp. 188, 298–9.
7  E. C. Büchner, 'Het verbruik van brood en vleesch te Amsterdam vergeleken met dat te

Parijs, Berlijn enz', *Tijdschrift voor Staatshuishoudkunde en Statistiek*, 1855, vol. 11, pp. 369–79, J. M. van 't Hoff, 'Onze voeding', *De Natuur*, 1886, vol. 6, pp. 134–8, 172–6; K. J. Carpenter, *Protein and Energy. A Study of Changing Ideas in Nutrition*, Cambridge, Cambridge University Press, 1994, pp. 88–99, 112–8.

 8  F. Nitti, 'The food and labour-power of nations', *The Economic Journal*, 1896, vol. 6, pp. 30–63, at p. 31; J. L. van Zanden, 'De mythe van de achterlijkheid van de Nederlandse economie in de 19e eeuw', *Spiegel Historiael*, 1989, vol. 24, pp. 163–7.

 9  S. Stockman, 'The development of meat inspection', *The Veterinarian*, 1899, vol. 72, pp. 847–58, at p. 857; R. Koller, *Saltz, Rauch und Fleisch. Theorie und Praxis des Pökeln und Räucherns*, Salzburg, Verlag Bergland, 1941, p. 34.

10  P. A. Koolmees, *Symbolen van openbare hygiëne. Gemeentelijke slachthuizen in Nederland 1795–1940*, Rotterdam, Erasmus, 1997, pp. 109–13.

11  R. Perren, *The Meat Trade in Britain 1840–1914*, London, Routledge and Kegan Paul, 1978; P. A. Koolmees, 'Meat in the past: a bird's-eye view on meat consumption, production and research in the Western World from antiquity to 1945', in W. Sybesma, P. A. Koolmees and D. G. van der Heij (eds), *Meat Past and Present: Research, Production, Consumption* (vol. 1), Zeist, The Netherlands, TNO Topics on Nutrition and Food Research, 1994, pp. 5–32.

12  J. G. van Logtestijn, P. A. Koolmees and D. A. A. Mossel, 'De onderkenning en preventie van vleesvergiftigingen', *Tijdschrift voor Diergeneeskunde*, 1987, vol. 112, 1037–46.

13  R. M. van Daalen, 'Nauwbehuisd en dichtbevolkt. Gemeentelijke voorzieningen en klachten uit de burgerij, Amsterdam 1865–1920', *Sociologisch Tijdschrift*, 1985, vol. 12, pp. 274–307, at 280–1.

14  A. Moreau, *l'Abattoir moderne, construction, installation, administration*, Paris, Asselin and Houzeau, 1916, (second edition), pp. 3–12; A. Fowler la Berge, 'The Paris health council, 1802–1848', *Bulletin of the History of Medicine*, 1975, vol. 49, pp. 339–52.

15  E. S. Houwaart, *De Hygiënisten. Artsen, Staat & Volksgezondheid in Nederland 1840–1890*, Groningen, Historische Uitgeverij, 1991, pp. 19–21, 107–17, 161–2, 193–6.

16  C. G. von Reeken, 'De geneeskunde der dieren in verband met staatsen volksbelang', *De Gids*, 1861, vol. 25, II, pp. 27–56; C. D. Morris, 'Meat inspection', *Journal of Comparative Medicine and Veterinary Archives*, 1895, vol. 16, pp. 71–8; R. von Ostertag, 'Der Tierarzt und die menschliche Gesundheit', *Zeitschrift für Fleisch – und Milchhygiene*, 1939, vol. 39, pp. 249–52, 269–74.

17  P. A. Koolmees, 'The professionalisation of medical professions in The Netherlands 1840–1940', in J. Schäffer (ed.), *Domestication of Animals; Interactions Between Veterinary and Medical Sciences. Report of the 30th Congress of the WAHVM and the 6th Conference of the Historical Division of the DVG*, Gießen, German Veterinary Medical Society, 1999, pp. 54–64.

18  J. de Loverdo, *Les Abattoirs Publics. Vol. 1. Construction et agencement des abattoirs*, Paris, Dunot et Pinat, 1906, pp. 691–859; A. Moreau op. cit., pp. 140–3.

19  P. A. Koolmees, 'The development of veterinary public health in Western Europe, 1850–1940', *Sartoniana*, 1999, vol. 12, pp. 153–79.

20  Koolmees, 1997, op. cit., pp. 206–11.

21  Koolmees, Fisher and Perren, op. cit., pp. 16–8.

22  D. F. van Esveld and L. van der Harst, *De Keuring van vee en vleesch in Nederland. Rapport uitgebracht door het Hoofdbestuur van de Maatschappij ter bevordering der Veeartsenijkunde in Nederland inhoudende de resultaten van het onderzoek naar den toestand der keuring van vee en vleesch hier te Lande*, Utrecht, Beijers, 1894.

23  Koolmees, 1997, op. cit., pp. 180–2.

24  Ibid., pp. 134–5, 180–2.

25  T. Dunlop Young, 'Meat inspection in England compared with other countries', *Veterinary Record*, 1932, vol. 12, pp. 1101–5; W. A. Lethem, 'Slaughterhouse practice at home and abroad: a comparison between the systems of administration of different countries, the

methods of meat inspection and the practice of home killing', *Journal of the Royal Sanitary Institute*, 1937–38, vol. 58, pp. 562–72, at 563.

26  Ministry of Agriculture, Fisheries and Food, *Report on the Animal Health Services in Great Britain 1966*, London, HMSO, 1968.

27  G. R. Leighton and L. M. Douglas, *The Meat Industry and Meat Inspection*, London, Educational Book Co., 1910, vol. 2, pp. 369–84; G. H. Collinge, T. Dunlop Young and A. P. McDougall, *The Retail Meat Trade: A Practical Treatise by Specialists in the Meat Trade*, London, 1927, pp. 185–90; Dunlop Young, op. cit. p. 1102; M. French and J. Phillips, *Cheated not poisoned? Food regulation in the United Kingdom, 1875–1938*, Manchester, Manchester University Press, 2000, pp. 86–7.

28  R. von Ostertag, *Handbuch der Fleischbeschau für Tierärzte, Ärzte und Richter*, Stuttgart, Verlag F. Enke, 1910 (sixth edition); Dunlop Young, op. cit.; M. Mammerickx, 'Histoire de la médecin vétérinaire belge, suivi d'un Répertoire bio-bibliographique des médecins vétérinaires belges et de leurs écrits', *Mémoire de l'Académie Royale de Médecin de Belgique*, Bruxelles, IIe Série, Tome V, No. 4, 1967, pp. 305–14; G. Theves, 'Les vétérinaires municipaux de la ville de Luxembourg', in R. Clesse (ed.), *Der Gemeinde-Schlachthof der Stadt Luxemburg*, Luxembourg, 1991, pp. 63–78.

29  J. R. Fisher, 'Not quite a profession: the aspirations of veterinary surgeons in England in the mid nineteenth century', *Historical Research*, 1993, vol. 66, pp. 284–302; Koolmees, Fisher and Perren, op. cit., p. 17.

30  Van Logtestijn, Koolmees and Mossel, op. cit.; D. A. A Mossel and K. E. Dijkmann, 'A centenary of academic and less learned food microbiology pitfalls of the past and promises for the future', *Antonie van Leeuwenhoek*, 1984, vol. 50, pp. 641–63.

31  T. M. Romano, 'The cattle plague of 1865 and the reception of the germ-theory in mid-Victorian Britain', *Journal of the History of Medicine and Allied Sciences*, 1997, vol. 52, pp. 51–80.

32  J. van der Hoeden, 'Tuberculose van dierlijken oorsprong bij den mensch', *Tijdschrift voor Diergeneeskunde*, 1937, vol. 64, pp. 1351–65; Koolmees, 1997, op. cit., pp. 124–9.

33  R. A. Packer, 'Veterinarians challenge Dr. Robert Koch regarding bovine tuberculosis and public health', *Veterinary Heritage*, 1987, vol. 10, pp. 7–11; L. Wilkinson, *Animals and Disease. An Introduction to the History of Comparative Medicine*, Cambridge, Cambridge University Press, 1992, pp. 112–3; M. Worboys, '"Killing and curing"; veterinarians, medicine and germs in Britain, 1860–1900', *Veterinary History*, 1992, NS vol. 7, pp. 53–71. For the British situation regarding pasteurisation see Chapters 3 and 5 of this book.

34  H. Huitema, *Tuberculosis in Animals and Man: With Attention to Reciprocal Transmission of Mycobacterial Infections and the Successful Eradication of Bovine Tuberculosis in Cattle in The Netherlands*, The Hague, Royal Netherlands Tuberculosis Association, 1993; Schwabe, op. cit., p. 41.

35  Jones, op. cit., pp. 379–401.

36  B. R. Berends and F. van Knapen, 'An outline of a risk assessment-based system of meat safety assurance and its future prospects', *Veterinary Quarterly*, 1999, vol. 21, pp. 128–34; Koolmees, Fisher and Perren, op. cit., pp. 19–20.

37  Schwabe, op. cit., pp. 83–6.

38  R. von Ostertag, *Handbuch der Fleischbeschau für Tierärzte, Ärzte und Richter*, Stuttgart, Verlag F. Enke, 1892.

39  Koolmees, Fisher and Perren, op. cit., p. 9.

40  A. M. Johnston, 'Animal disease and human health', in A. R. Michell (ed.), *The Advancement of Veterinary Science. The Bicentenary Symposium Series, vol. 1, Veterinary Medicine Beyond 2000*, Wallingford, C.A.B. International, 1993, pp. 169–78; Berends and Van Knapen, op. cit..

41  V. Robertson, 'Shifting goalposts and a government with a thin majority are the two elements currently causing grief to Britain's abattoir sector', *Meat International*, 1993, vol. 3, no. 4, pp. 24–5.

42  L. Thomas, *La privatisation des abattoirs publics*, PhD thesis, Ecole Nationale Vétérinaire d'Alfort, *s.l.*, 1979; Koolmees, Fisher and Perren, op. cit., p. 19.

43  P. Atkins and P. Brassley, 'Mad cows and Englishmen', *History Today*, 1996, vol. 46, pp. 14–7; Fisher, 1997, op. cit; F. van Dongen, 'Invloed Brussel op vleessector steeds groter', *De Keurmeester*, 1999, vol. 90, no. 4, pp. 31–2; B. van der Velden, 'Vleesoorlog gaat over principes' *Nieuwe Rotterdamse Courant*, 28 October 1999.

44  J. Rifkin, *Beyond Beef. The Rise and Fall of Cattle Culture*, New York, Dutton, 1992; A. H. van Otterloo, 'The development of public distrust of modern food technology in The Netherlands. Professionals, laymen and the consumers' union', in A. P. den Hartog (ed.), *Food Technology, Science and Marketing: European Diet in the Twentieth Century*, Tuckwell, East Linton, 1995, pp. 253–67.

45  R. G. Kauffman and L. J. M. Rutgers, 'The ethics of meat production: what man's relationship should be with animals and why', in: F. J. M. Smulders (ed.), *The European Meat Industry in the 1990s. Advanced Technology, Product Quality and Consumer Acceptability*, Nijmegen, Audet, 1991, pp. 247–70; C. S. Manette, 'Veterinary ethics and the changing role of the veterinarian: an historical review', *Veterinary Heritage*, 1998, vol. 21, no. 2, pp. 25–33; R. M. Ridley and H. F. Baker, 'Big decisions based on small numbers: lessons from BSE', *Veterinary Quarterly*, 1999, vol. 21, pp. 86–92.

# 5　The People's League of Health and the campaign against bovine tuberculosis in the 1930s

*L. Margaret Barnett*

Although tuberculosis remained the leading cause of death of Britons between the ages of eight and forty-five, there were some encouraging developments in the fight against this scourge during the inter-war years. The death rate fell by one-third, an upsurge of cases during the First World War proving to have been a temporary phenomenon, and the disease resuming its long retreat with the return of peace.[1] Following the creation of the Ministry of Health in 1919, efforts to increase the pace of the decline intensified, with both national and local governments taking a more aggressive stance. Funding for treatment and public health education increased, medical facilities expanded, and new controls to prevent the spread of tuberculosis came into force. One opportunity to reduce the incidence of the disease was missed, however, when the authorities failed to eliminate a known source of infection – milk from tuberculous cattle.

At the international congress on tuberculosis held in London in 1901, Robert Koch, the discoverer of the tubercle bacillus, had announced that it was well nigh impossible for humans to catch tuberculosis from cattle and that even if they did, they would experience only a mild version of the disease. Most species of the mycobacteria that cause tuberculosis are host specific, but not *Mycobacterium bovis (M. bovis)*, which can infect other animals as well as human beings. A Royal Commission confirmed the transmissibility of bovine tuberculosis in 1911, and Koch subsequently revised his views. His earlier statement about the trivial consequences for humans had already found fertile soil in Britain, however, contributing to a long-lived belief that drinking milk containing live tubercle bacilli was relatively harmless.[2]

The number of people actually sickened by *M. bovis* during the inter-war period reinforced such views and encouraged claims by farmers and others that the pasteurisation campaigners were overstating the dangers of raw milk. Indeed, tuberculosis of bovine origin formed a very small proportion of total tuberculosis cases. In 1928, for instance, it accounted for just 7 per cent of new cases and 5 per cent of deaths in England and Wales, and what made it seem even less significant in many people's eyes was the fact that it killed a mere 1 per cent of people suffering from pulmonary tuberculosis. Bovine infections were more common in Scotland, but again they accounted for only

4 per cent of pulmonary deaths. In pulmonary cases, it is the lungs that are primarily affected, and about four fifths of people suffering from tuberculosis in 1928 had this form of the disease. By far the majority of them were adults, and it was they who filled most of the beds in the new sanatoria and who were the focus of official efforts to stem the spread of infection. In the remaining 20 per cent of cases, the nodular lesions, called tubercles, might appear throughout the body (disseminated) or develop primarily in the intestines, the genito-urinary system, the bones and joints, the nervous system, the lymphatic glands, or other organs. Non-pulmonary cases were often treated in hospitals rather than sanatoria,[3] which perhaps made these forms of the disease seem less sinister in popular estimation, thus reducing the apparent need for government intervention. It was here, however, that pasteurisation could make the greatest impact, since bovine infections contributed much more frequently to non-pulmonary tuberculosis and accounted for nearly a quarter of all deaths from that cause (see Table 5.1).[4]

While tuberculosis of bovine origin played a minor role in terms of numbers, two factors raised its importance from the social point of view. First, even though its death rate was falling at a faster rate than that of tuberculosis in general – 30 per cent in the 1920s alone – the incidence of new infections remained stable. This meant that an increasing proportion of those infected were surviving and being disabled by the disease, which placed more strain on the public purse. The second and most dramatic point was that those most at risk were children. Two thirds of those who died from it in England and Wales in 1928 were under fifteen years of age, with the under-fives hit the hardest – not surprising, given the amount of milk in infants' diets. Aside from bacteriological proof, statistics provided compelling evidence of the need to address the matter of contaminated milk.[5]

*Table 5.1.* Deaths from bovine infection in England and Wales, 1928[a]

| Type of TB | Percentage of deaths caused by the Bovine Form | |
| --- | --- | --- |
| | *All ages* | *Children under 15* |
| Respiratory | 1.1 | 1.5 |
| Nervous system | 21.4 | 22.8 |
| Abdominal | 52.5 | 75.0 |
| Bones and joints | 6.4 | 22.0 |
| Skin | 10.0 | 0.0 |
| Lymphatic glands | 40.0 | 79.4 |
| Genito-urinary | 15.8 | 33.3 |
| Disseminated | 13.5 | 24.6 |
| Other organs | 8.0 | 15.0 |

[a] Source: Report of a Special Committee appointed by the People's League of Health Inc. to make a Survey of Tuberculosis of Bovine Origin in Great Britain, London, 1932, p. 17.

## The People's League of Health inquiry into Bovine Tuberculosis

By 1930, when the People's League of Health took up the issue, much had already been done to improve the cleanliness of the milk supply – on the farm, in transit, and at the wholesale and retail levels of sale. Although most Britons would still be consuming raw milk at the outbreak of World War Two, distributors, particularly in big cities, were increasingly adopting pasteurisation and other heat treatments to destroy bacteria, and over 90 per cent of the milk sold in London would be pasteurised by 1933.[6] In 1922, the government had introduced a licensing system, amended slightly the following year, which was designed to encourage higher standards in dairy farming. Producers could advertise, and charge a little more for, milk described as 'certified', 'grade A (tuberculin tested)', 'grade A', or 'pasteurised'. All four milks were limited as to the number of bacteria they could contain and the raw milk categories entailed quarterly inspection of herds for signs of tuberculosis and other diseases that could be transmitted to humans. The safest of the three raw milks, certified, not only had a lower permitted bacterial count than pasteurised milk but was bottled right at the farm, and grade A (tuberculin tested) left the farm in sealed churns.[7] Such measures did little to improve overall milk safety, however, because Britain's strong agricultural lobby had ensured that compliance with the scheme, as with too many other milk orders, was voluntary. Moreover, the licenses were expensive, rendering the scheme attractive only to owners of the largest herds although most of the country's 2.5 million cows lived in small herds of 12–14 heads. By 1930, only 480 of Britain's 200,000 producers owned certified or grade A (tuberculin tested) certificates.[8] To top things off, there was no national farm inspectorate and the checking of premises was left to over-burdened local authorities, whose frequently superficial efforts fell far short of the ideal.[9] What the People's League of Health and other interested parties wanted to see in the 1930s, therefore, was effective inspection of herds and the compulsory pasteurisation of all milk not already designated certified or grade A (tuberculin tested).[10]

The part played by the People's League of Health in this debate cannot be appreciated without knowing something about the organisation's early years and about its colourful founder, Olga Nethersole. Founded in 1917, the People's League of Health was a voluntary society, but unlike the majority of such bodies, which tended to focus on local problems or on the treatment of disease, the League aimed to be a national organisation that promoted prevention. In that it did not target a specific problem but took up a range of health issues, it also differed from other national groups such as those that focused on the prevention of tuberculosis or venereal diseases. Uniquely too, the League saw itself as a consumer advocate. Roles listed in its second general report included 'holding a watching brief for the people', and its ultimate goal was the creation of a consumer lobby consisting of the population in general – '"Public Opinion" manifesting itself in the individual vote', as Nethersole

on tuberculosis of bovine origin. Tippett's persistent efforts to interest the Ministry of Health, the British Medical Association, and the National Association for the Prevention of Tuberculosis had all been rebuffed, the BMA's Joint Tuberculosis Council voicing doubts in January that such a gathering would serve any useful purpose.[25] Tippett must have been delighted when just a few weeks later the members of the People's League of Health not only wholeheartedly approved the appointment of a special committee to look into bovine tuberculosis but were so enthusiastic that they drafted the committee's mandate immediately. At a follow-up session held on 24 March, representatives of a variety of other organisations proved just as eager, with H. B. Brackenbury, Chairman of the Council of the British Medical Association announcing the BMA's readiness 'to help the work of the League in every way' and everyone else present accepting an invitation to join the League's new Bovine Tuberculosis Committee.[26] The PLH had won recognition as a suitable agent through which organisations and individuals concerned with clean milk and bovine tuberculosis could work together.

Walter Fletcher was outraged by the participation of Georges Dreyer, the Chairman of the Medical Research Council's own Tuberculosis Committee.[27] Fletcher himself had refused an invitation from the League to participate in the project and successfully persuaded several other MRC members to do so as well. The People's League of Health, he told one, was 'becoming a great nuisance. It is sheer impertinence to ask you to waste your time ... with a mixed lot of charlatans and advertisers ... '.[28] The People's League of Health 'is an absurdity', he wrote to another, 'because it contains 30 or 40 persons of whom the great majority have no first-hand knowledge of the problems involved'.[29] Dreyer's response to Fletcher's plea to disassociate himself is instructive. Before making his decision to join the committee, Dreyer had scanned the names of every person on the League's Medical and Science Councils. '[I]f names ever are a guarantee', he told Fletcher, 'there was no indication that an acceptance could in any way embarrass the Medical Research Council'.[30] Far from being made up of charlatans, the League's two councils consisted of trained professionals, many of them eminent in their fields. Over the years, the People's League of Health had steadily increased its membership and was now in a position to act as a medical lobby.

Looking at the names of those involved in the tuberculosis inquiry, it is hard to understand Fletcher's objections. Of the sixty five participants, forty did not belong to the League and they represented a broad spectrum of professional organisations, health societies and agricultural interest groups. These included the British Medical Association, the Royal Colleges of Surgeons and of Physicians, the Royal Veterinary College, county medical officers of health, university professors of physiology and veterinary pathology, and voluntary societies such as the Save the Children Fund. Of the many other organisations involved it is worth highlighting the inclusion of the Highland and Agricultural Society of Scotland, the Royal Agricultural Society of England, dairy industry societies and companies such as the Certified and Grade A Milk Producers' Association, along with the British Dairy Farmers' Association, United Dairies and the Pure Milk Society. Wilfred Buckley, who headed the latter, was actually an opponent of pasteurised milk, but in light of the slow progress the licensing scheme was making in ending the sale of bacteria-laden milk he was temporarily prepared to join this effort to force the government into more decisive action.[31] So the bovine tuberculosis inquiry committee clearly amounted to rather more than just 'Miss Nethersole's organisation'.

The Bovine Tuberculosis Committee had two sub-committees, each with a specific task. The oddly named Sub-Committee A and B, chaired by Dr William Hunter, who represented the Royal College of Physicians of London, collected statistics on the extent of tuberculosis among cattle, the incidence of TB of bovine origin among humans, ways by which infection was transmitted, and factors affecting transmission, while Sub-Committee C, chaired by C. O. Hawthorne, who represented the British Medical Association, looked at ways by which tuberculosis in cattle could be reduced. These inquiries over, possible solutions were discussed by the general committee, which subsequently unanimously endorsed the final report written by William Savage, the Medical Officer of Health for Somerset.[32]

The longest section of the report was devoted to the findings of Sub-Committee A and B. Like the Ministry of Agriculture itself, the Committee could only estimate the extent of tuberculosis among cattle because although the debate over clean milk dated back decades, full statistics still did not exist, not even for one county, and both government and independent investigators had to rely on sampling. Samples taken by official inspectors would not have been truly random, however, the report stressed, since they were mainly taken from herds whose owners wanted them certified, meaning that visibly sick animals would have been removed beforehand. Official figures thus tended to understate the problem. In 1926 licensing inspectors had found only 17.5 per cent reactors to the intradermal tuberculin test used to detect tuberculosis among cattle. Yet three previously untested herds used for a Medical Research Council study published in 1925 contained an average of 53 per cent reactors, and one herd inspected by a member of the PLH Sub-Committee had no less than 61 per cent. A conservative average, it was concluded, was 40 per cent, which matched the average incidence of gross macroscopic lesions of tuberculosis found at the slaughter of 55,318 cows performed at three big-city abattoirs between 1924 and 1930 (39.5 per cent). The situation compared unfavorably to that in other countries, especially the United States, where an aggressive eradication program had reduced the number of reactors to the tuberculin test from 4.1 per cent of 329,878 cows tested in 1919 to just 1.8 per cent of nearly 12 million in 1929.[33]

Reaction to the tuberculin test only meant that an animal had picked up the bacillus, not that it had active tuberculosis, and the Sub-Committee estimated that only 0.2 per cent or two in every thousand animals were actually producing infected milk. However, since Britain had so many small producers, milk from several farms was often mixed together before processing for retail sale, which meant that one infected animal could contaminate a large amount of milk. The Sub-Committee examined data on 69,901 specimens of raw milk sold between 1918 and 1930 and discovered that the average contamination with tubercle bacilli was 6.7 per cent, although individual figures varied widely. Of the towns and counties examined, Blackburn and Somerset had the lowest average proportion of infected milk – 2.1 and 2.3 per cent, respectively – and Manchester and Brighton the highest – 12.9 and 11.1 per cent. The situation in Manchester had actually worsened in recent years, with levels of infection as high as 17.6 per cent in 1928 and 14.3 per cent in 1930. Also disturbing was the fact that the average proportion of infected milk in the country had remained steady for the past ten years, just like the number of people contracting new cases of tuberculosis of bovine origin.[34] After providing statistics for the incidence of this form of the disease in humans, Sub-Committee A and B concluded by reminding readers of the 'immense amount of suffering, invalidity and often permanent deformity... caused by this bacillus'.[35]

Sub-Committee C, tackling the issue of prevention, looked first at various ways by which tuberculosis among cattle could be reduced. The most obvious was to remove from the food chain all cattle that reacted positively to tuberculin testing. Responsible farmers were already slaughtering such animals, but the extent of the problem in Britain rendered a quick cull impossible, since if 40 per cent of cows were to be slaughtered in a short period this would result in a drastic temporary shortage of milk and other dairy products. Moreover, farmers would have to be compensated for their losses during the process, which the Sub-Committee acknowledged would place an inconceivable financial burden on the state. It was nevertheless possible to hasten the rate of the cull, the Sub-Committee advised, by closing loopholes in existing legislation, enforcing existing legislation, improving quality control in tuberculin production, introducing standardized methods of testing, testing cows before they joined herds, giving farmers more incentives to keep tuberculin tested herds, and creating an official register of accredited herds. Until these procedures had achieved their aim, meanwhile, the swiftest and surest way to prevent the spread of *M. bovis* infections among humans was pasteurisation.[36]

At the request of R. Stenhouse Williams, the director of the National Institute for Research in Dairying, who was one of several raw-milk advocates on the Sub-Committee, the report emphasised that pasteurisation was not intended to be an alternative to the production of clean milk containing a minimal amount of bacteria and it acknowledged that heat treatments did destroy vitamin C and cause certain other changes in the milk.[37] The anti-pasteurisation arguments are discussed in detail in this book by Peter Atkins, but they included the belief that heat treatment ruined the most effective form of immunising children against tuberculosis, and contributed to dental caries and general debility.[38] Citing Eli Metchnikoff's claims about the life-prolonging action of fermented milk products, some opponents even argued that forcing children to consume pasteurised milk would cheat them of time on earth.[39] Such 'controversial issues', Sub-Committee C declared, would be settled by future research. More positively, it emphasised the wealth of evidence that pasteurisation had reduced not only the incidence of tuberculosis of bovine origin in big cities in Britain and in other countries, but also the frequency of epidemics of other diseases carried by milk.[40]

The full report was finished by October 1931, and if this had been the early 1920s, the People's League of Health would have immediately dispatched it to the Ministry of Health via a deputation. The latter would have included too many speakers, thus obscuring the main points of the report, and the League would have made no effort beforehand to harness public support, making it easy for the ministry to ignore their findings. The tuberculosis report, however, was handled quite differently.

First, in January 1932, the League published the report and sent copies of the official-looking document to local authorities around the country with a request for comments and approval. Seventy two councils representing 11 million people endorsed the findings and eleven speaking for another 1.6 million gave conditional support: a list of these authorities would be included in the copy of the report later submitted to the government.[41] The League's next step, on 11 July 1932, was to hold a public meeting at the Mansion House, London, attended by what even a Ministry of Health official admitted was 'a large and influential gathering'.[42] After the Lord Mayor of London had obligingly opened the session with praises for the League's work, 'leaders of the medical and veterinary professions, members of Government departments, representatives of many municipalities, and persons interested in dairying and agriculture', reportedly listened appreciatively to Savage's precis of the Committee's findings. The Lord Mayor of Manchester, who moved to adopt the report, and the spokesman for the National Institute for Research in Dairying, who seconded it, both repeated the call for compulsory pasteurisation and amendment of the milk licensing scheme.[43]

Like the Bovine Tuberculosis Committee itself, the deputation that presented the report to the government on 24 November 1932 consisted not just of members of the People's League of Health but representatives of the numerous interest groups involved. Remarkably, only five of the thirty people in the deputation spoke, which kept attention on the main issues.[44] In addition to the Minister of Health, the Parliamentary Secretary of the Ministry of Agriculture and the Parliamentary Under-Secretary of State for Scotland were present. The session was very civil, but it did not result in any great changes to government policy. Officials from the Ministries of Health and Agriculture and the Departments of Health and Agriculture for Scotland had in fact already decided at a joint meeting held on 17 November to advise their chiefs to resist compulsory pasteurisation, citing a variety of reasons: farmers would have no incentive to produce clean milk, it constituted 'undue interference with the liberty of the subject' to make a person drink heat-treated milk, it was 'contrary to the principles embodied in the Public Health Act' not to destroy contaminated food, and it would bring economic ruin to milk producers.[45] Although an inquiry of its own soon confirmed the League's statistics, the government heeded the officials' advice and did not take effective measures to eliminate the threat to humans of tuberculosis of bovine origin until after World War Two. An attested herds scheme and changes to milk licensing categories hardly touched the problem before the war.[46] The last excuse given by the bureaucrats at their 17 November 1932 meeting for opposing compulsory pasteurisation was the main reason for this. As Gail Savage points out in her study of the inter-war English civil service, while the Ministry of Agriculture safeguarded its constituency during the inter-war years and regularly challenged legislation that would have hurt farmers' profits, the Ministry of Health frequently sacrificed the interests of the body it was supposed to protect – the public – to Treasury demands for economy, 'ministry officials interpret[ing] their role in light of their duty to control expenditure rather than relieve suffering', as she puts it.[47] Significantly, notes made by Ministry of Health officials about the PLH tuberculosis report all too often include the words: 'there are, however, financial considerations'.[48]

The PLH continued its efforts on behalf of safe milk in the years that followed, publishing a series of papers critical of government inaction, some of which were produced by a new veterinary council that like the earlier medical and science councils attracted highly qualified individuals, including previously unaffiliated people who had served on the Bovine Tuberculosis Committee.[49] Topics included cattle diseases, school milk, the attested herds scheme, and the government's 1937 white paper on milk policy.[50] Olga Nethersole continued to represent the League at conferences, and in September 1933 delivered a cogent paper arguing for attested herds and pasteurisation to agriculturists attending the annual meeting of the British Association. She remained at the helm of the People's League of Health until her death in 1951.[51]

What conclusions can one make about the League's campaign for clean milk? First, that Walter Fletcher was right: the 1930 investigation was a put up job. The same arguments had been raised, for example, at the British Medical Association's annual meeting in 1925, and in 1929 Savage had published a whole book on the subject, *The Prevention of Human Tuberculosis of Bovine Origin*.[52] Nevertheless, the inquiry effectively focused national attention on the issue, and co-ordinated the activities of, and helped form consensus among, a wide range of individuals and groups that were interested in the issue. The part played by the British Medical Association in the endeavor is also noteworthy. While the PLH contained people who belonged to the BMA, the latter largely ignored the League in the 1920s and rarely gave it a mention in its journal, but this aloofness changed with the tuberculosis inquiry. Dr Brackenbury's comments at the 24 March 1930 meeting undoubtedly went far to persuade non-PLH members, including Professor Dreyer, of both the PLH's and the project's validity, and plenty of good publicity in the *British Medical Journal* followed. In April 1932, for example, a lengthy editorial praised the PLH's newly published report as 'a compendium of the most up-to-date knowledge and opinions on the subject of bovine tuberculosis' that compared most favourably, the writer implied, with a Ministry of Health report on the same subject. This was described as having been produced too hastily in 1931, and in response to a request for information by one of the League's own members just two days after the decision to embark on the bovine tuberculosis inquiry.[53] How much guidance if any the British Medical Association as an entity provided as the campaign evolved is not clear. All that is sure is that the inquiry displayed a degree of sophistication, tactical skill and concentration not previously displayed by the PLH. The report on tuberculosis of bovine origin was the most significant achievement in the League's history.

Finally, another striking aspect of this campaign is that it corrects the suggestion that one of the reasons for the lack of effective milk legislation in the inter-war period was the absence of a consumer lobby.[54] If the dozens of professional organisations and voluntary societies that contributed to the production of the report and the millions of people whose local councils backed the report do not constitute a consumer lobby, then what does? Lack of success does not mean lack of existence. The People's League of Health had most certainly fulfilled its pledge to speak on behalf of the public.

## Acknowledgements

The research upon which this chapter is based was conducted with the assistance of a grant from the Burroughs Wellcome Fund.

## References

1 L. Bryder, *Below the Magic Mountain: A Social History of Tuberculosis in Twentieth-Century Britain*, Oxford, Clarendon, 1988, p. 7.
2 A. Stanley Griffith, 'The bovine tubercle bacillus in human tuberculosis', *British Medical Journal*, 1932, vol. 2, p. 501; Ministry of Agriculture, Fishery and Food, Factsheet A2, 'Tuberculosis in cattle and humans', 7 April 1999, p. 1.
3 Bryder, op. cit., p. 75.
4 The People's League of Health, *Report of a Special Committee Appointed by the People's League of Health Inc. to make a Survey of Tuberculosis of Bovine Origin in Great Britain*, London, 1932, pp. 17, 20.
5 People's League of Health, 1932, op. cit., pp. 15–7.
6 P. J. Atkins, 'White poison? The Social consequences of milk consumption, 1850–1930', *Social History of Medicine*, 1992, vol. 5, p. 225. By 1938, over 98 per cent of London's milk was pasteurised, and the death rate there from abdominal tuberculosis among children under five had fallen to less than 1 percent of the 1921 rate. W. A. Letham, Memo, 'Bovine tuberculosis', 11 February 1946, Public Record Office (hereafter PRO) FD1/1356.
7 J. Phillips and M. French, 'State Regulation and the hazards of milk, 1900–1939', *Social History of Medicine*, 1999, vol. 12, p. 379.
8 H. D. Kay, 'Future of the milk industry', *Nature*, 1942, vol. 150, p. 42; Phillips and

French, 1999, op. cit., p. 381; 'Tuberculous milk: conference on People's League of Health proposals', *Veterinary Record*, 1932, vol. 12, p. 859.

9  For more information about the agricultural lobby and difficulties surrounding the state regulation of food production, see Atkins, op. cit.; Phillips and French, 1999, op. cit.; F. B. Smith, *The Retreat of Tuberculosis, 1850–1951*, London, Croom Helm, 1988.

10  People's League of Health, 1932, op. cit., p. 39.

11  O. Nethersole, *The Inception of the League*, London, n.d. [1926], p. 9, PRO, FD1/1797; People's League of Health, *Second General Report 1922, 1923, 1924 and 1925*, London, 1926, p. 26.

12  O. Nethersole, *An Apologetic Defence (of my statement that a People's League of Health is Necessary and should be created as a means of raising the standard of health of the British Nation)*, London, 1917, p. 19.

13  For the Ministry of Health's approach to food regulations, see J. Phillips and M. French, 'Adulteration and Food Law, 1899–1939', *Twentieth-Century British History*, 1998, vol. 9, pp. 360–1.

14  People's League of Health, untitled pamphlet outlining objectives, n.d. [probably 1920], PRO, MH 58/153.

15  B. S. Townroe to Michael Heseltine, 26 January 1921, PRO, MH 58/153.

16  B. S. Townroe to Mr Gibbon, 27 November 1920, PRO, MH58/153.

17  Ibid.; see also Sir Bruce Bruce-Porter's comments, 'Minutes of a meeting of the People's League of Health', 26 February 1920, Contemporary Medical Archives Centre, Wellcome Trust Library, London (hereafter CMAC), SA/EUG.

18  B. S. Townroe, 'Precis of Correspondence between the Ministry of Health and the People's League of Health', 19 November 1920. PRO, MH 58/153.

19  'Olga Nethersole (1870–1951)' in W. C. Young, *Famous Actors and Actresses on the American Stage: Documents of American Theater History*, New York, R. R. Bowker, 1975, vol. 2, pp. 864–72; J. H. Reilly, 'A forgotten "Fallen Woman": Olga Nethersole's Sapho' in J. L. Fisher and S. Watt (eds), *When They Weren't Doing Shakespeare: Essays on Nineteenth-Century British and American Theatre*, Athens, GA, University of Georgia Press, 1989, pp. 106–20; J. H. Reilly, 'From wicked woman of the stage to new woman: the career of Olga Nethersole (1870–1951) actress-manager, suffragist, health pioneer', unpublished dissertation, Ohio State University, 1984; K. N. Johnson, 'Censuring "Sapho": regulating the fallen woman and the prostitute on the New York stage', *American Transcendental Quarterly*, (September 1996), pp. 167–86.

20  Even when the League's relations with the Ministry improved in the 1930s and 1940s, officials expressed their discomfort with Nethersole as a person. For example, in 1946 she was described as 'an eccentric woman with a tendency toward paranoia'. SFW [?] to Mr Hawton, 7 August 1946, PRO, MH 55/649.

21  Sir Aubrey Symonds to P. Barter, n.d., PRO, MH 58/153.

22  P. Barter to Sidney Greville [Prince of Wales' private secretary], 29 October 1920; LAN [?] to Mr Ward, 11 December 1931, PRO, MH 58/154.

23  SFW [?] to Mr Hawton, 7 August 1946, PRO MH 55/649.

24  In September 1906, she spoke at a fund-raiser in Edinburgh held by the Women's International Anti-Tuberculosis League, *The Times*, 29 September 1906, p. 12. She also represented the People's League of Health at TB conferences throughout the inter-war period; 'Tuberculosis of bovine origin in Great Britain', *British Medical Journal*, 1932, vol. 1, pp. 618–9; 'Tuberculosis and the milk supply: meeting at the Mansion House', *British Medical Journal*, 1932, vol. 2, pp. 117–8.

25  W. M. Fletcher to Georges Dreyer, 7 May 1930, PRO, FD 1/1797; Alfred Cox to Ernest Ward, 10 January 1930, and P. Strickland to G. C. Anderson, 13 January 1930, CMAC, SA/BMA.

26  People's League of Health, 1932, op. cit., pp. ix–xii.

27  People's League of Health, 1932, op. cit., p. xi.

28  W. M. Fletcher to A. Stanley Griffith, 17 March 1930, PRO, FD 1/1797.

29 W. M. Fletcher to A. S. McNalty, 7 May 1930, PRO, FD 1/1797.

30 W. M. Fletcher to Georges Dreyer, 7 May 1930, Georges Dreyer to W. M. Fletcher, 9 May 1930, PRO, FD 1/1797.

31 List of members of the General Committee, People's League of Health, 1932, op. cit., pp. xii–xiv; for more on Buckley's position, see W. Buckley, 'By what means can pure milk be obtained and at what cost: the point of view of the producer', *British Medical Journal*, 1925, vol. 2, pp. 248–9; Buckley also features in P. J. Atkins' chapter in this volume.

32 People's League of Health, 1932, op. cit., pp. xv–xvii; and see W. G. Savage, 'The League's safe milk campaign', People's League of Health advertisement, *The Times*, 5 April 1937, p. iii.

33 People's League of Health, 1932, op. cit., pp. 1–9.

34 Ibid., pp. 9–13.

35 Ibid., p. 23.

36 Ibid., 24–32 passim.

37 R. S. Williams to E. Mellanby, 15 June 1931, CMAC, PP MEL, B8/29.

38 Eric Pritchard, typed memoirs, chapter 'The Infants Hospital', pp. 1–6, CMAC, GC/49.

39 Ibid., p. 2.

40 People's League of Health, 1932, op. cit., pp. 33–5.

41 People's League of Health, *Deputation from the People's League of Health (Incorp.) To the Government of His Majesty King George V*, London, 1932, PRO, MH 58/154.

42 Unsigned Ministry of Health memo, 'Deputation of the People's League of Health on tuberculosis of bovine origin', n.d. [November 1932], p. 1, PRO, MH 58/154.

43 The Lord Mayor of Manchester told the gathering that the city had recently applied for government approval of a local bill to limit the sale of milk in the city to pasteurised or 'certified' or 'grade A (tuberculin tested)' milk. 'Tuberculosis and the milk supply: meeting at the Mansion House', *British Medical Journal*, 1932, vol. 2, pp. 117–8; 'Tuberculous milk: conference on People's League of Health proposals', *Veterinary Record*, 1932, vol. 12, pp. 859–60; see also 'Manchester Corporation. Part X milk supply. Draft clauses', n.d.[1932], PRO, MH 58/154.

44 Three of those five did not belong to the League: Sir Archibald Weigall, representing the Royal Agricultural Society of England; Professor F. T. G. Hobday, Principal of the Royal Veterinary College; and Dr Norman C. Wright, Director of the Hannah Dairy Research Institute. People's League of Health, *Deputation*, op. cit.

45 'Pasteurisation of Milk', 18 November 1932 [report of a meeting on 17 November], PRO, MH 58/154.

46 For brief details about the progress of the pasteurisation campaign after the onset of World War Two, see P. J. Atkins' chapter in this volume.

47 G. Savage, *The Social Construction of Expertise: The English Civil Service and Its Influence, 1919–1939*, Pittsburgh, University of Pittsburgh Press, 1996, p. 162.

48 Unsigned memo, 'Deputation of the People's League of Health on Tuberculosis of Bovine Origin', n.d. [November 1932], PRO, MH 58/154.

49 For example, Frederick Hobday, Principal of the Royal Veterinary College, and F. C. Minett, Professor of Pathology at the Royal Veterinary College and Director of its Research Institute.

50 These included: Special Committee of the Medical, Science and Veterinary Councils of the People's League of Health, Incorporated, *A Safe Milk Supply and the Report of the Committee on Cattle Diseases (Economic Advisory Council)*, London, 1934; Special Committee of the Medical, Science and Veterinary Councils of the People's League of Health (Incorporated), *Milk for School Children*, London, 1934; Report and Resolutions of a Special Meeting of the Original Bovine Tuberculosis Committee and the Veterinary Council of the People's League of Health (Incorporated), *A Safe Milk Supply and the Ministry of Agriculture and Fisheries Attested Herds Scheme*, London, 1935; Report and Resolutions of a Special Meeting of the People's League of Health's Veterinary Council and Special Bovine Tuberculosis Committee, *A Safe Milk Supply: Memorandum of the*

*People's League of Health on the Government's White Paper (Milk Policy) 1937*, London 1937; and People's League of Health, *A Safe Milk Supply: Memorandum of the People's League of Health on the Compulsory Pasteurisation of Milk*, London, 1943.

51  O. Nethersole, 'Discussion on milk production and distribution in relation to nutrition and disease', paper delivered to the Agricultural Section of the British Association Meeting, Leicester, 12 September 1933, Typescript copy in PRO, MH 58/154.

52  See 'British Medical Association. Proceedings of sections at the annual meeting, Bath, 1925. Section of Medical Sociology', *British Medical Journal*, 1925, vol. 2, pp. 241–53; W. G. Savage, *The Prevention of Human Tuberculosis of Bovine Origin*, London, 1929.

53  'Tuberculosis of bovine origin in Great Britain', *British Medical Journal*, 1932, vol. 1, pp. 618–9; Ministry of Health, 'A memorandum on bovine tuberculosis in man, with special reference to infection by milk' [by A. S. Griffith], *Reports on Public Health and Medical Subjects*, 193, No. 63.

54  Phillips and French, 1999, op. cit., pp. 386–7.

# 6 'Axes to grind': popularising the science of vitamins, 1920s and 1930s

*Harmke Kamminga*

In 1935 Leslie Harris, vitamin expert and head of the Dunn Nutritional Laboratory in Cambridge, published *Vitamins in Theory and Practice* – a book he hoped might be 'intelligible and of interest to the general reader', and also useful for those with a professional interest, including science students, medical men, household economists and social welfare workers.[1] In his final chapter, 'Dietetics – What to Eat?', Harris aimed to give 'the man in the street' information that would allow people to benefit practically from the latest nutritional knowledge. Under the subheading 'On the defensive', he commented:

> Maybe I shall be criticised by some of my professional colleagues, who hold that 'research workers should not be popularisers'. Enough to publish their results in technical form in the appropriate scientific journals! Leave the journalists to their job as best they may! To which criticism I think it is legitimate to reply that the public demand for knowledge cannot well be denied, and that it is better that it be supplied by those with intimate knowledge than by those whose information is second-hand and less accurate, or by those who have an axe to grind, or even worse by those whose primary interest is in the selling of some commercial foodstuff or preparation.[2]

Thus, in defending his foray into popular science writing, Harris presented himself as a disinterested scientist with intimate knowledge of vitamins, who considered it his duty to convey that knowledge, accurately and dispassionately, to his fellow-citizens. Setting himself apart from popularisers with less disinterested motives, he intimated that scientific experts like him were in the best position to make an objective selection of scientific facts for purposes of public education. This ideal view of popularisation as public education by disinterested experts, for the public's benefit, merits closer scrutiny.

Harris was unquestionably sincere in his efforts to help people benefit from the science he knew intimately, as were other vitamin researchers writing for a general readership in the same period. Furthermore, his conviction that the expert should play an active educational role seems reasonable in the light of the strongly mediated relationships between nutrition science and the foods people eat.[3] There was legitimate concern about the information on vitamins that was reaching the public from commercial sources, such as advertisements of vitamin preparations and vitamin-forti-fied foods, the packaging of these products, articles in magazines where they were advertised, and cookery books published by food companies. While these media served to spread information about vitamins widely, that infor-mation was biased in favour of the products being promoted.[4] Vitamins were used to grind other axes as well. As Rima Apple has shown, vitamins were enlisted in American popular culture to propagate an ideology of 'scientific motherhood', and to promote patriotism and military vigour during World War Two.[5]

In this chapter, I argue that vitamin researchers, too, had certain 'axes to grind' in taking their work out of the laboratory to broader readerships. It is not my intention to impute reprehensible motives, but to ask what functions popularisation served for scientists themselves. I take my cue from Ludwik Fleck's analysis of popular science, first published in German in the same year as Harris' book, which yields a perspective on popularisation that differs markedly from the ideal view expressed by Harris.[6] Drawing also on more recent theoretical work,[7] I approach the popularisation of vitamins as a multifunctional process involving many constituencies.

I focus on the 1920s and 1930s, the period in which vitamins were being consolidated – inside and outside the laboratory – and vitamin researchers increasingly published works aimed at non-specialists. I pay particular atten-tion to books because these, of all forms of publication, were intended to be non-ephemeral expositions of progress in vitamin research and its social import. Instead of viewing these general works as endproducts of scientific endeavour, however, I treat them as integral to the process of constructing vitamins as scientific facts and as everyday facts.

With reference to the earliest vitamin books, I draw attention especially to their authors' efforts to set up vitamin research as a distinct and coherent field of scientific endeavour, with its own community of experts; to promote and boost funding for vitamin research by enlisting different readerships; and to consolidate vitamins as undisputed facts. I then indicate how, as everyday facts, vitamins could in turn be enlisted for a range of other pursuits, includ-ing political agendas of different complexions, as illustrated by political appeals to vitamins made by science writers amidst the crises of the 1930s. The point is not that political appeals to vitamins were cynical in intent – far from it – but that they made vitamins even more robust as facts.

## Popularisation and the hardening of facts

In *Genesis and Development of a Scientific Fact*, Fleck drew attention to the cognitive importance of 'popular science'.[8] Defining it as 'science for non-experts', he stressed that popular science 'furnishes the major portion of every person's [scientific] knowledge': even the most specialised experts derive many scientific concepts, analogies and even their general viewpoint from popular science.[9]

Fleck's book consists of a lengthy and subtle answer to the question with which he opens the work, 'What is a fact?' Crucially, he presents scientific facts not as given objectively, but as created collectively: new concepts become accepted as facts only through social consolidation within and beyond the specialised community where they were first generated. The boundaries of specialist circles being open, there is a continuous exchange of ideas and experience between different communities, and in these exchanges facts are shaped, constrained and transformed in a series of feedback loops. Since the communities taking part in these exchanges range from fellow-scientists in neighbouring fields to the lay public, popularisation plays an important role in the consolidation of scientific facts.

More radically, Fleck argues that facts become *harder* the further they are taken away from specialist circles. At the cutting edge of research, facts are never absolutely fixed. As the specialist journals show, novel facts are invariably resisted by some fellow-specialists, some fact or other is always in dispute, and even facts that have become part of the consensual knowledge of a research community remain open to challenge. In that sense, all scientific facts are provisional in the context in which they are produced and guide further research. On the other hand, when facts are conveyed to neighbouring research communities in reviews or handbooks, or further afield in popular expositions, controversy gets toned down and facts get secured by linking them up with larger bodies of knowledge. Facts that are integrated with and shored up by an increasing range of knowledge and experience, up to and including everyday life, become increasingly difficult to contest. Once such facts are adopted in the popular domain, through the medium of popular science, they become incarnated as unquestioned objects of reality. As such, they shape public opinion, which in turn feeds back into research communities via education, policy decisions, and so on.

Popularisation, on this perspective, is a process that moves increasingly further outwards from small circles of specialists, but involves much more than a linear transfer of knowledge. Facts in the making can be taken in different directions simultaneously, ranging from closely connected peer groups to the lay public, and then back again in new forms. The toning down of specialist controversies in these exchanges has profound practical consequences. For example, chemists who tried to isolate and determine the structure of vitamin D in the 1920s were interested in the molecule because they had taken on board the message that vitamin D prevents rickets, although this matter was still hotly disputed among physiologists and biochemists investigating the aetiology of the disease. Sceptics in that circle were sidelined increasingly when chemists isolated and purified vitamin D and the compound was tested successfully for its antirachitic effects. On their part, chemists disagreed about the precise structure of vitamin D, but that controversy did not impinge on the therapeutic use of vitamin D by physicians or on the sale of commercially produced vitamin D preparations to consumers. The commercial success of these products stimulated industrial production of pure vitamin D preparations, and these were not only used therapeutically but as new tools for biochemists and physiologists investigating the role of vitamin D in metabolism.[10] At each stage, knowledge about vitamin D had been communicated to new communities and was put to new uses and refashioned. In the process, vitamin D was hardened as a fact.

This sketch of some of the movements of vitamin D across boundaries between different communities only hints at the intricacies of the process of consolidation. A full reconstruction, even for one vitamin, would require close attention to scientific, medical, industrial and dietary practices, as well as the policies that shaped these practices and were informed by them. My objective here is narrower. I explore Fleck's point that communication of facts is a necessary condition for their consolidation, and that the literature aimed at non-specialist readerships – from fellow-scientists to lay communities – plays a vital role in that process. It is this literature I examine for the case of vitamins (in the form of books), looking especially at the purposes for which different readerships were addressed.

In this last respect, I move beyond Fleck, whose prime concern was the epistemological function of popularisation in the hardening of facts. More recently, sociologists of science have highlighted other functions served by the wider dissemination of scientific facts by specialists, especially the promotion and legitimation of particular research endeavours by seeking the support of broader communities.[11] I draw on these insights, integrating them with Fleck's perspective.

## Turning vitamins into popular facts

The earliest books to introduce vitamins were *Die Vitamine* (1914) by the Polish-born biochemist, Casimir Funk, and *The Newer Knowledge of Nutrition* (1918) by Elmer McCollum, the American biological chemist.[12] Although far removed from what is conventionally regarded as popular science, these works can be seen as first steps in the process of popularisation: written by insiders, they were aimed at conveying specialist knowledge of a new subject to broader scientific and medical readerships. The books exemplify a point made by Richard Whitley, that in new fields of research there is not even a cohesive community of specialists in the first place. Even closely connected peer groups are yet to be persuaded that a distinct new field is under construction, and those engaged in the research need to put in much effort to be seen as 'experts' in the area of specialisation that is in the making.[13]

Besides disseminating new knowledge, an important function of these works was to stake out a new field. At that stage, it was not even agreed among participants what that field should be called. Funk had introduced the term 'vitamine' only two years before his book appeared,[14] but it was resisted strongly by workers doing related research. McCollum, for one, did not use the word, writing more neutrally about 'factors'; yet his book, which went through numerous editions under the same title, has come to be seen as a classic statement of how work on *vitamins* had transformed perspectives on nutrition. I shall come back to the issue of terminology.

Both Funk and McCollum brought together a multitude of observations from heterogeneous investigations in a systematic way, so that the reader gets the impression of a coherent research effort. Moreover, by linking the new nutritional findings with work in biological chemistry, physiology, pathology, medicine, veterinary science and agriculture, these authors strove to bring home the significance of research on the new food factors to a range of expert readerships beyond those immediately involved in that research.

While both books were addressed at scientific and medical readers, McCollum reached out further: he also made extensive links with dietary practices, as is announced in his subtitle, 'The Use of Food for the Preservation of Vitality and Health'. This form of linking became the primary method of making vitamin research relevant to the experiences of more general readerships: most books written subsequently by vitamin researchers included at least one chapter giving dietary advice, with information about the distribution of specific vitamins in different foods.

In the early 1920s, some vitamin books appeared that were aimed explicitly at a general readership as well as scientists in cognate fields and other professionals. In fact, fellow-scientists were still the primary target and the less scientifically literate reader would have found these works forbidding. Their authors presented the 'current state of knowledge' concerning vitamins with detailed arguments drawing on technical evidence, as would have been required to convince colleagues in other fields.

I consider three of these works, by authors engaged in vitamin research. While the authors worked in different countries and different institutional contexts, their books have significant features in common, as I aim to show. *Vitamins* by Ragnar Berg originated in Germany; *Vitamins and the Choice of Food* by Violet and Robert Plimmer came from Britain; and *The Vitamins* by Henry Sherman and S. L. Smith from the United States.[15]

The different origins of these books did result in differences in emphasis to which I shall refer. Most pertinently, in Germany Berg felt himself to be outside the main centres of activity in vitamin research, that is, Britain and the US. Moreover, while writing his book, this respected physiological chemist was dismissed from Lahmann's Sanatorium, a homeopathic institute in Dresden, whose directors did not value his scientific approach to nutrition.[16] Robert Plimmer, a highly regarded and senior British biochemist, also unexpectedly faced institutional difficulties after his move in 1919 to the Rowett Research Institute in Aberdeen, which was being built up as a major centre for research in animal nutrition. John Boyd Orr, who assumed a managerial role, was a sceptic about vitamins at this time and discouraged Plimmer's research, aimed at estimating vitamin requirements in fowl by means of feeding experiments. Conflicts came to an end in January 1922, when Plimmer took up the chair of chemistry at St Thomas's Hospital in London.[17] The book written with his wife Violet was based on three public lectures he gave in Aberdeen, to an audience beyond his immediate colleagues.

While for Berg and Plimmer institutional problems may have formed part of the motivation for reaching out to broader readerships, that was not the case for Sherman, Professor of Food Science at Columbia University in New York. He and his co-author, who worked as a specialist in biological and food chemistry for the US Department of Agriculture, wrote their book on the invitation of the American Chemical Society for its new monograph series, which was explicitly intended to promote chemical research.

One obvious feature the three books have in common is the use of the term 'vitamins' in the titles. Yet in every case the authors expressed reservations about it. The term had been coined by Funk as a contraction of 'vital amine' when he thought he had isolated the substance that prevents beri–beri and classified it chemically as an amine. He proposed that 'vitamines' constitute a class of dietary substances that are needed to prevent specific 'vitamine deficiency diseases', which he brought together under a new disease category.[18] Funk's peers judged his chemical interpretations to be premature and resisted his terminology, especially when it became clear that the substances they investigated were not amines. Insiders used a whole array of terms, none of which was adopted unanimously. At the same time, the term 'vitamine' was circulating widely in less specialised literature, including medical journals, and in 1920 Jack Drummond proposed the compromise of 'vitamin', to loosen the connection with the chemical category of amines.[19]

The authors considered here all devoted critical attention to the problem of nomenclature and mentioned the wide currency of the term vitamin(e). The Plimmers were most reticent, but placed their discussion pointedly in a chapter on 'The discovery of accessory food factors, or vitamins', giving all credit to Cambridge biochemist Frederick Gowland Hopkins. Funk's name is not mentioned once in the book, but insiders would have recognised the following statement as a curt dismissal of Funk:

> The word 'vitamine' has, however, crept into general use and is now spelled 'vitamin', the terminal *e* having been dropped, as it implied that the substances had a known chemical constitution.[20]

Sherman and Smith not only had problems with the chemical connotations of 'amine', but pointed out that 'vita' might claim too much, carrying 'an exaggerated implication of unique responsibility for life and vitality'.[21] Discussing Drummond's proposal, they commented: 'In view of the wide currency which the term vitamin has attained, this suggestion seems as practical as any and will be employed when convenient in the present work'.[22] Still they thought it desirable 'to make sufficient use of the physiological designations' and important to 'avoid habits of thought or expression which might prejudice the interpretation of experiments now in progress or yet to be made …'.[23]

These rather reluctant concessions to public usage suggest that public opinion was feeding back into the inner circle of vitamin researchers. Berg still tried to turn the terminological tide, unsuccessfully as it turned out. He reserved the term 'vitamin' strictly for the antineuritic substance supposedly isolated by Funk, and gave the term 'Ergänzungskörper' or 'accessory food factors' (which he judged satisfactory in principle but too colloquial) his own 'scientific rendering' of 'complettins'. He also coined the term 'acompletti-noses' for the deficiency diseases associated with the different complettins, A, B and C.[24] While Berg used this idiosyncratic nomenclature throughout his book, he gave it the title of *Vitamins* because the public was not yet suffi-ciently familiar with 'complettins'. Hence, Berg was aware that nobody would buy or read a book with complettins in the title, because people would have no idea what it was about!

It comes as no surprise that Funk, by contrast, was deeply satisfied by the popularity of the term he had introduced. In the 1922 edition of his book, he wrote:

> In our opinion, the name 'Vitamine', proposed by us in 1912, contributed in no small measure to the dissemination of these ideas. The word, 'Vitamine', served as a catchword which meant something even to the uninitiated, and it was not by mere accident that just at that time, research developed so markedly in this direction.[25]

Given the inner circle's opposition to his term over the previous decade, Funk's implied claim on credit for the expansion of vitamin research was impudent. Yet he surmised correctly that unification of terminology helps communica-tion and dissemination. For our reluctant authors, too, it was much easier to bring together many separate lines of investigation by translating them all into the language of vitamins. While they expressed dissatisfaction that public usage had forced their hand, they drew considerable benefit from that pressure.

The authors did bring together evidence from many disparate investiga-tions over a long period. Their emphasis on technical evidence was necessary because vitamins were still contested in scientific and medical circles at the time. In their selection of evidence, the authors resorted to a great deal of reinterpretation and translation of much earlier investigations as revealing the existence and actions of vitamins, long before vitamins had been thought of. The books by Sherman and Smith and by Berg, as well as the vastly expanded second edition of Funk's book, had huge bibliographies, with some 1000 entries in the first case, and over 1500 entries in each of the other two. Placing vitamin work in the context of evidence from so many sources helped to suggest that the facts presented were supported by an enormous number of lines of investigation, thus anchoring vitamins more securely as facts.

As insiders, the authors themselves were convinced of the importance of vitamin research and its beneficial practical implications, but at the time it was not a foregone conclusion that others would be similarly persuaded. One of the functions of their books was to promote vitamin research by efforts to recruit others to the field. Accordingly, the authors specified lines for further research and emphasised the need for support of new investigations. This dual aspect of the promotion of vitamin research helps explain the authors' choice of targeted readerships: they aimed to attract readers with scientific credentials who might join the vitamin research community and also prospective patrons and policy makers among a more general readership.

In terms of research priorities and recruitment efforts, the emphasis differed in accordance with the authors' own research interests. Sherman and Smith called for more chemical studies of vitamins at many points. Their book was organised in a way suited to a predominantly chemical readership: each of their main chapters deals with a different vitamin, that is, a different chemical substance, albeit of unknown chemical composition and structure at that stage. Clearly, there was much work to do for chemists.

The Plimmers stressed the need for investigations of the metabolic and physiological role of vitamins in health and disease. The call for basic research of this kind would have appealed to the wider community of biochemists. This was consistent with Robert Plimmer's commitment to the young science of biochemistry, which he promoted through his active involvement in the Biochemical Society, which he had helped to found, and as co-editor (with F. G. Hopkins) of the *Monographs on Biochemistry* series. By presenting their material at a somewhat lower level of technicality and using the vitamin deficiency diseases as a major organising theme, the Plimmers also adapted their book to a medical readership. Emphasis on the medical significance of vitamins may have been directed most specifically at Robert Plimmer's new colleagues at St Thomas's Hospital.

Appeal to a wider readership was made most obviously by emphasis on the social importance of vitamin research, in all cases especially in final chapters that included extensive tables with qualitative information on the distribution of vitamins in different foods. These chapters were presented explicitly as being of special relevance to the general reader; Sherman and Smith even advised the 'non-technical reader' to read the last chapter first, so as to get an initial idea of the 'true significance' of vitamins.[26]

Berg was most explicit in addressing lay readers to mobilise funding and institutional support for vitamin research. In his conclusion, directed clearly at policy makers, he deplored how far Germany lagged behind in the new biochemical research in nutrition, blaming the unavailability of British and American journals during the war. In his final paragraphs he put in a plea for the foundation, by the state, of large multidisciplinary institutes dedicated to nutritional research, and institutes of nutritional hygiene to ensure that the findings of the transformed science of nutrition would find application in daily life. He ended with the exhortation, 'The consciousness of the masses must be permeated with a practical knowledge of the new science of dietetics'.[27]

In Britain, books soon began to appear that took the new science of dietetics as a whole to the public at large, presenting new biochemical insights into the nutritional value of all components of food, not just vitamins. While the Plimmers had focussed on vitamins throughout *Vitamins and the Choice of Food,* they placed food first in their next title, *Food, Health, Vitamins,*[28] broadening their scope and potential readership. Even more clearly aimed at a popular market, in the same year, was *Food and the Family* by Vernon Mottram, Professor of Physiology at King's College of Household and Social Science, London.[29] Mottram sought to present 'to the lay reader, in terms as intelligible as they may be made, the broad outlines of the results of modern scientific research into the values of foodstuffs, with especial reference to economy in food compatible with health'.[30] Vitamins were given much attention, but not singled out especially in this book. Here, they were placed firmly in an everyday context – that of the family meal.

In 1928, vitamins made their appearance in a book that would be classified as popular science by any criteria, *Hunger Fighters* by the very widely (and internationally) read US science writer Paul de Kruif.[31] With this book, written to entertain as much as to convey messages about the excitement, fascination and fruits of science, vitamins were placed on the map of popular culture. I shall say more about this book and its author in the next section.

By the late 1920s, vitamins had been brought to the attention of a highly diverse range of readerships. As facts, vitamins had been taken out of the research laboratory to colleagues with related expertise in physiology, biochemistry, chemistry and more, to physicians, public health officials, policy makers, dieticians, students, housewives, and the reading public more generally. As new communities took up vitamins, new interests came into play and vitamins were put to new uses.[32] As a result, vitamins as facts acquired new connotations. Used therapeutically, vitamins became medical facts; exploited industrially, they became commercial facts; and chosen as components of everyday diets, they became household facts.

Once vitamins had been turned into popular facts, they were indeed unquestioned objects of reality. As such, they could be used for a range of other purposes, away from the special contexts of the research laboratory, the clinic, the industrial plant and the dinner table. By way of example, I now turn to the enlistment of vitamins for political change.

## Turning vitamins into political facts

Vitamins were given a new, political identity amidst the deprivations of economic depression and mass unemployment in the 'hungry thirties'. Vitamin researchers themselves helped to forge this identity, through their participation in debates about nutritional policy and the links between poverty and ill health through deficient diet. At least until the mid-1930s, there was no expert consensus on the quantitative requirements for vitamins in humans, nor on the extent and causes of malnourishment, and these issues were hotly disputed.[33] While the debates and their translations into policy are beyond the scope of this chapter, I want to consider briefly their impact on books by vitamin researchers for the general public. Indeed, one reason for writing such books was to set the terms of the debates.

A common theme of books written by experts was the importance of the qualitative composition of diet, not just the quantity of food required to still hunger. While the scientific basis for this message was not new in the 1930s, there was a new emphasis on the dangers of hidden malnourishment and the need for optimum vitamin intakes: extrapolating from animal studies, insiders invariably stressed that diets even mildly deficient in vitamins were a common cause of general ill health which, over time, could cause severe damage.

Taking account of the relatively high cost of foods recommended for their vitamin content, many authors identified widespread poverty as the major obstacle to the implementation of scientifically informed nutritional practices. Not all vitamin researchers agreed, some seeing widespread public ignorance of sound dietary principles as the root problem.[34] Notably, the Plimmers maintained that it was possible to eat properly on a very low income if foods were selected and prepared sensibly; they included inexpensive menu suggestions in their books, with detailed costing, up to the late 1930s.[35] Most insiders writing for the general public at this time, however, emphasised the link between faulty diet and poverty, adding comments on inequalities in income and the political necessity to alleviate or eradicate poverty.[36] Such comments were made out of genuine concern for human suffering, and if they seemed to have a stronger political content than any statements by authors who did not challenge the status quo, including the Plimmers, it is because any criticism of the social order was seen as politically loaded. The stance of authors who were content with the status quo was, of course, equally political; they just did not need to use the language of politics overtly. Hence, while vitamins were politicised by supporters and critics of the social order alike, as facts they were given a specific political content largely by the latter, within and beyond the vitamin community.

The transformation of vitamins into political objects, which made them even more robust as facts, shows up particularly clearly in writings about vitamins by authors outside the vitamin circle. A striking illustration is provided by two books in which de Kruif highlighted vitamins, published eight years apart. De Kruif had abandoned a career in medical bacteriology at the Rockefeller Institute in New York for scientific journalism, so that he could propagate the marvels of medical science to a wide public.[37] His popular science books, inaugurated in 1926 with the famous *Microbe Hunters,* told vivid adventure stories about scientific pioneers whose discoveries had changed the world. Always stressing the 'human interest' angle, de Kruif excelled at integrating science and everyday life.

De Kruif introduced vitamins in his second book, *Hunger Fighters* of 1928, and returned to them in 1936 in *Why Keep Them Alive?*[38] In the interval, he had undergone a conversion about which he was very explicit: where he had extolled scientific progress before, he later felt compelled to protest vehemently about an economic order that placed the fruits of scientific progress beyond the reach of many. His presentation of the science of vitamins changed radically as a consequence.

The subject of *Hunger Fighters* was the heroic fight against hunger by scientists who had transformed plant and animal breeding, soil science, veterinary science and nutrition science in the US. After sections on 'Wheat', 'Meat' and 'Maize', vitamins took up the final section, entitled 'The Hidden Hunger', in three stories of discovery.[39] First came Stephen Babcock's discovery that certain diets, which do not make animals – or people – feel hungry, can cause a 'hidden hunger' that eventually manifests itself in disease and even death.[40] For de Kruif, this 'finder of the hidden hunger' and prime mover behind the research at Wisconsin that brought world renown to 'ambitious' Elmer McCollum and 'serious' Harry Steenbock, was 'the father of the vitamins'.[41]

The hero of the next story was Steenbock himself, the 'sun-trapper' who gave antirachitic activity to foods normally low in vitamin D,[42] by irradiating them with ultraviolet light; and who assigned his patent rights on the process to a non-profit making research foundation at Wisconsin, newly established for that purpose.

The final tale concerned Joseph Goldberger's compassionate struggle against pellagra,[43] which he found to be a vitamin deficiency disease, or hidden hunger, that could be held at bay by a meat-rich diet. As meat was beyond the means of the poor blacks in the south who suffered most from the disease, Goldberger searched desperately for a cheaper dietary solution, eventually discovering the beneficial effects of dried yeast.

In each case, de Kruif very skilfully presented discovery as a drawn-out process involving many steps and stages. Realisation of the true facts did not dawn on his heroes in one leap, but there was a build-up of insights and a lot of hard work, as well as wrong turnings and happy accidents. Invariably, the heroes also had to overcome resistance and obstruction from others. By the end of the stories, however, vitamins and vitamin deficiencies had become incontrovertible facts, and facts of enormous social import.

Eight years later de Kruif used these facts for very different purposes in *Why Keep Them Alive?* The result of a collaboration with his wife Rhea, this book was a passionate indictment of an economic order that allowed thousands of children to suffer poverty, hunger and disease in a country full of riches. De Kruif was furious that the fruits of science, which he himself had propagated with such enthusiasm, were not being used to create a world of plenty for all, as they could and should be, but to support gross social inequalities.[44] In a way that is structurally akin to his accounts of scientific discovery, de Kruif vividly related how he became aware, in stages, of social injustices and of the impotence of science in the face of them when the political will to set them right is lacking.

The chapter headings alone are suggestive of de Kruif's process of discovery, and of the tone of sarcastic outrage that pervades the book:

I.      Why should they die?
II.     Discovery that children are forgotten.
III.    Discovery that it's dollars or children.
IV.     The power of science without money.
V.      The people's death-fight.
VI.     Drought is a blessing.
VII.    Who owns our science?
VIII.   Observation of children of the shadows.
IX.     Should children eat?
X.      Children can live!

De Kruif's discovery began with a hard-hitting letter from the poet Ezra Pound, who alerted him to poverty as the biggest killer of all, the 'man-made cause of dying that was more murderous than all the swarming subvisible billions of man-killing microbes put together'.[45] At Rhea's instigation, the couple travelled through the country to see for themselves the human misery wrought by poverty and hunger. Via harrowing descriptions of failures to combat easily preventable disease through sheer lack of money, de Kruif worked up to a climax of indignation by returning to the hidden hunger theme, in his chapter 'Should children eat?'[46] This time he wrote that the details of the science of vitamins 'shouldn't detain us', since they had become common knowledge. In a few brief paragraphs he recapitulated what we all knew about vitamins A, B, C and D, using phrases such as 'it is old stuff', 'it is nothing new', 'school kids now know'.[47] Vitamins were everyday facts that required no further explanation.

De Kruif introduced just one new scientific element: recent observations of the cumulative effects of low-vitamin diets. The discovery that the hidden hungers can gnaw away perniciously before any clinical damage becomes manifest made it imperative that people, especially growing children, should eat diets with the full range of vitamins in higher quantities than had been thought necessary before.[48]

For de Kruif, there was no excuse for children suffering malnourishment and hidden hungers. The solution was well known and it was simple: dietary vitamins. No more scientific research was needed here, and de Kruif was scathing about scientists who retreated to their laboratories in search of cheap solutions to malnourishment instead of joining him in his outcry against poverty. What was needed was the political will to make healthy diets available to all, and that meant changing the economic order.[49] His general message was that science was already capable of producing a world of plenty, a world in which all children would be able to live decently. Yet want and misery were still rife, and that situation could only be changed by political means. In de Kruif's conversion from the cause of science to the cause of poverty, he used vitamins as political facts.

For all his savage criticisms of US capitalism, de Kruif did not spell out a positive route for change, insisting that he was a reporter, not an economist. His books of the 1930s indicate that his political sympathies veered largely, if erratically, towards the left. Above all, he developed a compassionate commitment to the underdog. In *Why Keep Them Alive?* he was particularly taken with the Social Credit theory of the British engineer Major Clifford Hugh Douglas,[50] whose books he had read avidly on the recommendation of Ezra Pound. ('I was that suggestible', he later wrote in his memoirs.[51]) The economic mechanisms and political ramifications of the Douglas scheme were highly contentious,[52] but de Kruif never showed any awareness of these intricacies in his writings. The central message he drew from his reading, and the pervading theme of *Why Keep Them Alive?*, was that wealth could and should be redistributed more fairly.

In the same year that de Kruif's book appeared in the US, John Boyd Orr published his *Food, Health and Income* in the UK,[53] which was taken up widely to argue for the necessity to redistribute wealth. Orr's book was not a work of popular science, but its conclusions were very clear and disseminated widely. It is a sober report of Orr's investigations of expenditure on food by families in different income groups and his comparisons of these findings with the minimum cost of an adequate diet, in accordance with optimum standards set in the US. He found a strong correlation between income and nutritional quality of diet and, extrapolating from his study, concluded that nearly half the British population lived on a diet deficient in one or more classes of nutrients, especially vitamins and minerals. (Orr was, by this time, a convert to vitamins.)

This shocking conclusion about the extent of malnourishment, and its link with poverty, had a major impact on public debates about nutrition policy. In consequence, vitamins featured even more widely in arguments for the alleviation of poverty through increased state benefits, higher wages for workers and food subsidies. Indeed, Orr, as a progressive conservative who favoured state planning, used such arguments himself.[54] More radically, vitamins were invoked in arguments for the eradication of poverty by means of a revolutionary transformation of society, among others by scientists with an overt leftwing agenda.

The depression and the rise of fascism in Europe radicalised a significant number of British scientists who were already appalled at the uses to which science had been put in the Great War.[55] Convinced of the rationality of science and of the social benefits science could bring if used responsibly, they put their hopes in a scientifically planned society along socialist lines.[56] Convinced, too, that rational planning required scientifically educated citizens, many of them were actively engaged in workers' education and wrote popular works of science.[57] Using everyday examples, they set out the social functions of science, coupled with political messages about the conditions under which the full potential of science could be realised and about the transformation required to achieve those conditions. Vitamins, and their link with poverty, featured in many of these writings, not just as popular facts, but as political facts.

To illustrate this point, I use an example from *Science and Everyday Life* by J. B. S. Haldane, geneticist, outspoken Marxist and prolific author of popular works.[58] The essays in this collection, published originally in the communist newspaper *The Daily Worker*, include four on vitamins. After succinctly discussing the basic scientific information and the medical and social significance of each of the vitamins A, B, C and D, Haldane ended with a political message directed against capitalism, fascism, or colonialism. The essay on vitamin B ('aneurin') concluded:

> There is no question but that millions of people in India are terribly short of aneurin. Beri-beri is common in children and pregnant mothers in the rice-eating districts of Southern India, and is likely to continue so until real wages are raised, though this condition is partly due to the introduction of factory methods of rice-milling, which remove all bran. Since the British introduced these methods, along with other features of capitalism, they are responsible for this disease, and should either take steps to remedy it or make way for others who will do so.[59]

In Haldane's hands, then, vitamins became socialist facts.

## Conclusions

I have here tried to illustrate some functions of the popularisation of science that are not captured by the ideal view of popularisation as public education, by disinterested experts, for the public's benefit. Expressing this view in 1935, Harris implied that it is the duty of experts to convey to the lay public, accurately and without axes to grind, the hard facts produced in their laboratories. In contrast, Fleck argued that the expert's facts are not hard at the point of production but, on the contrary, are made hard in the process of popularisation. Fleck's perspective also undermines perspectives on popularisation by experts as a disinterested process. The hardening of facts is crucial for the continuation of the research of specialist circles, and requires the wider dissemination of facts among communities whose support is being enlisted.

The example of vitamins has shown up the role played by the wider dissemination of contested facts in the creation, promotion and consolidation of a new field of research. Vitamins became harder in the process of popularisation, not because they were simplified, but because they became increasingly difficult to contest as they were integrated in larger bodies of knowledge and experience. Put to new uses and supported by new interests, vitamins were given new layers of meaning by different publics, initially enlisted in support of vitamins by insiders themselves.

On this perspective, popularisation is not a unidirectional transfer of knowledge from expert to lay public, but a series of exchanges in which facts are shaped and used for purposes selected by all participants. The process benefits scientific insiders in making their objects of research increasingly robust, but insiders do not have sole control over the fate of these objects outside the research laboratory. As vitamins became entrenched as popular facts, they could be enlisted in the pursuit of a whole range of agendas, up to and including the transformation of the social order. Even these uses served a useful function for insiders, however, by making vitamins even more pervasive as popular facts and even more important as objects of scientific investigation.

Although they deplored appeals to vitamins for prejudiced purposes, popularisers among vitamin researchers, too, had axes to grind. Their engagement with disputes about nutrition policy in the 1930s is a case in point. Harris himself highlighted the links between poverty and faulty diet in this politically charged context. That context not only helps to explain the incentive he had for writing his popular book, but also his careful positioning of himself as a disinterested expert: it would not have done for the director of a laboratory funded by the Medical Research Council to be seen to be engaging in political activities.[60] Yet it was inevitable that the facts he – as a vitamin expert – presented to the public would contribute to the pool of facts available to political activists.

The attempts of Harris and other vitamin researchers to influence policy debates were entirely honourable. My point is that they did have an axe to grind, and we gain historical insight into the enterprise of popularisation if we can identify the particular axes that were being ground in specific cases.

## Acknowledgements

I would like to thank the conference participants for very helpful comments on the first version of this paper, most particularly Sally Horrocks and Kelly Loughlin. For constructive suggestions and encouragement with this expanded version, I am especially grateful to David Smith, Bernard Harris and Andrew Cunningham. I thank the Wellcome Trust for financial support.

## References

1  L. J. Harris, *Vitamins in Theory and Practice*, Cambridge, Cambridge University Press, 1935. Page references here are to the second edition, 1937.
2  Ibid., p. 188; for a similar statement, see pp. xiii, xiv.
3  R. D. Apple, *Vitamania: Vitamins in American Culture*, New Brunswick, NJ, Rutgers University Press, 1996; H. Kamminga and Λ. Cunningham (eds), *The Science and Culture of Nutrition, 1840–1940*, Amsterdam, Rodopi, 1995; D. Maurer and J. Sobal (eds), *Eating*

*Agendas*, New York, de Gruyter, 1995; D. F. Smith (ed.), *Nutrition in Britain: Science, Scientists and Politics in the Twentieth Century*, London, Routledge, 1997.

4  R. D. Apple, '"They need it now": advertising and vitamins, 1925–1940', *Journal of Popular Culture*, 1988, vol. 22, pp. 65–83; Apple, 1996, op. cit.; S. M. Horrocks, in Kamminga and Cunningham, op. cit., pp. 235–58; S. M. Horrocks, in Smith, op. cit., pp. 53–74.

5  R. D. Apple, 'Constructing mothers: scientific motherhood in the nineteenth and twentieth centuries', *Social History of Medicine*, 1995, vol. 8, pp. 161–78; R. D. Apple, this volume, chap. 9.

6  L. Fleck, *Genesis and Development of a Scientific Fact*, transl. F. Bradley and T. J. Trenn, Chicago, Chicago University Press, 1979.

7  R. Cooter and S. Pumfrey, 'Separate spheres and public places: reflections on the history of science popularization and science in popular culture', *History of Science*, 1994, vol. 32, pp. 237–67; S. Hilgartner, 'The dominant view of popularization: conceptual problems, political uses', *Social Studies of Science*, 1990, vol. 20, pp. 519–39; and especially R. Whitley, 'Knowledge producers and knowledge acquirers: popularisation as a relation between scientific fields and their publics', in T. Shinn and R. Whitley (eds), *Expository Science: Forms and Functions of Popularisation*, Dordrecht, Reidel, 1985, pp. 3–28.

8  Fleck, op. cit., pp. 111–25.

9  Ibid., p. 112.

10  On the rickets controversy, see D. F. Smith and M. Nicolson, 'The "Glasgow School" of Paton, Findlay and Cathcart: conservative thought in chemical physiology, nutrition and public health', *Social Studies of Science*, 1989, vol. 19, pp. 194–238; on chemical investigations and industrial production of vitamin D, see H. Kamminga, 'Vitamins and the dynamics of molecularization: biochemistry, policy and industry in Britain, 1914–1939', in S. de Chadarevian and H. Kamminga (eds), *Molecularizing Biology and Medicine: New Practices and Alliances, 1910s–1970s*, Amsterdam, Harwood, 1998, pp. 83–105.

11  Hilgartner, op. cit.; Whitley, op. cit.

12  C. Funk, *Die Vitamine*, Wiesbaden, Bergmann, 1914; E. V. McCollum, *The Newer Knowledge of Nutrition: The Use of Foods for the Preservation of Vitality and Health*, New York, MacMillan, 1918.

13  Whitley, op. cit.

14  C. Funk, 'The etiology of deficiency diseases', *Journal of State Medicine*, 1912, vol. 20, pp. 341–68.

15  R. Berg, *Vitamins: A Critical Survey of the Theory of Accessory Food Factors*, transl. E. Paul and C. Paul, London, Allen & Unwin, 1923; V. G. Plimmer and R. H. A. Plimmer, *Vitamins and the Choice of Food*, London, Longmans, 1922; H. C. Sherman and S. L. Smith, *The Vitamins*, New York, Chemical Catalog Company, 1922.

16  Berg, op. cit., p. 28; for biographical information, see *Lexikon bedeutender Chemiker*, Leipzig, Bibliographisches Institut, 1988, pp. 38–9.

17  D. F. Smith, 'The use of "team work" in the practical management of research in the interwar period: John Boyd Orr at the Rowett Research Institute', *Minerva*, 1999, vol. 37, pp. 259–80.

18  Funk, 1912, op. cit.

19  J. C. Drummond, 'The nomenclature of the so-called accessory food factors (vitamins)', *Biochemical Journal*, 1920, vol. 14, p. 660.

20  Plimmer and Plimmer, op. cit., p. 51.

21  Sherman and Smith, op. cit., p. 15.

22  Ibid., p. 16.

23  Ibid., pp. 16–17.

24  Berg, op. cit., pp. 21–4; see also translators' discussion, pp. 9–11.

25  C. Funk, *The Vitamins*, transl. H. E. Dubin, Baltimore, Williams and Wilkins, 1922, (second edition) p. 18.

26  Sherman and Smith, op. cit., p. 1.

27 Berg, op. cit., p. 337.

28 R. H. A. Plimmer and V. G. Plimmer, *Food, Health, Vitamins*, London, Longmans, 1925 (and many subsequent editions).

29 V. H. Mottram, *Food and the Family*, London, Nisbet, 1925.

30 Ibid., p. x.

31 First published in the United States in 1928; page references here are to an inexpensive European edition: P. de Kruif, *Hunger Fighters*, Leipzig, Albatross, 1940.

32 Kamminga, op. cit.

33 On contests in dietary standard setting in the 1930s in Britain and by international bodies, respectively, see D. F. Smith, 'The social construction of dietary standards', in Maurer and Sobal, op. cit., pp. 261–78; P. Weindling, 'The role of international organizations in setting nutritional standards in the 1920s and 1930s', in Kamminga and Cunningham, op. cit., pp. 319–32.

34 D. F. Smith and M. Nicolson, 'Nutrition, education, ignorance, and income: a twentieth-century debate', in Kamminga and Cunningham, op. cit., pp. 288–318.

35 R. H. A. Plimmer and V. G. Plimmer, *Food, Health, Vitamins*, London, Longmans, 1938, (eight edition), chap. 13, and pp. 206–9.

36 For examples in books written by insiders for the general public, see W. R. Aykroyd, *Vitamins and Other Dietary Essentials*, London, Heinemann, 1933, chaps 15–18; A. L. Bacharach, *Science and Nutrition*, London, Watts, 1938, chaps 18, 19 (and also Preface by Jack Drummond); L. J. Harris, op. cit., chap. 9; V. H. Mottram, 'Medicine', in D. Hall and others, *The Frustration of Science*, London, Allen & Unwin, 1935, pp. 79–97.

37 For biographical information, see J. Kutulas, 'Paul Henry de Kruif (1890–1971)', *Dictionary of American Biography*, New York, Scribner, 1994, Suppl. 9, pp. 225–6; P. de Kruif, *The Sweeping Wind: A Memoir*, London, Hart-Davis, 1962.

38 First published in the US in 1936; the edition used here is P. de Kruif, *Why Keep Them Alive?*, Leipzig, Albatross, 1937.

39 De Kruif, 1928, op. cit., pp. 227–311.

40 Ibid., pp. 227–54.

41 Ibid., p. 254.

42 Ibid., pp. 254–81.

43 Ibid., pp. 282–311.

44 De Kruif, 1936, op. cit., p. 10.

45 Ibid.

46 Ibid., pp. 193–220.

47 Ibid., p. 199.

48 Ibid., pp. 200–2.

49 Ibid., pp. 207–10.

50 Ibid., pp. 30–2.

51 De Kruif, 1962, op. cit., p. 187.

52 C. H. Douglas, *Economic Democracy*, London, Palmer, 1920; C. H. Douglas, *Social Credit*, London, Palmer, 1924. For criticisms, see F. Henderson, *Foundations for the World's New Age of Plenty*, London, Gollancz, 1933; W. R. Hiskett, *Social Credits or Socialism: An Analysis of the Douglas Social Credit Scheme*, London, Gollancz, 1935.

53 J. B. Orr, *Food, Health and Income: Report on a Survey of Adequacy of Diet in Relation to Income*, London, MacMillan, 1936.

54 J. B. Orr, 'Nutritional science and state planning', in J. B. Orr and others, *What Science Stands For*, London, Allen & Unwin, 1937, pp. 11–29. See also Smith, this volume, chap. 7.

55 See G. P. Werskey, *The Visible College: A Collective Biography of British Scientists and Socialists of the 1930s*, London, Free Association Books, 1988 (first published 1978).

56 The classic source is J. D. Bernal, *The Social Function of Science*, London, Routledge, 1939.

57 Probably the greatest bestseller was L. Hogben, *Science for the Citizen: A Self-Educator*

making during both world wars. He concluded that there is little evidence of professional interests of scientists being set aside in wartime.[5] During the First World War, however, there may have been a 'strategic consensus' which helped scientists to gain a foothold in policy. In contrast, it was suggested that the Second World War was an opportunity for scientists to press longstanding claims for influence in food policy, resulting in a scramble for position. The role of the Scientific Food Committee was mentioned very briefly. The current chapter presents the results of more recent research on the Scientific Food Committee, providing further insights into the role of science and the dynamics of food policy making in Britain during the Second World War.

## Scientific data, food policy, and policy culture

It has been suggested that certain research findings on the food consumption of the population, produced by a project supervised by Orr immediately before the war, played an important role in the formulation of wartime food policy.[6] These are data from a large-scale dietary survey and nutritional experiment which began in 1937, supported by the Carnegie United Kingdom Trust. Orr had hoped that the results of this project would break resistance by the government to the conclusions of his earlier report, *Food, Health and Income*, published in 1936. The latter showed how the quality and quantity of diet, and health and physique, deteriorated with decreasing income.[7] Orr saw this as a powerful case for costly state intervention in the food system in the interests of improving the diet of the poor, but this failed to materialise. When the war began, the Carnegie survey was complete, but little progress had been made with writing up its findings. During the autumn of 1939, some of the data were rapidly analysed and submitted to a long-term ally of Orr, Walter Elliot, then Minister of Health, in the hope that they would help the minister to intervene in policy making. Elliot was a member of the Food Policy Committee of government ministers with responsibilities for different aspects of food. This committee was formed at the end of November 1939 to oversee food policy. It was chaired by the Lord Privy Seal, a senior member of the government who assisted the Prime Minister in co-ordinating the activities of other ministers.

The archival record shows that Elliot's use of the Carnegie data was hardly decisive. In a memorandum discussed in December 1939, Elliot referred to Orr's data on consumption by income group and argued that variation of diet by income could be overcome by pegging the price of essential foodstuffs. In the case of milk he suggested that it was so important nutritionally that the price should be reduced.[8] Elliot's memorandum made little impact, but it was agreed that the Ministry of Health should hold consultations with other ministries on the supply of milk to mothers and pre-school children. The Ministry of Health then suggested that cheap milk could be made available for these groups without a means test.[9] The latter proposal was remitted to a committee of chief civil servants of the ministries represented on the Food

Policy Committee, chaired by Sir Horace Wilson, permanent secretary to the Treasury. Wilson was a close adviser and confidant of Neville Chamberlain, Prime Minister of the conservative-led National government that was in power at the outbreak of war. Five months later, in April 1940, the inter-departmental committee reported that the cheap milk proposal could not be implemented immediately and called first for consideration of general questions regarding the principles of differential pricing.[10] But wider pressures forced the pace of change. Rationing, introduced in January 1940, inevitably involved some teething problems and these, along with price rises, resulted in increasing popular discontent with the government's food policies.[11] One consequence was the replacement of the Minister of Food, W. S. Morrison, by Lord Woolton on 4 April 1940. Morrison had occupied the position since September 1939, when the ministry was set up, and had earlier been responsible for the department that undertook pre-war food planning. Because of the public criticism of food policy, as well as broader shifts in government policy resulting from the end of the 'phoney war' period,[12] the ministerial committee now wanted action, and as a result a cheap milk scheme was rapidly devised for introduction at the beginning of July 1940.[13] The demands for action on food policy in the Spring of 1940 were encouraged by the publication of a book entitled *Feeding the People in Wartime* by Orr and his colleague, David Lubbock, who had co-ordinated the Carnegie survey.[14] The book, which like *Food, Health and Income* was published by Macmillan, included data derived from the survey, and a further consequence of the political pressure generated during this period was the formation of the Scientific Food Committee.

The Carnegie data were certainly used in internal government documents, in additional to those already mentioned,[15] but the sequence of events briefly outlined illustrates the point that the link between scientific findings and policy decisions is by no means straightforward. It cannot be argued, for example, that the presentation of the Carnegie data to the government led to the formulation of the welfare milk scheme. On the other hand, this chapter will show that active lobbying by scientists can have broader effects. The 'effect of science on policy', may be looked at not only in terms of the application of scientific findings, but also in terms of changes in the 'policy culture' or the broad principles of policy making. Berridge and Stanton have referred to such shifts as 'changes in climates of debate and policy agendas'.[16] Such changes may be indicated, for example, by a shift from emphasis upon preserving the *status quo* towards an interventionist approach, or shifts in the balance of power between government ministries. Looked at in this way, we can see more clearly the contribution of scientists such as Orr to wartime food policy – not as passive providers of data, but as activists with long-term aims, intervening tactically in a thoroughly political process.

## The formation of the Scientific Food Committee

From the beginning of the war occasional voices criticised the government's food policies, but at the end of March 1940 an intense debate began in *The Times*. This was launched by an article by A. P. McDougall, livestock commissioner for Scotland during the First World War, and a letter by A. D. Hall, former director of Rothamsted Experimental Station. McDougall argued that a major feature of the government's food production campaign – the ploughing up of grassland – would have little effect on the 1940 harvest, and advocated a comprehensive scheme involving all methods of increasing production.[17] Hall commented on the announcement that 40,000 tons of home-grown wheat would be made available as animal feed. Did the government not understand the basic science of 'conversion factors', he wondered? This was a reference to the fact that passing grain through animals results in the loss of a large proportion of the food energy originally available. The 'most disturbing feature' Hall thought, was that it '... raises a doubt of whether the Ministry ... are receiving proper advice on matters of this kind, which should be determined by science and not what particular groups of the community would like'.[18] If scientific advice was followed, said Hall, the diversion of human food to cattle would have been forbidden. The suspicion was that the Ministry of Agriculture and Fisheries was leading food policy in the interests of farmers rather than the population.[19]

In *Feeding the People in Wartime*, reviewed in *The Times* around this time, Orr and Lubbock argued that if the endurance of the population was to be maintained, then food policy should aim to eliminate the dietary deficiencies of the poor. They advocated a comprehensive system of subsidies of home produced foods of high nutritional value.[20] After about ten days of debate, a *Times* editorial concluded that some authority was needed 'with the power to organise this section of the economic front from one end to the other'. It approved of a rumour that this responsibility would fall to Sir Kingsley Wood, a beneficiary of a government re-shuffle which aimed to bolster failing support for Chamberlain's administration.[21] Wood had become Lord Privy Seal and chair of the ministerial Food Policy Committee. A few days later, Wood initiated discussion with the Ministries of Food and Agriculture about the appointment of a scientific advisory committee. The Ministry of Agriculture's attitude was defensive. Donald Ferguson, the chief civil servant, warned that farmers would 'resent any idea that a group of scientists were going to produce some grandiose plan regardless of the circumstances of each district and farm'.[22] Within the Ministry of Food, however, the attitude was quite different. One senior official welcomed the proposed committee because he thought it would tend to deflect criticism away from the Ministry of Food and towards the Ministry of Agriculture.[23]

The Ministry of Food officials were relatively favourably disposed to the proposed new committee, because it could potentially help them in their dealings with the Ministry of Agriculture. The Ministry of Agriculture, in contrast, made further attempts to dissuade the Privy Seal's office from pressing ahead. They argued that the only result would be to create 'a mess for our Minister, whoever he may be', a hint that the Minister of Agriculture might resign over the issue.[24] The minister at this time was Reginald Dorman Smith. As shown in Peter Atkins' Chapter, Dorman Smith had been associated before the war with groups that favoured a return to traditional ways of farming and whose opposition to scientific agriculture was manifested by opposition to pasteurisation of milk. The Ministry of Agriculture and Privy Seal's office were deadlocked when the Chamberlain government fell at the beginning of May. Winston Churchill became Prime Minister and the Labour Party now joined the Wartime Coalition. Clement Attlee, leader of the Labour Party, became Lord Privy Seal and chair of the Food Policy Committee. A new Minister of Agriculture was appointed, Robert Hudson, and Elliot lost his job as Minister of Health.

The debate in *The Times*, and discussion of the question of the establishment of a scientific food committee, coincided with attempts by the Ministry of Food to exert greater influence upon the programme of the Ministry of Agriculture. As part of this process the Ministry of Food was already beginning to deploy scientific data provided by its chief scientific adviser, Jack Drummond, and his colleagues. Drummond, who was professor of biochemistry at University College, London, had been recruited by the Ministry of Food early in the war as adviser on gas contamination of food. His remit was expanded in January 1940 after the first rationing arrangements were introduced. At that time the Minister of Food was planning a movement to guide the public on the best use of the foods available. Drummond, it was envisaged, would advise on the food economy campaign and act as general scientific co-ordinator for the ministry. He would recommend who, in other departments, might be consulted on particular problems. He was appointed Scientific Adviser from 1 February, initially with a staff of five, and soon began to develop a much more autonomous role than had been envisaged.[25]

Drummond and his colleagues produced a paper entitled 'A Survey of War-time Nutrition with Special Reference to Home Production of Foods and Import Policy', dated 12 May 1940.[26] This was attached, as an appendix, to the first draft of the Ministry of Food's programme for the second year of war. In late 1939, however, when Drummond had attempted to expand his role by compiling an estimate of national food requirements, his activities had met with disapproval from Ministry of Food officials. He told Edward Mellanby, secretary of the Medical Research Council, that he been 'given to understand – quite informally – that it might raise rather a delicate position if I were to assist in compiling this survey unofficially whilst holding an official position at the Ministry of Food'.[27] The 'Survey' of May 1940 therefore represented an important advance in the position of scientific advice in the Ministry of Food. Having successfully established a wider remit, Drummond might have viewed the prospect of the formation of a new committee of outside scientific experts with some ambivalence.

A few days after Drummond and his colleagues produced their survey, consideration of the proposed scientific committee restarted, when Hall sent a memorial to Churchill signed by about twenty 'men of science connected with nutrition and agriculture'. This called for 'the formation of a food policy on scientific lines' and outlined a policy similar to that in Orr and Lubbock's *Feeding the People in Wartime*. In conclusion, the memorial argued for the appointment of a scientific committee to formulate principles of adminis- trative action on food and agriculture.[28] The officials of the Ministry of Agriculture were unimpressed. Ferguson prepared a long memorandum for the new minister, which repeated all the arguments he made previously. He asserted that nothing would convince farmers 'that they do not know how to farm their land better than people in Whitehall or eminent scientists'.[29] Hudson told a deputation of scientists that they could not be aware of all the factors involved in food policy. On Orr's aim of increasing home food production to the largest possible extent, he suggested that it pre-surmised that the country was in a state of siege and emphasised '... for various reasons, of which the scientists could not be aware, it was desirable and even essential to continue our policy on the assumption that we should be able to continue to maintain our imports as long as possible'. This was a hint that there were political, economic and military risks involved in the premature disruption of trade with allied and neutral countries, which might threaten the effective pursuit of the war, but which the single-minded scientists were unable to appreciate. He appealed to the deputation to realise that

> ... whilst the scientists could undoubtedly play a very useful part in the food production campaign it was not their function to advise on policy. That function must remain in the hands of the Ministers of the Crown who alone possessed the full knowledge which was necessary to enable the needs of the situation to be assessed.[30]

Nevertheless, Hudson admitted that scientists could help in advising on 'definite remits' and mentioned his intention to establish a 'Joint Scientific Advisory Committee' to advise his ministry and the Ministry of Food. At the end of May a proposal to appoint a scientific food committee was finally agreed by the ministerial Food Policy Committee.[31]

The Scientific Food Committee, as constituted, was chaired by physicist Sir William Bragg, president of the Royal Society. The nutrition experts were Edward Cathcart, regius professor of physiology of Glasgow University, Edward Mellanby, secretary of the Medical Research Council and Orr. The agricultural side included professors from Aberystwyth, Oxford, and Cambridge, and the secretary, who was a member of the Agricultural Research Council.

## The first report of the Scientific Food Committee – the basal diet

The first meeting of the Scientific Food Committee took place on 7 June 1940. It was agreed that Cathcart, Mellanby and Orr would draw up a memorandum on requirements in terms of biochemistry and food but instead Orr seized the initiative and prepared a document entitled 'Notes on nutritional aspects of War Food Policy'.[32] Orr argued that the basic objectives should be the provision of a 'basal diet good enough for health' for the entire population, and additional foods to maintain those in work in the 'highest possible state of physical efficiency'. He outlined a 'basal diet' consisting of bread, fats, potatoes, oatmeal, milk and vegetables, which should preferably remain unrationed. For psychological reasons, he suggested that tea and sugar should be part of the basal diet, but should be rationed. The basal diet envisaged would provide 2000 calories per head, with the rest of the diet made up from a list of 'supplementary foods', arranged in order of priority, according to calorie content and availability. A sub-committee of the Scientific Food Committee prepared a report based on Orr's document, but when it was discussed at the ministerial committee, the objections the Ministry of Agriculture had raised previously were again articulated. It was noted that the proposal to reduce the livestock population and increase the acreage of vegetables and potatoes could have serious repercussions: the fertility of the land 'might be gravely damaged'. The ministers decided to submit the report to an *ad hoc* interdepartmental committee of civil servants.[33]

While the interdepartmental committee was considering the basal diet report, the Scientific Food Committee began to worry about the fate of its document. Its minutes record that there seemed to be confusion as to whether the diet was a 'desperate expedient' or an 'immediate objective'.[34] Bragg wrote to Attlee about the matter and Orr wrote to Drummond and arranged to speak to Woolton. Orr told Drummond:

> Some of us are a little perturbed as to whether or not the recommendations of the Committee are going to be put into action or merely looked upon as suggestions of impracticable woolly-headed scientists.[35]

If the latter were the case, Orr told Drummond, it would not be worth attending meetings. To Woolton, Orr sent a five-page memorandum on 'The meaning of the "National Basal Diet"', which Woolton distributed to his Cabinet colleagues.[36] Orr explained that it was not intended that anyone would live only on the seven foods or eat the hypothetical amounts stated – but it was intended that the foods would form the basis of food policy. If sufficient quantities of these foods were within the purchasing power of everyone, there would be no malnutrition, health and physique would improve, and the government would be taking the first step towards social and economic reconstruction. Orr warned that if the recommendations were accepted merely in principle instead of being accepted as the basis of immediate action, a dangerous delay would result.

The interdepartmental committee consisted of representatives of the Ministries of Agriculture and Food. The Ministry of Agriculture was altogether unsympathetic and prepared a memorandum on milk which concluded:

> ... however desirable it may be on scientific grounds to provide 0.6 pint of milk per head per day as part of a basal diet under siege conditions, it must be recognised that it is extremely unlikely that under these conditions ... this quantity, or indeed the 0.4 pint per head per day which is at present consumed, could in fact be secured.[37]

Drummond, for the Ministry of Food, also expressed some doubts about the Scientific Food Committee's policies. He was particularly unhappy with the low priority that the Scientific Food Committee had accorded to sugar and pointed out its advantages as a cargo and the fact that it was often eaten with other foods such as oatmeal.[38] Drummond's sensitivity to the food habits of the population, which has been much commented upon, was probably developed though his study of English food history, first published in 1939 as *The Englishman's Food*.[39] His arguments were visible in the report of the interdepartmental committee, which emphasised the 'desirability of paying regard to existing habits of consumption on the one hand and the practical possibilities of importation and home production on the other'.[40]

The next meeting of the Scientific Food Committee took strong exception to the interdepartmental committee's criticisms. The scientists thought that it was the civil servants' duty to consider what practical steps needed to be taken, not to criticise the scientists. Mellanby drafted a letter to Attlee which explained:

> Scientists recognise only too well the emasculating effect of asking inter-departmental committees to report on any of their suggestions. This process has been going on in government circles for many years and is undoubtedly responsible for the sense of complete frustration that all scientific men ... have as regards the adoption of new knowledge and new principles therefrom by Government Departments.[41]

Bragg made these points to Attlee rather more subtly, leading to a meeting of members of the Food Policy Committee, the Scientific Committee and the chief officials.[42] Woolton told the scientists that it was necessary to go beyond the basal diet if the people were to be maintained in a happy and contented frame of mind, but he also stated that

> ... in drawing up the import programme ... he had taken careful account of the order of priorities recommended by the ... (Scientific Food Committee) and he had asked the Minister of Agriculture to produce the crops required to provide the basal diet.[43]

Woolton's statement, made in the presence of the Minister of Agriculture, indicates the success that the Ministry of Food had achieved in pressing its claim to 'prescribe what foodstuffs shall be grown at home'.[44] The establishment of the Scientific Food Committee in the face of opposition from the Ministry of Agriculture, and the outcome of the debate over the 'basal diet', had played a role in this shift in the relative positions of the two ministries. In August 1940 the Cabinet adopted a memorandum that accepted the principle that

> ... both agricultural and import policy shall take note of the findings of the Scientific Committee in order to ensure that, so far as practicable, the foods comprised in its basal diet shall be made available.[45]

The Ministry of Food's attempts to exert greater control over food production policy were strengthened by the outside scientists' agitation. Despite further attempts by the Ministry of Agriculture to resist change and to preserve the shape of British agriculture as far and as long as possible, from August 1940 the government began to pursue increasingly interventionist policies in managing the food system. We have seen, however, that the views of the outside scientists were not entirely in line with the Ministry of Food's internal scientific advice. Drummond was not entirely convinced by all the principles of the 'basal diet'. As the Scientific Food Committee turned their attention to a series of specific problems over the coming months, the relationship between the committee and the Ministry of Food's scientific adviser's division became increasingly problematic.

## The later relationship between the Scientific Food Committee and the ministries

In October 1940, the Scientific Food Committee recorded that substantial effect had been given to its principal recommendations.[46] It had now prepared reports on bread, milk, agricultural prices, potatoes and vegetables, but there seemed to be an endless range of problems that it could take up. One Ministry of Food official commented on a Scientific Food Committee paper which amounted to a comprehensive 'shopping list' of questions:

> ... every item ... forms part of the normal work in war time of some Government Department, and work on it has been carried out ... during the last 12 months ... the systematic examination proposed ... will merely duplicate work already done, or in the process of being done, thus occupying officials whose full time and attention are required for urgent work in Departments.[47]

The official realised that it was impossible to 'brush aside' the Scientific Food Committee and the only response would be to let it do as it wished even though this would mean extra burdens for the civil servants. The Ministry of Food should attempt, he suggested, to arrange for the committee to concentrate firstly on agricultural policy, to shift the pressure on to the Ministry of Agriculture, and to provide the Ministry of Food with a few weeks 'breathing space'.

The Scientific Food Committee was still helpful in the Ministry of Food's campaign to control the Ministry of Agriculture. The Committee's recommendations met with approval whenever they were in line with the Ministry of Food's own policies, and directed towards the Ministry of Agriculture. In mid October 1940 Drummond welcomed a memorandum that set out the basic science of agricultural production. He thought this would at least put pressure on the Ministry of Agriculture although he was pessimistic about whether it would have the intended effect:

> Clearly this note is another move in the frontal attack by the Scientific Committee on the Ministry of Agriculture, but I do not feel great confidence that it will force them [the Ministry of Agriculture] to abandon some of the positions they have held so tenaciously.[48]

This was a reference to the Ministry of Agriculture's desire to maintain the beef herd and its reluctance to implement the Ministry of Food's policy of prioritising milk production. The position of the Ministry of Food on this issue may be illustrated by an incident in December 1940. After a meeting with officials of the Ministry of Agriculture, Drummond received a warning from a colleague. Apparently the Minister of Agriculture was preparing a scheme for the elimination of diseased cattle from the dairy herd which would reduce the number of milk cows and therefore reduce milk production. The high priority given by the Ministry of Food to milk production is signalled by the concluding remark of Drummond's colleague: 'Surely dirty milk is better than no milk?'[49] Drummond commented, 'Your news is frightening. We simply must take a firm stand'. Drummond thought, however, that the support of the Scientific Food Committee could be expected. He felt sure that the Scientific Food Committee would 'take the strongest possible line if the Ministry of Agriculture and Fisheries refuse to abandon their suicidal policy'.[50]

Although the Scientific Food Committee continued to have uses in struggles with the Ministry of Agriculture, negative views about the Scientific Food Committee soon came to predominate at the Ministry of Food. At the end of October 1940 Drummond commented on a report by the committee on 'Requirements, supply and utilisation of edible fats and oils'. This had been written by Benjamin S. Platt, an MRC scientist who acted as Mellanby's assistant with regard to nutritional matters. Platt had joined the secretariat of the Scientific Food Committee and became responsible for preparing several of the committee's memoranda. In keeping with Drummond's awareness of established food preferences, he thought that Platt's suggestion that vegetable oils could be used more in cooking was unrealistic. According to Drummond it would be better to import fats, than to attempt to '"put across" an entirely new idea to the English housewife'. He considered Platt's memorandum 'rather an amateurish effort'.[51] To Drummond the exercise had been superfluous: he and his colleagues already understood the problem and its solution. His comments on Scientific Food Committee activities became increasingly vociferous. In March 1941 Drummond remarked to his colleagues:

> Can nothing be done to prevent such a waste of time as occurred this morning when seven of us ... gave the best part of two hours to discussing a series of figures prepared, I submit, in a most amateurish fashion by Dr B. S. Platt ... Either the Ministry of Food has on its staff people competent to estimate food requirements and import programmes or, if not, steps should be taken to obtain them. Why should this quite unnecessary duplication of effort be allowed to waste valuable time?[52]

## The Jameson Committee and debate on the future of the Scientific Food Committee

The rapid decline in standing of the of the Scientific Food Committee during early 1941, occurred at a time when another committee, chaired by Wilson Jameson, Chief Medical Officer of the Ministry of Health, was gaining more influence. This shift was partly the result of the activities of the Cabinet's Scientific Advisory Committee, the role of which was to co-ordinate science on behalf of the war effort. The latter committee, set up in the autumn of 1940, was chaired by senior statesman Lord Hankey, and consisted of representatives of the Royal Society and of the Research Councils, including Mellanby. In May 1941, the Scientific Advisory Committee held a discussion, in which Drummond participated, on 'health and nutrition'. Significantly, there is no mention of the Scientific Food Committee in the record of the meeting. The key intervention was made by Mellanby, who argued that there was 'a serious lack of co-ordination in the formulation and execution of policy on nutritional matters'. In Mellanby's view:

> ... the controlling influence should lie with the Ministry of Health, which on the administrative side would work where necessary through the Departments  ... while on scientific subjects they would keep in close touch with the Medical Research Council and the Agricultural Research Council.[53]

Mellanby's intervention is probably best interpreted not so much as an attempt to raise the status of the Ministry of Health, as an attempt to control Drummond and the Ministry of Food, and to enhance the role of the Medical Research Council.[54] After the meeting, Mellanby and Hankey prepared a memorandum together. During the drafting process it emerged that Jameson had already begun to convene informal meetings on food problems attended by representatives of the Ministries of Health, Labour and Food, the Department of Health for Scotland, the Board of Education and MRC. Hankey's final document recommended that this committee should be formalised and expanded to include representatives of other interested departments.[55]

While the discussion on the enhancement of the 'Jameson Committee' was underway, the future of the Scientific Food Committee was under consideration at the Privy Seal's office. It was realised that the committee was becoming ineffective. Possible ways of strengthening the committee were considered, as well as the possibility of letting it lapse. Despite the Ministry of Agriculture's earlier objections to the committee, Ferguson now advised against its abolition. He thought this would probably 'cause a recrudescence of the agitation among the scientists'. Although the committee 'duplicates the work that is being done by other people', it had become 'fairly innocuous and is more and more occupied in matters of minor importance'.[56] The Minister of Agriculture therefore advised Attlee to maintain the committee in its ineffective and harmless state and to 'let sleeping dogs lie'.[57]

At the beginning of June 1941, Attlee's officials advised that if Jameson's committee was given more formal status, two committees would be operating, with one covering part of the remit of the other. In negotiations with the war cabinet's office, Attlee agreed to wind up the Scientific Food Committee. The cabinet secretary prepared letters for ministers announcing the decision, but then had an attack of 'cold feet', as he put it, feeling that Bragg should be informed first.[58] Meanwhile the scientists got wind of their probable abolition and began to make representations. Finally, Attlee invited Bragg to a meeting, after which Bragg set out his views in a long letter arguing that there was a need for 'the broad view of non-departmental science' which could give a 'selfless and uninfluenced view'.[59] As a result of his encounter with Bragg, Attlee weakened and came to the conclusion that to abolish the committee would 'lead to complaints that the advice of scientists was being ignored'.[60] For this reason the Scientific Food Committee survived, but was sidelined. It met only four times between August and December 1941, and only once each year in 1942 and 1943.[61] Nutritional advice was thereafter covered almost entirely by the Jameson Committee. Of the ministers concerned, only Woolton favoured the alternative strategy of adjusting the membership and strengthening the Scientific Food Committee.[62]

## Discussion and conclusions

In conclusion, to return to the theme of science and scientists in policy making, it may firstly be observed that there is no evidence that the circumstances of war made the application of science to food policy particularly direct and unproblematic. From a longer term perspective, however, in view of the prolonged lobbying by nutrition scientists and their allies which produced relatively minor results during the 1930s, wartime policy making and implementation might be regarded as rapid in comparison. This point is made by Richard Titmuss, in his volume on social policy in the official *History of the Second World War*. He characterises the expansion of school meals and milk during the war as representing a 'revolution'. This was in reference to the attitudes of parents, teachers and children rather than civil servants and politicians, but he also claims that the adoption of the national milk scheme in the summer of 1940 occurred 'without dispute or financial argument'.[63] Certainly the milk scheme was introduced speedily, but as was shown earlier in this chapter, the final decision was preceded by months of prevarication, and was conditioned by political considerations.

The volumes on food and on agriculture in the official history both mention the Scientific Food Committee. Neither consider that the basal diet report had much influence, because it was regarded as impractical by the civil servants. Both also feel that the impact in general of the committee was unimportant. K. A. H. Murray, writing on agriculture, and R. J. Hammond, writing on food, both ascribe the weakness of the committee to its 'remoteness' from day to day problems.[64] The official historians have failed to consider, however, the contribution of the scientists to the broader changes in policy during the 1940s. In this light, the key contribution of the scientists who lobbied for, or who became members of the Scientific Food Committee, was not the precise scientific advice that they gave. Rather, they helped to effect a shift in the balance of power away from the Ministry of Agriculture with its emphasis on retaining the support of farmers, and towards the Ministry of Food which favoured a greater degree of planning and interventionism. No doubt the military situation, mentioned earlier in connection with the formulation and implementation of the welfare milk scheme, was important in forcing the move towards greater intervention. And the success of the German navy in sinking ships carrying food gave greater impetus to this trend in late 1940 and early 1941. It was at this point that the Battle of the Atlantic, at Hitler's command, was intensified, with the monthly volume of lost shipping steadily increasing in February, March and April 1941, prompting Churchill to order that details of sinkings be suppressed.[65] Nevertheless, it may be fairly suggested that from the summer of 1940 the outside scientists also helped the Ministry of Food to assert the function that it aspired to: that of prescribing the food that was to be produced by the Ministry of Agriculture. And the key contribution of Orr, for example, may be seen not so much as the provision of scientific data, but his active and effective lobbying.

The fate of the Scientific Food Committee also provides a useful reminder that it is inappropriate to speak of 'scientists' as if scientists constitute a unified group. This is highlighted by the criticisms of the Scientific Food Committee by Jack Drummond of the Ministry of Food, the lack of support for the committee from Edward Mellanby in early 1941, and the eclipse of the Scientific Food Committee by the Jameson Committee. Hammond suggests that had the Scientific Adviser's division been more integrated with the rest of the Ministry of Food when the Scientific Food Committee was established, the committee might have been more effective.[66] The evidence presented in this chapter suggests, in contrast, that had the position of the Scientific Adviser's division been more established, the division may have actively opposed the establishment of the committee. In connection with policy making, scientists are likely to be united only at certain points of time, such as when they all feel equally excluded from decision-making.

However, most of time there will be scientists who are relative insiders and those who are relative outsiders to the policy making process, who have differing interests, and who are unwilling or unable to act together.[67]

For the scientist who wants to intervene in policy making today, the main implication of this exploration of wartime policy making may be that there has never been a time when scientists could simply provide data to be applied by others. In other words, there has probably never been a substitute for either becoming an insider like Drummond, or staying on the outside and engaging in popular writing, courting press publicity, and actively lobbying politicians and civil servants. The main and most important result of recent lobbying in Britain, in which scientists have been involved, may be the creation of the Food Standards Agency. The main criticism that has led to this innovation in food policy is similar to the criticism levelled against the Ministry of Agriculture and Fisheries during early 1940. In recent years it has been frequently alleged that the Ministry of Agriculture, Fisheries and Food (MAFF),[68] has placed excessive emphasis upon the interests of producers, at the expense of consumers and health issues. As during the war, a shift of power in food policy making within government may prove to be the most significant outcome: in this case towards the new Agency and away from MAFF. It may also be informative to observe, during the years ahead, the activities and performance of newly created 'insiders', and their interaction with the advisory committees that have been created.[69]

## Acknowledgements

The author wishes to thank the Wellcome Trust for the financial support of the research upon which this chapter is based. Jim Phillips and others at the Department of Social and Economic History of Glasgow University, are thanked for their comments on an earlier version of the chapter delivered as a seminar paper in November 1998. The author is also grateful for the comments of Andrew Hull, the discussant for this paper at the Aberdeen conference, and to Bernard Harris.

## References

1 V. Berridge and J. Stanton, 'Science and policy: historical insights', *Social Science and Medicine*, 1999, vol. 49, pp. 1133–8, at 1133.
2 J. B. Orr, *As I Recall*, London, MacGibbon & Kee, 1966.
3 See this volume, Chapter 13.
4 J. Burnett, *Plenty and Want. A Social History of Diet in England from 1918 to the Present Day*, London, Nelson, 1966, pp. 258–9.
5 D. F. Smith, 'Nutrition Science and the Two World Wars', in D. F. Smith (ed.), *Nutrition in Britain: Science, Scientists and Politics in the Twentieth Century*, London, Routledge, 1997, pp 142–66.

6  D. Harvey, 'Family diet and health in pre-war Britain', in D. P. Cuthbertson (ed.), *Progress in Nutrition and Allied Sciences*, London, Oliver and Boyd, 1963, pp. 323–8, at p. 325.

7  J. B. Orr, *Food, Health and Income*, London, Macmillan, 1936; Rowett Research Institute, *Family Diet and Health in pre-war Britain*, Dunfermline, Carnegie Trust, 1955; D. F. Smith, in A. Fenton (ed.), Order and Disorder. *The Health Implications of Eating and Drinking in the Nineteenth and Twentieth Centuries,* East Linton, Tuckwell, 2000, pp. 64–80.

8  W. E. Elliot, 'Present food position in the UK', 20 November 1939, Public Record Office (hereafter PRO) CAB 74/10.

9  Minutes, 5 December 1939, PRO CAB 74/8; 'Interdepartmental Conference on Milk 'Report on Milk Policy in relation to free and cheap milk schemes', PRO CAB 74/3;

10  'Milk Policy in Relation to Free and Cheap milk schemes', 20 April 1940, PRO1 CAB 74/3.

11  Early wartime conditions also set back much of the progress that had made with school milk and meal schemes during the later 1930s. See B. Harris, *The Health of the Schoolchild*, Buckingham, Open University Press, pp. 155–60.

12  For the background history of this period see, for example, A. Calder, *The People's War: Britain 1939–45*, London, Cape, 1969 and P. Addison, *The Road to 1945: British Politics and the Second World War*, London, Cape, 1975.

13  'Cheap Milk Scheme' Memorandum by Secretary of State for Scotland, Minister of Health, Minister of Food, 3 June 1940, PRO CAB 74/4.

14  J. B. Orr and D. Lubbock, *Feeding the People in Wartime*, London, Macmillan, 1940.

15  One such document is J. Drummond, I. Dennehy, and A. N. Duckham, 'A Survey of War-time nutrition with special reference to home production of foods and import policy', 12 May 1940, PRO MAF 98/46.

16  Berridge and Stanton, op. cit., p. 1133.

17  A. P. McDougall, 'Food supplies a critic of home production government figures examined', *The Times*, 26 March 1940, pp. 9f–10a.

18  A. D. Hall, 'Feeding stuffs diversion of wheat to cattle scientific advice to ministry', *The Times*, 27 March 1940, p. 9a.

19  For convenience, the Ministry of Agriculture and Fisheries will be referred to in this chapter as the Ministry of Agriculture.

20  Orr and Lubbock, op. cit.; 'Books of the day food in wartime diet and production', *The Times*, 2 April 1940, p. 11f.

21  'Land and food' (editorial), *The Times*, 6 April 1940, p. 7b.

22  D. Ferguson to F. Floud, 13 April 1940, PRO CAB 118/43.

23  Minute of a meeting of the Secretary's Committee, 25 April 1940, PRO MAF 151/408.

24  Ferguson to Floud, 26 April 1940, PRO MAF 53/158.

25  P. J. Wheelson to P. D. Proctor, 22 January 1940, PRO MAF 127/49; Ministry of Food Memorandum, 4 April 1940, PRO CAB 118/43; 'Permanent record of operations: rationing', PRO MAF 75/68; 'Permanent record of the work of the Scientific Adviser's Division', PRO MAF 75/74.

26  Drummond, Dennehy and Duckham, op. cit.

27  J. C. Drummond to E. Mellanby, 26 October 1939, PRO FD 1/5393.

28  Memorial sent with Hall to Floud, 14 May 1940, PRO MAF 53/158.

29  Ferguson to Minister, 15 May 1940, PRO MAF 53/158.

30  'Note of a deputation, headed by Sir Daniel Hall', 25 May 1940, PRO MAF 53/158.

31  Food Policy Committee, Minute of Meeting, 30 May 1940, PRO CAB 74/2.

32  Minute of the Scientific Food Committee, 7 June 1940; 'Notes on nutritional aspects of war food policy', PRO CAB 74/11.

33  Scientific Food Committee, Minutes of Meeting, 20, 25 June 1940, PRO CAB 74/11; Food Policy Committee, Minute of Meeting, 4 July 1940, PRO CAB 74/2.

34  Scientific Food Committee, Minute of Meeting, 18 July 1940, PRO CAB 74/11.

35  J. B. Orr to J. C. Drummond, 24 July 1940, PRO MAF 98/254.

36  W. H. Bragg to C. R. Attlee, 22 July 1940, PRO CAB 118/43; J. B. Orr to Woolton, 24 July 1940, J. B. Orr 'The meaning of "National Basal Diet"', PRO MAF 98/254.

37  Note by Ministry of Agriculture, 'Milk Production', 17 July 1940, PRO MAF 98/254.

38  J. C. Drummond to J. R. Oake, 18 July 1940, PRO MAF 98/254.

39  J. C. Drummond and A. Wilbraham, *The Englishman's Food*, 1939, Burnett, op. cit., pp. 260.

40  'Report of the Interdepartmental Committee to consider the Report of the Scientific Sub Committee', 23 July 1940, PRO CAB 74/4.

41  Draft letter to Lord Privy Seal, PRO FD1/9056.

42  W. H. Bragg to C. R. Attlee, 22 July 1940, PRO CAB 118/43.

43  Food Policy Committee, Minute of Joint Meeting, 7 August 1940, PRO CAB 72/2.

44  'Policy of the Ministry of Food. Memorandum by the Minister of Food', 31 July 1940, PRO PREM 44/2/2.

45  Quote from War Cabinet Memorandum, 19 August 1940, in 'Note by Professor D. M. S. Watson', 24 August 1940, PRO CAB 74/11.

46  Scientific Food Committee, Minute of Meeting, 23 October 1940, PRO CAB 74/11.

47  Quintin Hill to French, 7 October 1940, PRO MAF 83/180.

48  J. C. Drummond to Mr Maud, 16 October 1940, PRP MAF 98/254.

49  R. Cohen to J. C. Drummond, 19 December 1940, PRO MAF 98/254.

50  J. C. Drummond, 20 December 1940, PRO MAF 98/254.

51  J. C. Drummond to E. C. Wilson, H. Davis, J. Van den Bergh, 28 October 1940, PRO MAF 98/254.

52  J. C. Drummond to E. M. H. Lloyd, 27 March 1941, PRO MAF 98/254.

53  Minute of the Scientific Advisory Committee meeting, 2 May 1941, PRO FD 1/6570.

54  Mellanby's behaviour throughout the war supports this view. Examples include his uncooperative response to a letter from Orr suggesting collaboration early in the war, and his response to the initiative of nutrition workers in holding informal meetings to discuss government policies. See Smith, op. cit., pp. 154–7.

55  Scientific Advisory Committee, 'National Health and Nutrition Second Report', 5 June 1941, PRO CAB 90/2.

56  Ferguson to Hudson, 23 May 1941, PRO MAF 53/158.

57  Hudson to Attlee, 30 May 1941, PRO CAB 118/44.

58  E. E. B. to Attlee, 9 September 1941, PRO CAB 118/44.

59  Bragg to Attlee, 24 July 1941, PRO CAB 118/46.

60  D. J. W. R. to Secretary, 23 July 1941, PRO CAB 118/44.

61  See PRO CAB 74/12.

62  Woolton to Lord Privy Seal, 8 August 1941, PRO CAB 118/44.

63  R. Titmuss, *Problems of Social Policy*, London, HMSO, 1950, pp. 510–11.

64  K. A. H. Murray, *Agriculture*, London, HMSO, 1955, p. 318; R. J. Hammond, *Food: The Growth of Policy*, London, HMSO, 1951, p. 96.

65  A. Calder, *The People's War*, London, Jonathan Cape, 1969, p. 267; A. Marwick, *A History of the Modern British Isles*, Oxford, Blackwell, 2000, p. 148; Hammond, op. cit., chap. XII.

66  Hammond, op. cit., p. 222.

67  For an example, concerning conflicts about the role of the Nutrition Society during the Second World War, see Smith, 1997, op. cit., pp. 157–60.

68  The Ministry of Agriculture, Fisheries and Food was formed in 1955 from the merger of the Ministry of Food and the Ministry of Agriculture and Fisheries and Food.

69  The Food Standards Agency, which began work on 1 April 2000, has set up a web site, and has proclaimed that, in the spirit of openness, and in order to win public confidence, minutes of its Board meetings and other information will be added regularly. See the Food Standards Agency homepage. Online. Available HTTP: http://www.foodstandards.gov.uk (4 April 2000).

# 8   The food supply in The Netherlands during the Second World War[1]

*Gerard Trienekens*

Could The Netherlands feed itself if it was cut off from imported supplies from abroad for a prolonged period? That was the question in the 1930s, as it became clear that a war between Nazi Germany and other major European powers was probable. While hoping that The Netherlands would remain neutral as in 1914–18, the Dutch government began preparing plans for self-sufficiency in food provision in 1934. These plans were developed on the assumption that The Netherlands would be physically isolated as it had been by the end of the First World War.

There was no simple answer. The Netherlands routinely exported large amounts of butter, cheese, condensed milk, veal, bacon, eggs, vegetables and fruit, mainly to the surrounding industrialised countries. However, even larger amounts of cereals, both for human and animal consumption, tropical fats and fodders like soy, maize and oilcakes, were imported from all over the world. In 1939, for example, farm-chickens consumed as much grain as the whole Dutch population. More generally, home grown rye was used as animal fodder and most cereals for bread were imported. This pattern of food exports and imports had existed since the last quarter of the nineteenth century, when the international agrarian crisis forced Dutch farmers to expand dairy cattle farming, horticulture and factory farming (pigs and poultry).[2] These changes accompanied and shaped the industrialisation of The Netherlands, with a strong growth of the population. Towards the end of the First World War, in 1917–18, when the submarine war cut off all shipped imports to The Netherlands, food shortages stimulated severe popular disquiet and protest. After the war the population continued to rise, from 6.5 million to 8.7 million in 1939, further complicating the question of how to maintain food supply without imports.

After lengthy consideration the planners concluded that self-sufficiency would be possible, but only if a number of severe conditions were applied. These included converting a substantial part of production for export to production for domestic consumption, a compilation of stocks that would bridge this period of conversion until the first new harvest became available, the development of a nation-wide rationing system comprising all foodstuffs and, last but not least, the shaping of an organisation or apparatus with sufficient powers to regulate and control the whole process of production, distribution and exchange. This most important final pre-condition was met largely due to the efforts of a single official, the head of the public agricultural crisis organisation, S. L. Louwes, an agricultural engineer by background, who possessed a substantial personal capacity for administrative organisation. By May 1940, when The Netherlands were occupied by the Germans, the details as well as the principles of policy were in place, with all the necessary legal orders ready for execution. Even unleavened bread, for example, used in the Catholic celebration of the Holy Communion, would be available.[3]

## The German occupation and effects on the food supply

On 10 May 1940 the Germans attacked The Netherlands. After five days of fighting and the bombing of Rotterdam the surrender took place. While the Queen and her ministers fled to England to function in London as a government in exile, in The Netherlands Hitler installed a civil administration headed by the *Reichskommissar*, Dr A. Seyß-Inquart. This administration was very small and its main function was supervisory. The routine daily business of government was conducted by pre-existing Dutch civil servants, directed by the college of Secretary-Generals, the highest officials of the ministerial departments. They had been ordered by the Dutch government, in the event of military defeat, to stay in office as long as they could serve the interests of the Dutch people more than those of the enemy. In the light of subsequent developments there has been much discussion, including discussion among historians, about the extent to which the civil servants interpreted these orders correctly.

Neither the German occupiers or Seyß-Inquart's civil administration did much to disturb the Dutch food supply policy, which remained the province of Dutch officials until September 1944, whereafter the population of the western part of The Netherlands suffered the 'Hunger Winter' which is discussed in the second half of the chapter. Until this point only minor deviations from the pre-war plan were effected, in order to accommodate the food requirements of the German forces of occupation. The Germans had little interest in abandoning or redrafting these plans, for it suited the occupiers to maintain nutritional well-being, public health and hence peace and order and the economic and industrial capacities of the Dutch civilian population.[4]

Nevertheless, the Dutch civil servants had to work hard to ensure that the volume and character of the civilian diet was maintained. Although the experts in Berlin understood the difficulty of the Dutch food supply, the authorities in Germany continued to press for a substantial volume of imports from The Netherlands. Hence the need for covert resistance by the Dutch administrators, who managed the situation so that while it looked on paper as if a substantial part of Dutch agricultural produce was going to Germany, in reality no more than 3 per cent of the annual calorific value of food produced was actually exported.[5] All the same, at the beginning of the occupation a big part of the enormous reserves of fats, coffee and cocoa were forcibly exported to Germany, although payments were at least received by the Dutch owners. Crucially, however, the strategic stock of cereals, amounting to seven months' human consumption in peacetime, deemed necessary under the pre-war plans to bridge the period of conversion in agrarian production to a war-time footing, was undisturbed.[6]

Execution and administration of policy were conducted by the same Dutch officials who had prepared the plans before the war, including S. L. Louwes, now General Director of the Food Supply, under the formal guidance of the Secretary-General of Agriculture, and naturally with the assent of the *Reichskommissar*. From 1941 the organisation of the food supply was conducted by the 'Rijksbureau voor de Voedselvoorziening in Oorlogstijd', (RBVVO), part of the Department of Agriculture, on the one hand, and a cluster of statutory trade organisations on the other. In the trade organisations, which each represented separate agricultural sectors like corn and pulses, livestock and meat, milk and dairy produce, vegetables, and fish, all categories of participant (farmers, processors and traders) were represented. The organisation was completed by a kind of police or inspectorate organisation, the 'Centrale Crisis Controle Dienst' (CCCD), and an agency to administer justice and secure compliance with the law. All parties involved in food production and distribution were obliged to join the organisation, and to observe its rules. Penalties for trangressing these rules ranged from fines to most severely, exclusion from the organisation and hence loss of business and livelihoods.

Retrenchment was secured in three main areas of production. First, a 20 per cent reduction of the horned cattle-livestock was effected, so that part of the arable meadows situated in the higher regions of The Netherlands could be ploughed. Second, there was a scaling down by 70 per cent of pig-livestock, so that principally only those animals necessary for breeding and to resume production as soon as possible were retained. In the meantime there would be some pork production for domestic use by farmers and for consumption by priority groups, including coal miners and the German Army in The Netherlands, with a little left over for general distribution. Even this limited degree of pork production was dependent on the availability of farm and kitchen offals, required for the feeding of pigs. Third, a 90 per cent diminution of chicken-livestock was secured. In fact, only breeding material and some chickens for home consumption were left. Eggs were a privilege the rationing system only allowed to the sick.[7]

In place of livestock, on the ploughed meadows and on the fields formerly used for the cultivation of foddercrops, vegetable and grain production was significantly extended. Potatoes were emphasised, and rye cultivated more than wheat, because rye produced a better average harvest in The Nether-

five in 1944.[18] Many enterprises were closed and labourers were summoned to Germany for work – *Arbeitseinsatz* – or taken by razzias. In this manner a total of 420,000 people lost their job in The Netherlands and were required to move to Germany, although in reality only an estimated 242,000 actually went. The remainder, along with around 60,000 students, went underground.[19] Later on a small part of the productive machinery was also transported to Germany. Nevertheless, in 1945 industrial capacity in The Netherlands was greater than in 1940.

For factory and other industrial workers who remained in The Netherlands, the situation was relatively unchanged, despite the fall in domestic production. Most enterprises retained their personnel on the pay-roll even if there was little or no work in the short-term. And many of the workers who had gone underground, refusing to go to Germany, were able to secure some form of employment and income.[20] In obtaining food these workers were assisted by resistance organisations, who were aided in this pursuit by the Dutch food authorities. So much was this the case that one resistance leader later said, 'It was for us more difficult to prevent undergrounders getting more than one portion than to supply everybody with food'.[21]

Access to the black market, which provided on average some 25 per cent of food consumed, depended not only on the possession of money. People in the country could easily go to the farmers who normally charged only a little more than the official price. Later on in the war high prices were paid for products like meat, fats and rapeseed oil. Around 20 per cent of the population worked in the agrarian sector, so many urban inhabitants had family in the countryside. Even urban dwellers without rural connections could enhance their formal provisions informally. Some contemporary witnesses were convinced that working class people had much more knowledge about the methods and means of the 'scratch-economy' than the higher classes.[22] Also a lot of non-food products were involved in the grey and black market, so much could be done by barter.

The Netherlands had many small farmers and market gardeners, who all derived more income after 1940. Similarly, many retailers, certainly if they possessed some old stocks, had better times. Working class people were on average better off by having more work, good rations and access to the 'scratch-economy'. The capitalists saw their profits rise. So the only group which did not benefit from the new situation were white collar workers who had no connections with the countryside. In terms of social class differentials there was some degree of equalisation of income through the war-time introduction of a national health insurance system and a new taxation system, but the extent is unknown.[23]

So when reviewing the social distribution of food during that part of the German occupation which preceded the 'Hunger Winter' in 1944, the conclusion must be that the produce available was, on average, more equitably divided between social classes than it had been before the war. In this sense, despite the fact of the German occupation, the Dutch planners framed a programme of rationing and distribution with social levelling results which closely resembled developments in war-time Britain, where rationing and increased real wages combined to secure improved working-class nutrition.[24] According to doctors who worked in The Netherlands during the war, the cross-class range of the bodyweights of people narrowed. And as a result of the efforts of illegal organisations, combined with the support of the Dutch food authorities, even those people living underground were generally able to secure food.[25]

The composition of the food basket changed much more than the volume and the calorific value. Apart from the farmers who ate only slightly less than before the war, the population generally consumed less meat (40 g per person per day on average, including farmers) and fats and hardly any eggs and white bread. The supply of fish was very irregular. It was used by the German Army and distributed in Amsterdam, to keep the capital quiet. On the other hand there were lots of potatoes (800 g per person per day), which consequently had a low value on the black market. There were abundant supplies of other vegetables, and consumption in this area rose by some 50 per cent. Besides potatoes, bread remained the main staple, with around 300 g available per person per day. It was baked by official order from a mixture of cereals, milled to flour containing 80 per cent of the corn germ, with some potato and pulse meal, and called 'government bread'. This was greyish in colour, and not enjoyed by many people, although it would probably not be dark enough for modern Dutch tastes. With milk there was increased consumption of 'standard' milk, which consisted of 2.5 per cent of fat solids, along with skimmed and butter-milk. The rationing of pulses was obviously in excess of demand, given that these coupons were never fully redeemed. This presumably stemmed from the shortage of pork, with which pulses were typically prepared in The Netherlands. In summary there was no lack of proteins or vitamins and food was more fibrous than before.[26]

## The health situation

The facts about the health situation confirm the optimistic conclusions about the total availability of food and the more equitable social distribution until September 1944.[27] There were indications that in the first year of the new policy and diet, some people had problems. Some of these were possibly psychological. Many people, for instance, visited their family doctor to inform him about 'flatulence'. Most people lost some weight after rationing became general, but after some months the losses were partly restored.[28]

An overview of the health situation is provided in Table 8.1. Perhaps the most remarkable feature of the table is the growth of the birth-rate in wartime, rising by 17 per cent between 1939 and 1944. The increase probably resulted from the increase in employment and improvement of incomes, particularly among formerly unemployed people, small farmers and retailers. On the other hand, in Belgium, where the food supply and the industrial

*Table 8.1.* Birth-rates, death-rates and infant mortality (per thousand live-born children) in The Netherlands, 1939–1946[29]

| Year | Birth-rate | Death-rate | Violence[a] | Infant mortality |
|------|------------|------------|-------------|------------------|
| 1939 | 20.6 | 8.6 | | 33.7 |
| 1940 | 20.8 | 9.9 | 0.6 | 39.1 |
| 1941 | 20.3 | 10.0 | 0.1 | 43.6 |
| 1942 | 21.0 | 9.5 | 0.2 | 39.5 |
| 1943 | 23.0 | 10.0 | 0.4 | 40.1 |
| 1944 | 24.0 | 11.8 | 1.4 | 46.3 |
| 1945 | 22.6 | 15.3 | 2.4 | 79.7 |
| 1946 | 30.2 | 8.5 | | 38.7 |

[a] Increase due to death by violence per thousand inhabitants.

supply of raw materials were less effectively organised, the birth-rate decreased substantially.[30] So it is possible to conclude that the presence of a good food situation had at least some indirect bearing on the birth-rate. It might be speculated that Dutch people, after some hesitation, generally had more optimistic life expectations than they themselves had before 1940, and than the Belgians did during the war. Larger families were the result of these increased expectations.

In evaluating death-rates, it should be emphasised that Table 8.1 does not include the 110,000 or so Jews, who with other Dutch citizens were deported and murdered or died in the concentration camps in Germany and other parts of Europe.[31] These figures only apply to the deaths which took place in The Netherlands. The direct influence on mortality of the war by military conflict, bombing, executions and suicide is set apart in Table 8.1 under the heading 'violence'. The growth in these death-rates before the Hunger Winter had no connection with food problems arising from the war. This proposition is supported by several arguments. First, the most typical deficiency diseases like night-blindness, beriberi, scurvy, rachitis, oedema and childhood anaemia remained as rare as before the war, or became even less prevalent, in the case of anaemia,[32] although oedema was a problem in prisons.[33] It seems that illness did not arise from shortage of particular nutrients, although it could be suggested that wartime diet lowered resistance to infectious diseases, a question to which I will return later.

Second, the rise in death-rates was linked to an epidemic of influenza in February 1941 and, more generally, to a strong increase of contagious and infectious diseases, like diphtheria, scabies, dysentery, tuberculosis, scarlet fever, venereal diseases and malaria. At the same time, a number of illnesses diminished in scale, including stomach ulcers, some kinds of cancer, diabetes, appendicitis, kidney, urethra and bladder stones, and pregnancy-related diseases, and thrombosis was reduced by more than half. The number of still-born children fell from 25.1 per thousand births in 1940 to 18.5 in 1943 and 1944. The possibly favourable impact of improved diet on heart and vascular diseases was partly offset by the rise and impact of stress-related illnesses in the conditions of war and military occupation.[34] It might be suggested that these various trends were the result of deficiencies in the provision of food supply. But it could more convincingly be stated that a healthy supply of food was simply unable to outweigh wider factors, notably the worsening hygienic situation from 1940. The main features of this hygienic deteroration included a lack of soap, evacuations, dirty and clandestine slaughtering of pigs, life underground, people working in Germany and coming home infected, living close together to save coal for heating and even the impact on public health of increased sexual promiscuity along with other forms of unrestrained personal behaviour, like tuberculosis patients freely entering public spaces instead of being confined at home or in sanatoria.[35]

Third, the rise of the death-rate was also strongly linked to the rise of the infant mortality as Table 8.1 makes clear. Infants were the most vulnerable group in the situation of deteriorating personal and public hygiene. The rise of infant mortality is unlikely to be directly connected to problems in the food supply because the average birth weight remained stable until some months after the beginning of real scarcity in October 1944.[36] There also exists no reason to think that mothers could not normally feed their children after confinement.

Fourth, the spread of illness and rising death-rates, for infants and others, is also probably not the result of changes in the diet of the population. Mortality had already risen in 1940 under rather traditional food conditions, and the higher level of infant mortality continued in 1946. The rise of both also happened in provinces like Groningen and Limburg and small villages, where it was very easy to supplement rations with additional supplies.[37]

Last but not least, there is the evidence of the rate of lethality, the number of deaths for every thousand cases of potentially fatal diseases. This did not increase but diminished, even after correcting the data from falsifications made to get extra food rations and still more to prevent people from being transported to Germany, either to the concentration camps or as forced labourers.[38] That human resistance to disease was not impaired but strengthened also becomes clear by the decreasing numbers of post operative complications.[39] So there are also direct indications for rejecting the suggestion that diminished resistance was the reason for the increase in the death rate during the occupation. The deteriorating hygienic situation with all its consequences provides a sufficient explanation.

## The 'Hunger Winter', 1944–5

The great disturbance, to food policy and practical supply and consumption, took place after 17 September 1944, when allied airborne troops landed near Eindhoven, Nijmegen and Arnhem, and the Dutch government in London ordered a railway strike to support the allied advance. The allies' attack, known as Operation Market Garden, failed to achieve its goal of securing the Rhine at Arnhem, and the Germans retained control of the country to the north of the Maas and the Rhine until April 1945. As an act of revenge in response to the railway strike, the German authorities stopped all shipping traffic, at the time the most important means of food transportation. These measures resulted in the blockade of the western half of that part of The Netherlands which remained under German occupation. This mainly urbanised, lowland pasture area contained 4.5 million inhabitants, half the Dutch population, including the three largest cities of Amsterdam, Den Haag and Rotterdam. As only a very small part of the surplus of cereals and potatoes had already been transported from the still occupied eastern provinces, famine was an imminent threat in these blockaded western provinces. Because the occupiers wanted to avoid living among a starved and diseased population, the shipping blockade was finally discontinued on 8 November. But supply remained severely disrupted by a combination of continuing transport problems, frozen waters and renewed war operations during the spring. On the last day of April, just before the liberation on 5 May, the final supplies of bread were distributed. From that moment every delay in the delivery of relief would have caused disaster. Immediately prior to the German surrender air-drop took place and, more importantly, convoys of allied trucks, loaded with food, were on standby at the border of the starving area.[40]

Starvation during the 'Hunger Winter' was not only the result of absolute food shortages, worsened by the cold weather and the lack of fuel, but also reflected the fact that the available quantities of food were divided less equitably than before. The railway strike and the allied attack had precipitated a decisive shift in the character of the occupying regime, as the SS enlarged its influence significantly at the expense of the officials of the *Reichskommissariat*. High scarcity, in combination with the disappearance of the necessary support by the German authorities for the Dutch food supply organisation, led to the malfunctioning of the central gathering and rationing system. The black market and prices expanded, and it cost individual consumers a lot of energy to visit the farms in the unusually cold winter. In this respect the 'Hunger Winter' arguably has much in common with famines in developing countries since the 1970s. These have been commonly explained as the result of politically-related or even politically-motivated failures of distribution rather than failures of harvesting and production.[41] In the Dutch famine there existed in the affected area absolute food shortages, but it is possible that nobody at all would have died if the food that was still available had reached the people more equitably and with less effort.

In the 'Hunger Winter' calorific intake was very low. Officially only between 600 and 800 calories per person per day were rationed, partly through public soup kitchens because of the lack of coal for personal consumption. Most people succeeded in augmenting this quantity by purchasing from sometimes profiteering farmers – there also were saints –

or by buying on the black market. Goods like the family gold, silver and linen were more welcome to the sellers than money, given the obvious doubts about the value and validity of currency after the war, which was dragging to a foreseeable end.[42] Vegetables continued to be amply available, but contained little energy. People in towns survived mainly on the extra consumption of sugarbeets, possibly as much as 60 kg per person in about 120 days, which could not be processed into sugar because of the lack of fuel. Tulip bulbs were also consumed and tasted much better than sugarbeets, although it is something of a myth that the survival of 4.5 million people was secured by these alone. The available quantity was in reality insufficient to provide consumers with anything more than a few hundred grammes per person. Another potent myth is that of the Swedish Red Cross's white bread, popularly remembered in biblical terms as the 'manna from heaven'. Far from dropping as loaves from the heavens, or even the sky, this actually came as flour imported by boat, and was delivered to bakeries for normal processing and distribution through rationing. Arguably this 'manna' contributed more to survival in psychological than physical terms, diminishing the besieged population's sense of isolation.[43]

Given this perilous reliance on sugar beets, and the minor physical impact of tulip bulbs and Swedish flour, the 'Hunger Winter' exacted terrible physical strains on the population. By the time of liberation the loss of weight was, on average, 15–20 per cent. Around 50 per cent of women had stopped menstruating. Oedema affected 5 per cent of the total population and 18 per cent of persons aged more than sixty years. Other common diseases were emaciation (cachexia), papillare atrofia (tongue ulcers) and paraesthesias (abnormal skin sensations), although the typical deficiency diseases, as mentioned above, were rare because of the high vegetable consumption. The diseases which did take root stemmed from an absence in the food supply of energy and proteins, and were soon diminished once normal supplies were restored. The hardest situations were seen in institutions, such as psychiatric hospitals and children's homes, where the inmates could not help themselves.[44]

One peculiar feature of the 'Hunger Winter' was the fact that most contagious and infectious diseases, except diarrhoea, continued retreating, a process in train well before 1944.[45] There was no influenza epidemic, and new virulent infections only came after the liberation when labourers returned from Germany.[46] The good health situation at the beginning of the winter and the isolation of the hunger area are the likeliest explanations of this unexpected phenomenon; unexpected because contagious diseases are key characteristics of famine. Estimates for the total number of deaths range from 16,000 to 22,000.[47] Two main groups were affected. First, there were the very young. Table 8.1 indicated the huge rise in infant mortality in 1945, up to 79.7 per 1,000 from 46.3 per 1,000 in 1944. Infant mortality also rose in the eastern and liberated southern provinces, and reached its summit in the summer of 1945 after the surrender of Germany.

referring to the hunger of war-time. Myths about the war also preserved the good conscience of the Dutch people, deflecting discussion about their own responsibilities for developments. What, for example, is the explanation for the fact that of all the German-occupied countries The Netherlands delivered the highest percentage of Jews?[57] This a complex and under-researched question that will require extensive and prolonged investigation and discussion by historians. Among the factors that these historians will have to consider are the Dutch government's effective administrative organisation, the bourgeois honesty and obedience and also the relatively minor resistance of the people and, last but not least, the pacifying impact of the good economic and food situation. Why did these optimistic expectations exist, which led to a such high birthrate in wartime? It seems a bit like the story of Adam and Eve in Paradise, eating from the forbidden apple. The most comforting personal approach is to deny all responsibility and pin the entire guilt on the serpent. Exploring the scientific evidence about the character and outcome of food policy is an important part of this process of demythologisation.

## Acknowledgements

I wish to thank Jim Phillips for redrafting the text I sent to the editors.

## References

1 This chapter is based on research about food production and consumption in The Netherlands during the Second World War. The results are published in: G. M. T. Trienekens, *Tussen ons Volk en de Honger. De Voedselvoorziening 1940–1945*, Soest, 1985 and ibid., *Voedsel en Honger in Oorlogstijd 1940–1945. Misleiding, Mythe en Werkelijkheid*, Utrecht/ Antwerpen, Kosmos-Z&K Uitgevers, 1995.
2 J. Bieleman, *Geschiedenis van de Landbouw in Nederland 1500–1950*, Meppel, Boom, 1992, pp. 215–21.
3 In analysing government food supply 1934–45, the author used two main sources: the archives of the Ministry of Agriculture at The Hague, particularly the 'Archieven betreffende de voedselvoorziening in verband met de oorlog van 1939–1945' (RBVVO), and the archives of the Dutch Institute for War Documentation (NIOD) at Amsterdam, notably the 'Archief van het Generalkommissariat für Finanz und Wirtschaft, Hauptasteilung, Ernährung und Landwirtschaft' (E und L). For the war-preparations relating to food see RBVVO, 'Archief van het rijksbureau voor de voorbereiding van de voedselvoorziening in oorlogstijd' (1936–1940).
4 Trienekens, 1985, op. cit., pp. 85–9.
5 Ibid., p. 202.
6 S. L. Louwes, 'De voedselvoorziening', in J. J. van Bolhuis (ed.), *Onderdrukking en verzet. Nederland in oorlogstijd*, vol. II, 605–47, Nijmegen, Arnhem, Van Loghum Slaterus, 1947–54, pp. 611, 612. See also: NIOD, E und L, Port. 44, omslag I, stukken d.d. 9 en 12 juli 1940.
7 M. J. L. Dols and D. J. A. M. van Arcken, 'De voedselvoorziening in Nederland tijdens en onmiddelijk na den tweeden wereldoorlog 1940–1945', *Voeding*, vol. 6 1946 pp. 193–207 and Louwes, op. cit.
8 Detailed statistics on agriculture are published by the Centraal Bureau voor de Statistiek

(CBS), *Jaarcijfers voor Nederland*, 1943–1946, Utrecht, De Haan 1948 and *Economische en sociale Kroniek der oorlogsjaren*, 1940–1945, Utrecht, De Haan 1947.

9  See note 12.

10  Louwes, op. cit., p. 632.

11  The archive of the Archbishopric Utrecht contains some Pastoral Letters urging farmers to do their duty (these begin on 8 September 1941). Dr M. J. L. Dols, head of the 'Voedingsvraagstukken' of the RBVVO declared that Louwes and he more than once visited the Archbishop and the Secretary-General of the Synod of the Dutch Reformed Church to discuss their position and to keep their support; interview by the author, 10 May 1976.

12  Result of the calculations by the author published in Trienekens, 1985, op. cit., p. 359. These calculations are based on existing and reliable data of the CBS concerning the acreages of the crops, the number of the full-grown dairy cows, the sows and hens. CBS figures for yields of arable fields and animal procreation and production, all too low, conform with the official statistics made and used in the war. The arable production was reconstructed by combining the acreages with 'the state of the crops', the noted maturation data, the harvest conditions, and the yield figures known for the normal years 1930–9. The 'state of the crops' (figures between 10 and 100, normally given with some comment five times a season for the crops on the fields) were calculated by the Department of Agriculture to indicate for external consultants the quantity of cereals required by Dutch importers. Animal food production was reconstructed separately for every product, such as milk, beef, pork, horse, mutton, goat, chicken and eggs. This was done by calculations relating to mother-animals and also in relation to procreation and production in the 1930s. To control the surprisingly high result a balance-sheet was reckoned, encompassing energy and protein requirements and the availability of fodder. Human consumption was calculated by reconstructing the food-balances made by the food supply organisation in wartime. The calculations included stocks, production, industrial use, animal consumption, the consumption of the German army, the exports and the official rationed home consumption. All calculations are published in Trienekens, 1985, op. cit.

13  Of the warrants made by the CCCD, 8,000 were analysed to get an impression of the impact of both government policy and the black market. See Trienekens, 1985, op. cit., pp. 171–9.

14  See note 12; the estimation of pre-war consumption was based on several separate studies in the 1930s concerning municipalities and groups. See ibid., pp. 362–3.

15  Dols en van Arcken, op. cit., pp. 196–7.

16  The discussion of economic data and interpretations is based on H. A. M. Klemann, '"Belangrijke gebeurtenissen vonden niet plaats....". De Nederlandse industrie 1938–1948', *Bijdragen en Mededelingen betreffende de Geschiedenis der Nederlanden* (BMGN), 1999, vol. 114, part 4, 506–52. Klemann's important recent studies represent a new and rather optimistic view of economic life in The Netherlands during the first years of the German occupation.

17  *Malnutrition and Starvation in Western Netherlands, September 1944 to July 1945*, The Hague, General State Printing Office 1948, Part I, p. 67.

18  Klemann, op. cit., p. 519, Table 1.

19  Ibid., p. 527.

20  Ibid., pp. 528–9.

21  Interview with A. Hendriks, organiser of the TD resistance group, by the author, Amersfoort, January 1994.

22  Dr M. Wilhelmij, family doctor in war-time Utrecht, has three explanations for the small number of emaciated patients who he treated before the Hunger Winter: extra rations; allotment-gardens; and black market purchasing, especially among factory workers; M. Wilhelmij, 'The Average Diameter of the Erythrocytes in cases of Emanciation in Times of War', *Acta Medica Scandinavica*, 1947, vol. CXXVII, Fasc. III–IV, p. 284.

23  CBS, *Economische en sociale Kroniek*, pp. 278–80.

24  Angus Calder, *The People's War*, London, Jonathan Cape, 1969, pp. 438–47.

25  H. J. de Koster, organiser of the illegal food supply, to the state committee examining Louwes' conduct during the occupation, 7 September 1945, RBVVO, Archief Ir. S. L. Louwes, doos 13, no. 356, Bijlage D. Interviewed by the author on 19 February 1985, C. J. van Schelle, war-time official of the RBVVO, observed that Louwes authorised him personally to supply the underground with food ration coupons and to inform the Dutch government in London over the wireless. The transmitter was on his bicycle.

26  Trienekens, op. cit., 1985, pp. 361–73.

27  The discussion of the health situation is mainly based on several sources: *Verslagen en Mededelingen betreffende de Volksgezondheid, 's-Gravenhage*, vols 1942–1948 (Department of Public Health official series); Commissie tot onderzoek van de voedings- en gezondheidstoestand der Nederlandse Bevolking (z.g. Polscommissie van de voedingsraad), *Rapport Betreffende het Onderzoek naar de Voedings- en Gezondheids Toestand van de Nederlandse Bevolking in de Jaren 1941–1945, Uitgezonderd de z.g. Hongerwinter (1944–1945)*, vols I and Ia, 's-Gravenhage, Voorlichtingsbureau voor de Voeding, 1953; I. Boerema (ed.), *Medische Ervaringen in Nederland Tijdens de Bezetting, 1940–1945*, Groningen, Wotters, 1947.

28  *Malnutrition and Starvation*, Part I, p. 66; flatulence is discussed by Boerma, op. cit., pp. 76 and 264. Dr Wilhelmij attributed the initial emaciation to 'psychical influences' in 'The Average Diameter of the Erythrocytes', p. 281.

29  CBS, *Zestig jaren statistiek in tijdreeksen, 1899–1959*, Zeist, 1959.

30  E. W. Hofstee, *Korte Demografische Geschiedenis van Nederland van 1800 tot Heden*, Amsterdam, 1981, Grafiek 4 (contains comparison of the Dutch and Belgium birth-rates).

31  J. Presser, *Ondergang. De Vervolging en Verdelging van het Nederlandse Jodendom 1940–1945*, 's-Gravenhage, Staatsuitgeverij, 1965, vol. II, pp. 509–10.

32  Boerema, op. cit., pp. 18, 97, 266 and 289; analysis of starvation victims based on World Health Organisation, *Prevention and Treatment of Severe Malnutrition in Times of Disaster*, WHO Technical Report Series No. 45, Geneva, 1951.

33  *Verslagen en Mededelingen*, 1947, p. 347.

34  Boerema, op. cit., pp. 75–92, 127, 275, 393; see also CBS, *Zestig Jaren Statistiek*, Tabel: 'Sterfte in Nederland, 1910–1950'.

35  Boerema, op. cit., pp. 11–16; C. Banning, 'De volksgezondheid', in Bolhuis, Onderdrukking en Verzet, pp. 329–46.

36  Boerema, op. cit., pp. 131–57.

37  Trienekens, op. cit., 1985, Table LXIX, 'Tuberculosesterfte in 1939 en de stijging in 1941, 1942 en 1943 ten opzichte van 1939 in de provincies en groepen van gemeenten'.

38  *Verslagen en Mededelingen*, 1946, contains figures for mortality per 100 diseases. The author made a selection of 'non-political' diseases. See Trienekens, 1985, op. cit., Table LXXI).

39  Boerema, op. cit., pp. 100–3.

40  Louwes, op. cit., pp. 642–4. For delivery of relief, see W. H. Van Baarle, *Slag om B2. Een herinnering in woord en beeld aan het Commissariaat Noodvoorziening*, Den Haag, Mouton 1945.

41  For an engaging historian's discussion of contemporary famine in developing countries see E. P. Thompson, 'The moral economy reviewed', in *Customs in Common*, Penguin, Harmondsworth, 1991.

42  G. J. Kruyer, *Sociale Desorganisatie. Amsterdam tijdens de Hongerwinter*, Meppel, Boom 1951, examines the 'hongertochten', food-gathering expeditions to farms by citizens.

43  Trienekens, 1985, op. cit., pp. 106–11.

44  The research of the international medical teams, who arrived in the hunger area immediately after liberation, was published by 'The Editorial Committee' (G. C. E. Burger, J. C. Drummond and H. R. Sandstead), in *Malnutrition and Starvation* op. cit. The influence of the famine on people born in or shortly after the Hunger Winter is still the subject of

research conducted by 'The Dutch Famine Birth Cohort Study' of the Academisch Medisch Centrum in Amsterdam and by the Medical Research Committee of the University of Southampton.

45  Boerema, op. cit., p. 106.

46  Banning, op. cit., pp. 332–3.

47  See Dols en van Arcken, op. cit., and CBS, Kroniek, p. 332.

48  Trienekens, op. cit., 1985, p. 406.

49  The reactions are analysed by the author in Trienekens, 1995, op. cit., pp. 102–21.

50  J. Presser, op. cit., vol. II, pp. 509 –10.

51  P. Arnoldussen and Jolanda Otten, *De Borrel is Schaarsch en kaal Geworden. Amsterdamse horeca 1940–1945*, Amsterdam, Bas Lubberhuizen, 1994. p. 8.

52  Trienekens, 1995, op. cit., pp. 111–14.

53  L. de Jong, *Het Koninkrijk Der Nederlanden in de Tweede Wereldoorlog*, vols I–XIII, 's-Gravenhage, 1969–1988. The economic developments, the food supply and health situation are the subject of 'Deel 7, eerste helft, Hoofdtuk I', pp. 1–280. In the 1960s de Jong was the author and presentator of the television series, 'De Bezetting'. Books under the same title accompanied this series.

54  G. M. T. Trienekens, 'Het Koninkrijk der Nederlanden in de Tweede Wereldoorlog van L. de Jong, getoetst op het terrein van de voedselvoorziening', *Bijdragen en Mededelingen betreffende de Geschiedenis der Nederlanden*, 1990, vol. 105, no. 2, pp. 231–43.

55  M. T. Knibbe, 'De Nederlandse landbouw tijdens de Tweede Wereldoorlog', *Tijdschrift voor Geschiedenis*, 1998, vol. 111, pp. 75–94 at p. 77 see also Klemann, *Belangrijke Gebeurtenissen*, p. 506. Dr Knibbe writes: 'In the economic history community the thesis of Trienekens was recognised as a standard work .... as it ten years later still fully rightly appears to be'. Unfortunately for the author, not one historical journal reviewed his thesis.

56  Reactions to lectures by the author.

57  See note 31.

# 9 Vitamins win the war: nutrition, commerce, and patriotism in the United States during the Second World War

*Rima D. Apple*

Vitamins and victory: for the United States during the Second World War the two were alliteratively, positively, and profitably linked. Throughout the 1920s and 1930s, the media loudly and often announced that scientists had identified a new vitamin; that researchers had isolated and then synthesised another of these micro-nutrients; that clinicians had discovered the benefits, if not miracles, of these wondrous elements. Vitamins were found in foods, of course. But in the pre-war era in the United States, innovative entrepreneurs created alternative sources as well. They added vitamins, some would say frivolously, to a wide array of foods, of soaps, of cosmetics, even of pet foods. And pharmaceutical firms concocted a dizzying range of vitamin products. The Second World War, however, proved a major catalyst in popularising vitamins in American culture.

Very quickly, vitamin usage was associated with patriotism as, according to manufacturers, pharmacists, and advertisers, the war presented the American population with fearful conditions that only the increased use of vitamins could diminish. Of course, the United States needed a healthy fighting force; so the diets of soldiers received much attention, but so too did the nutritional needs of the civilian population, especially those enlisted in the defence industries in support of the war effort. Building on the research and discoveries of previous decades, researchers, industrialists, unions, manufacturers, and pharmacists considered vitamins vital in the creation and maintenance of the healthiest possible work force. Their focus on the nutritional well-being of the home-front fostered the use of vitamin supplementation in the United States.

## Vitaminised foods

The vitamin frivolity evident in the 1920s and 1930s grew to a veritable 'craze' in the years shortly before the United States entered the war. Despite the medical profession's vehement claims that the populace simply needed to eat appropriate foods in the appropriate quantities, many manufacturers and advertisers believed that Americans could be persuaded otherwise. Miles Laboratories with its popular One-A-Day Brand would dominate the market by the end of the 1940s, but with the release of its initial formulation at the beginning of the decade, it was one of many options available to consumers interested in vitamin capsules. Pharmaceutical and chemical firms such as Squibb, Eli Lilly, International Vitamin Corporation, National Oil Products Company, and Parke–Davis typically produced a line of vitamins which they sold to the public and they also provided vitamins to other manufacturers who wanted to join the market. Consequently, regional chain groceries such as Kroger's and major department stores like Macy's, as well as speciality companies such as Vitamins Plus, all promoted their brands of vitamin capsules. For those unwilling or unable to swallow a capsule, vitamins were added to milk, to chewing gum, to cosmetics, and even to Lydia Pinkham's Vegetable Compound, a popular nineteenth-century patent medicine that continued to enjoy a profitable life in the twentieth century. One of the most interesting examples of this 'enrichment' was a patent issued to Andrew Viscardi in 1940. He developed a process for the 'impregnation of tobacco with vitamin $B_1$', declaring that with such tobacco cigar and cigarette smokers would 'secure therapeutic benefit'.[1]

Another item that received much publicity was vitaminised candy. Baker's Chocolate produced a half-pound candy bar fortified with vitamins A, $B_1$, and D; Smith Brothers added vitamin A to their famous cough drops. As the spectre of war crossed Europe, concerned and enterprising Americans saw vitaminised candy as one part of a nutrition solution. By late 1940, a subsidiary of the Life Savers Corp. unveiled a new product, Vita-mints, sold in packages of ten for 10¢ with the promise that they supplied the 'daily requirements of vitamins $B_1$, $B_2$ (G), C and D for an adult or child'. Dr Philip Newton, a 1910 graduate of Georgetown University Medical School and member of the Vitamins for Britain Committee, a group of physicians who also served on the nutritional advisory committee of the US National Research Council, endeavoured to improve the product. In early 1941, he devised a formulation that incorporated vitamin A into the candy (see Figure 9.1). For export the confection was called 'Vitamin Sweets' and was distributed by the British–American Ambulance Corps in packages of fourteen carrying the legend 'approved by British Ministry of Health'. The media promoted 'Vitamin Sweets' and urged donations to cover the costs of manufacturing and distribution, which the company estimated at $8.55 per child per year. Enthusiasm for 'Vitamin Sweets' waned, however, as researchers began to question the stability of the vitamins in candy and especially after the *Journal of the American Medical Association* criticised the plan, pointing out Newton's previous experience with the less reputable wing of the patent medicine business.[2]

Ideas such as vitaminised candy did not spring full-blown from the minds of manufacturers and advertisers. They were inspired by decades of reports in the popular media documenting that the diets of many, if not most, Americans were insufficient and innutritious. Medical organisations such as the American Medical Association and public health officials such as adminis-

# VITAMINS FOR BRITAIN

**NUTRITIOUS CANDY**

At left—Dr. Philip Newton, a member of the Medical Advisory Committee of the British American Ambulance Corps "Vitamins For Britain" fund drive, is shown at the pill press in his laboratory in New York City, where he devised the formula for the vitamin tablets which the corps is sending to England. Dr. Newton's contribution was the first successful incorporation in a sugar candy of vitamin A. Previously, there had been placed on the market in this country a vitamin candy which contained vitamin B, C, D and G, but not vitamin A.

Each tablet contains 500 I.U. vitamin A, 50 I.U. vitamin B-1, 33 gammas riboflavin (vitamin G), 5 mg. ascorbic acid (vitamin C), 50 I.U. vitamin D and cane sugar, flavored with cinnamon. Each child is to eat six of the candies daily. Cost for 156 packages estimated to be enough for one child for one year, is $8.55. The tablets are being made at cost price by the Life Savers Corp.

*Figure 9.1*   Philip Newton, who devised a vitamin A candy (from *Drug Topics*, 27 January 1941, p. 13).

trators at the Food and Drug Administration derided these reports, staunchly maintaining that all Americans needed to do was eat a moderate, well-balanced diet. Many others could and did point to deficiencies in the American diet. Some blamed modern food and agricultural processes for 'denaturing' foodstuffs, stripping vital micronutrients before the food ever arrived at the table. Others claimed that the problem lay in deficient education; people needed better knowledge of healthful cooking methods. For whatever reasons, popular magazines and newspapers were filled with stories about the insufficiency of most American diets.[3]

One alternative to this dilemma was enrichment, a topic widely discussed in the popular media. Some proponents of enrichment sought simply to replace the vitamins lost in processing; others preferred fortification, which involved adding extra micronutrients to target known nutritional deficiencies, a pattern established with the vitamin-D enrichment of milk and the addition of iodine to salt. Nutritionists and other scientists typically supported fortification on pragmatic grounds while at the same time decrying the need for such programmes. According to Agnes Faye

Morgan, one of the leading nutritional scientists of the day, 'To combat in the general population the perverse use of vitamin-poor foods, such as sugar, white flour, polished rice, alcoholic and soft drinks, fortification of these foods may be desirable until the slow process of education relegates the demand for them to the background'. Others resisted altering the nutritional value of foods, considering enrichment programmes 'shotgun prophylaxis' and 'wasteful, inefficient, and possibly harmful'.[4] Ultimately, though, the pressures of war impelled implementation of enrichment programmes.[5]

In the early years, much of the attention focused on enriching flour and flour products such as bread and pasta, in particular the loss of vitamin B through modern milling processes.[6] By 1940, Britain's Ministry of Food required that all British millers fortify their flour and United States scientists and physicians, such as Dr Russell M. Wilder of the Mayo Clinic and the National Research Council, extolled the virtues of vitaminised flour.[7] Food processors saw the advantages of promoting fortified products, too. Journals carried articles about the need for enriched flour products as well as advertisements for them. *Hygeia*, the popular health magazine produced by the American Medical Association, followed a story outlining the deleterious consequences of the modern diet on health, 'Refinement of food and its effect on our diet', with a full-page, text-rich advertisement by General Mills for its new vitamin-enriched VIBIC flour. According to the company, its flour 'has the enthusiastic unofficial (sic) endorsement of many leading physicians and nutritional specialists'. A few months later, in a back-cover, colour advertisement for its popular cereal Kix, the company advised mothers to use the product to end 'deficient breakfasts', announcing that 'National Defence begins at *Breakfast!*' As the advertisement reminded mothers, quoting from a government publication, 'defense is plants and guns – but it is also building the health and fitness of all our people ... Hungry people, undernourished people, ill people do not make for strong defense'.[8]

This invocation of 'health and fitness' in part explains the focus on fortifying flour products. For one thing, modern milling processes were the most frequent targets of nutritionists who complained that contemporary diets were insufficient; they wrote often on the loss of vitamin $B_1$. Also, flour products were dominant components in the typical American diet. Moreover, by 1939 researchers had developed a crystalline form of thiamine, vitamin $B_1$, making it feasible to consider fortification. Most significantly, lack of vitamin B had been and continued to be linked with a host of worrisome, though not life-threatening conditions. *Milling*, a British journal, was quoted in the American press, linking dietary deficiency with the 'moral and physical weaknesses' observed in Germans in the First World War.[9] *Hygeia* deplored the 'relationship between the decreasing vitamin B content of modern diets and the increasing malnutrition, nervousness, constipation, and possibly other gastro-intestinal disturbances in children'.[10] Wilder was more pointed and colourful: 'A little thiamine deficiency is associated with irritability, but much or long-continued deficiency is more likely to result in depression, exhaustion and feelings of inferiority'. Citing examples from Europe and Canada and his own research out of the Mayo Clinic, he concluded that 'insufficiency of vitamins $B_1$ (thiamine) is a principal cause for the majority of the nervous and mental abnormalities that are associated with or responsible for the psychological states, commonly spoke of as loss of morale'.[11]

## The powers of vitamins

This concern over the vitamin $B_1$ content of the American diet had several results. On the one side, it stimulated practical efforts to mitigate potential problems; for instance, the enrichment programmes in the United States were significantly expanded.[12] On the other side, it could, and did, lend itself to comic interpretations.[13] If depression and anxiety resulted from a deficiency of vitamin $B_1$, what would result from an excess? Just such a throw-away line is heard in the 1942 musical, *The gang's all here*. It occurs in the conversation of a society couple: he is a staid, even stodgy husband played by Edward Everett Horton; the wife is played by Charlotte Greenwood. Horton is unaware of his wife's previous career as a chorus girl. When Greenwood meets and flirts with the man with whom she used to dance, Horton is frustrated by her increasingly flippant behaviour. As he gets more and more agitated, he announces that 'I absolutely forbid you from getting within 20 feet of that man again, you understand me, 20 feet'. She responds: 'Won't you accept 10 [feet]?' He settles for no less than fifteen and claims that her 'irresistibility' is the result not of her personality but her diet: 'It's that vitamin $B_1$. I told you, you were taking too much. You're overdoing it'. The moral is clear: if too little vitamin $B_1$ makes you irritable, too much makes you 'irresistible'. Viewers in the early 1940s would have been very familiar with the concept from their daily newspapers.

Some researchers tried to go beyond anecdotal evidence to investigate the power of vitamins, particularly thiamine. In Toronto, Dr W. J. McCormack looked at the micronutrient's ability to increase stamina. He found ten test subjects whose diets were 'rich in $B_1$' and determined that they could hold their arms horizontal for between forty-three minutes and two hours; four subjects with 'more refined diets' could hold their arms horizontal for only thirteen to thirty-six minutes. These latter subjects received daily doses of thiamine for one week, after which their endurance increased to over two and a half hours. McCormack claimed that he also worked with swimmers and that their speed performance improved with vitamin supplementation.[14] An obvious application of such test results would be vitamin supplementation for soldiers and other service personnel. In addition, these test results were used to promote vitamin supplementation for industrial workers.

Once again, at the forefront of this effort was Dr Russell M. Wilder. Over and over again in the popular press, he is quoted arguing that thiamine deficiency had resulted in physical and psychological ill-health, that the US diet was 'grossly deficient' in vitamin $B_1$, which he called the nerve and morale vitamin. His arguments were echoed by others who linked lack of sufficient thiamine with 'numberless undesirable symptoms affecting our daily living', including 'fatigue, lack of zest, discouragement, depression, irritability, constipation, poor appetite'. Most worrisome in these times of national emergency:

> ... striking studies made recently in connection with our defense program have emphasized again the fact that the average American is not getting as much of the B complex or 'morale' vitamin as he needs. We should have made use of this knowledge long ago; now, when we much hold ourselves ready in a world at war, it is a fact we must face and deal with.[15]

The general problem was malaise, irritability; the specific problem could be labour unrest. Wilder's research disclosed the damaging effects that a deficiency of vitamin $B_1$ could have on munitions workers and their miraculous improvement once the vitamin was restored their diet. He studied a group of female volunteers who were 'sociable, contented workers'. They were fed an 'acceptable, palatable diet', but one without thiamine. In a few weeks, Wilder reported, their personalities had changed drastically; they quarrelled, became depressed, and tired easily: 'They even went on strikes'. Once thiamine was restored to their diet, it took only two days for them to become 'their old selves again'.[16]

Stories such as this spurred the adoption of vitamin supplementation in several industries, though the justification was not usually so specific. One of the earliest examples was in a Continental Machines plant in Minneapolis, Minnesota. Wilkie, the vice-president, was impressed with reports he had heard of the beneficial effects of vitamin supplementation, particularly the increased resistance to colds and influenza. Consequently, in early 1941, he had vitamin capsules distributed to all company workers daily during a five-minute recess. Despite a mild influenza epidemic during the early weeks of the experiment, he found work attendance was 50 per cent better than the same period the year before. Moreover, 95 per cent of the workers declared that they felt healthier, slept better, had increased appetites, and even saw better at night. So successful was the campaign that the company determined to repeat the distribution plan each winter and spring. Though company officials were not willing to claim that this experiment proved the efficacy of vitamin supplementation, they were convinced 'it was worth $150 a month to them, for the cost of the vitamins, to keep their highly skilled men on the job, and they [didn't] really care whether it's health building or psychology which turns the trick'.[17] This was a telling illustration of the Hawthorne effect.[18]

Soon other industries instituted similar vitamin distribution programmes. They emphasised that supplementation was necessary to protect the health of vital defence workers, 'to step up efficiency and cut down on absences', rather than as specifics against cold and 'flu or low morale. William T. Thompson, a chemist, reported that his firm developed a 'Vitamins for Victory' plan, three tablets daily, costing three cents, which his firm distributed to half a dozen concerns including Northrop Aircraft, Vultee Aircraft, and North American Aviation.[19] Nor was it just company officials who promoted vitamins in the workplace. In the spring of 1942 the United Electrical, Radio and Machine Workers, an affiliate of the Congress of Industrial Organizations, which remained in war-time a more forceful advocate of improved labour conditions than its rival the American Federation of Labor, successfully demanded two vitamin pills a day in their contract negotiations.[20]

In a few instances, researchers attempted to measure more directly the immediate and long-term benefits of vitamin supplementation for workers. One case, often-cited in the popular press, sent investigators from California Institute of Technology to study workers at the Burbank plant of Lockheed Aircraft Corp. The subjects were healthy young men with 'a fairly standard diet', that included meat, eggs, and milk but was slightly deficient in fruits and vegetables. The workers were divided into three groups: one received vitamin supplementation five days a week; the second received a placebo; and the third was given no pills. Researchers reported little difference among the groups during the first six months, though evidently those who received pills did better psychologically than those who did not. By the second 6-month period, however, starker differences began to appear. Workers who had received vitamins demonstrated 19 per cent less absenteeism, 27 per cent less turnover (fewer were fired or quit), and they scored 2.6 per cent higher in the company's merit ratings. The researchers found that these effects were more psychological than physical. That is, vitamin takers were sick as often as the other test subjects, but were absent less and seemed happier. According to press stories: 'The investigators figured that the pills had added the equivalent of ten and a-half working days a year to each man's output'.[21]

## Vitamins go to Hollywood

The general idea that vitamins increased pep and energy was frequently described in the popular media of the day as well. Extreme examples could provide fascinating material for Hollywood comedy screenwriters, as evidenced in the 1944 RKO film, Danny Kaye's first feature movie, *Up in Arms*.

Danny Kaye plays Weems, a hypochondriac, who is very careful about everything he puts into his body. In one of the many scenes that establish his character traits, Weems is having dinner in an elegant New York restaurant, along with his best friend, Joe Nelson (played by Dana Andrews), and two women, Virginia Merrill (played by Dinah Shore) and Mary Morgan (played by Constance Dowling). Merrill is a nurse and is in love with Weems; Weems is in love with Morgan; Morgan and Nelson are falling in love; in other words, the usual 1940s romantic mix-up. As the scene opens, a haughty waiter brings Weems a glass of milk, which he accepts and then smells. With a quizzical look on his face, he asks the waiter, 'What kind of milk is this?' The waiter smells it also and announces nonchalantly that it is cow's milk. 'Cow's milk?' Weems responds, 'I didn't order cow's milk. Haven't you got any goat's milk?' 'No', replies the disdainful waiter, 'our goat is out shooting pool with some friends'. As an alternative, Weems asks for vitaminized milk. The evermore arrogant waiter retorts, 'My friend, this is the Chalet San Moritz; you want the Polyclinic Hospital, perhaps'. The scene escalates and when Weems' friends attempt to intervene, the maitre d' approaches and pompously insists that they must be careful how they treat waiters. To deflect the tension, Merrill invites Weems to come with her, tempting him with the promise that she 'know[s] a place that specialises in vitaminized milk'. 'It is', she tells him with a wink toward their friends, 'one of the hot spots in town'. Weems, torn between staying with Morgan and procuring his health drink, vitaminised milk, finally agrees to leave with Merrill who closes the scene with a breathless, satiric, 'Oh, I can hardly wait. You know, I'm just crazy about vitaminized milk'.

*Up in Arms* presents Weems as a man totally obsessed with his physical health, for which he takes extreme measures. Though madly in love with Morgan, he is so committed to his vitamins that he is lured away from her with the promise of vitaminsed milk. Milk with vitamins D and A added was generally available in the United States by the 1940s, but the extent to which Weems hungers for it is played broadly for the comic effect.

Despite his obsession, Weems' health concerns have no effect when he appears before the draft board and he is drafted into the armed forces. Soon he finds himself on board a ship headed for the south Pacific. His shipmates tease him unmercifully about his hypochondria and all his vitamins and tonics. Also on board are Nelson in uniform, Merrill as a nurse, and Morgan who is now also a nurse. Typical Hollywood musical complications ensue. Ultimately Weems is thrown into the brig for his actions and denied his vitamins.

He remains incarcerated once they land at their station on a Pacific island. All this time he has been without his vitamins. He becomes increasingly agitated, shouting to the sentries, pleading: 'You've got to get it for me, fellows. It's been weeks now. I'm going crazy. I warn you, I warn you. If I don't get my vitamins, it will over-excite my thyroid and', he screams, 'anything can happen'. The sentries, not surprisingly, ignore his cries. And, 'anything' does happen. Sometime later, a sailor informs the Captain that Private Weems has escaped. They rush over to find the brig in shambles. The Captain is astounded: 'You mean to tell me that Weems did this all by himself?' 'Yes, sir. But I can't figure it out, sir', reports the sailor, 'He was a man with no muscles at all'. Merrill, also observing the destruction, remarks: 'Well, one thing. He's got his health back, anyhow'. (In the end, the audience learns that a troop of Japanese soldiers destroyed the brig and released Weems; ultimately he captures them all.)

## Experts, pharmacists, and vitamins

Through the comic skill of Danny Kaye, Weems personifies the commonly circulated belief that one does not actually need those vitamin supplements. Physicians and other health officials of the period publicised a similar image of the vitamin supplement as misguided, as swayed by commercial products and irrational fears.[22] *Hygeia*, unambiguously proclaimed 'The chances of increasing industrial production by feeding vitamin pills to workers ... are not very great'. The journal quoted unnamed physicians to the effect that 'Industry would better spend the money on research than on vitamin pills'.[23]

In order to establish some scientifically credible resolution to the controversy over vitamin supplementation, especially its use in the defence industry, a New York State senator surveyed a number of leading nutritional scientists. They did not unequivocally condemn the practice. Several feared that the focus on synthetic vitamins would deflect attention from other nutrients and would detract from the importance of a nutritionally sound and well-balanced diet; to them, the appropriate response to war-time needs was stepped up nutritional education. According to Dr Wilbur A. Sawyer, of the Rockefeller Foundation:

> The crying need for better nutrition can be answered only with food. Giving synthetic vitamins is a stopgap procedure, of great value to some of the ill or depleted but having little or no value for the normal working individual needing better nutrition.[24]

For others, however, the war presented extenuating circumstances that demanded drastic new measures. Vitamin supplementation was a pragmatic choice to Dr Howard W. Haggard, Yale University, who believed that:

> There was time for education before the war; there will be time after the war; and it can go on during the war. But at the present, our attention is focused not upon normal, logical and rational conditions but upon the abnormal, illogical and irrational conditions of wartime.[25]

He had considered the results of several experiments in defence plants and regarded their findings as decisive; vitamin supplementation increased production and decreased absenteeism, fatigue, and spoilage. Thus, he concluded: 'increasing the vitamin intake of the American worker would be highly beneficial in production for the war effort'.[26]

In light of this lack of consensus, industry officials and druggists continued to publicise the benefits of vitamin pills for the defence industry. One enterprising pharmacy in Tulsa, Oklahoma, advertised vitamins as 'a work pick up'. The pharmacist advised workers 'to avoid a work let-down by religiously remembering those vitamin pick-up pills'. This promotion was linked directly to the war effort: 'Ill health means less work ... less work means weaker fighting power! Help win the war – and better health for yourself by giving your body proper vitamin intake'.[27] Clearly, many were convinced. By 1943, vitamin sales in the United States had reached nearly $180 million (up from about $136 million in 1942). A significant proportion was due to industrial sales, including vitamins purchased by plants for resale to employees at nominal cost, vitamins bought by plants for free distribution to workers, and vitamins sold at retail in company stores and commissaries. Though in 1942 industrial sales accounted for only 1.5 per cent of vitamin sales, by 1943, they were 7.9 per cent.[28]

Some pharmacists may have worried that the ready availability of vitamins outside the drug store would detract from their bottom line. However, while not enthusiastic over the principle of industrial sales, during the war they did not feel comfortable, 'to criticise (sic) the present practice and its aim: elimination of absenteeism'. Others, looking ahead, considered the contemporary practice a potential boon, 'since it gets workers into the habit of using vitamin products. The time will come, say these dealers, when the workers may not be able to get the vitamins where they work; and will have to turn to the druggist for their supplies'.[29] *Drug Topics*, the leading retail pharmacy journal, was reassuring on this matter. Studies, it reported, showed that

> ... in towns where factory employees were given free vitamins, sales through local drug stores increased at a greater rate than they did in other towns where there was no such gratis distribution. In other words, the factory users actually proved to be persuasive salesmen for vitamins among friends and relatives who, perforce, had to get their concentrates at the drug store.[30]

Soldiers represented another large group of vitamin users who did not purchase their pills in the drug store. As with defence workers, manufacturers and druggists assumed that when soldiers returned from service, they would continue to take vitamins.[31]

Not that pharmacists ceded all their vitamin business to the defence industry and the military. The national defence became an important motif of advertising directed to civilians, even before the United States entered the war. Vitamins for victory was a theme repeated in drugstore windows and displays and in newspaper and radio advertisements. Abbott Laboratories was one of the pharmaceutical firms to announce a new product, V-Kaps, the Victory Vitamin Capsule, heavily promoted in drugstores. Pharmacists proclaimed that 'It's your duty to keep fit for victory' and 'Just by keeping well you can win the war', with vitamin supplementation, of course.[32] (See Figures 9.2 and 9.3.)

Moreover, war-time emergency measures instituted on the home front provided further indication of the need for vitamin supplementation. Rationing was one such war-time measure, designed to maximise the production and distribution of foodstuffs at home and abroad among soldiers and citizens in countries affected more directly by the war. Americans considered the

## FOR DEFENSE

Right — Done in a color scheme of red, white and blue to carry out the d e f e n s e theme, this vitamin window was recently installed in the Rose Drug Store, 10205 Madison Avenue, Cleveland. Store owner S. Rose reports a "substantial increase in our vitamin sales." Vitamin products of several well known manufacturers were shown in the display.

*Figure 9.2*   Vitamins for health's defense (from *Drug Topics*, 8 December 1941, p. 25).

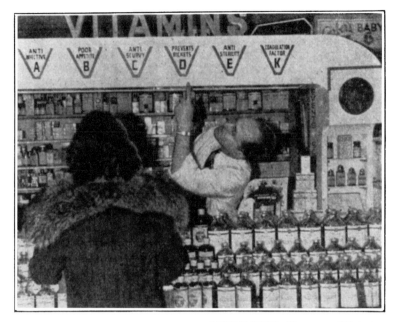

**VITAMINS** Above — "V is for vitamins as well as for victory", manager Henry Schoemehl tells a customer in the Katz Drug Store, St. Louis, Mo. This vitamin bar, featuring large sizes and massed display of liquid and capsule goods, has brought a rapid sales increase and much repeat business, reports Mr. Schoemehl.

*Figure 9.3*   Vitamins for victory (from *Drug Topics*, 9 February 1942, p. 27).

sacrifices that rationing represented as a demonstration of their patriotism and support for the war. It is not clear, however, that rationing dramatically altered the American diet. Most critical for understanding the popularity of vitamin supplements in this period is food historian Amy Bentley's insightful conclusion that, 'evidence suggests that while Americans' eating habits and the structure of their meals did not change significantly, wartime food rationing had a significant psychological effect'. Regardless of the measurable or negligible physiological or nutritional effects of rationing, Americans were concerned that it could mean food shortages and could most crucially result in poor nutrition.[33]

Druggists and drug companies used these anxieties over food shortages and the restrictions imposed by rationing to stimulate interest in vitamin supplementation among apprehensive consumers. The pharmaceutical manufacturer, Lever Brothers, launched a national advertising campaign for its popular product Vimms, to tell 'the nation that food rationing need not deprive them of essential vitamins and minerals'. *Drug Topics* suggested that pharmacists place reminders in their windows and throughout their stores with advice such as: 'Butter hard to get: These capsules will help make up for the vitamins you'd otherwise miss'; 'If you can't get all the fruit you need, you can still get the vitamins found in fruit by taking these products'; 'Food rationing may unbalance your diet. Help to make up the deficiency with vitamins'; and the pithy 'Enjoy robust health. Take more vitamins'. Though we have no clear measure of the impact of these campaigns, there is some anecdotal evidence showing that such promotions were followed by a boost in vitamin sales.[34]

What we do know is that vitamin sales increased dramatically during the war years. Between 1931 and 1939, the figure grew from slightly more than $12 million to over $82.7 million. According to *Drug Topics*, just three years later, the United States pharmaceutical industry could boast of sales of over $130 million. Even allowing for inflation, this meteoric rise continued: in 1943 the amount stood at over $179 million, and over $182 million a year later. *Fortune* magazine's statistics were slightly different, but its break-down is instructive. Approximately $200 million in vitamin sales was accounted for in capsules and other preparations sold over the counter. In addition to sales to food manufacturers for enrichment of milk, flour, and margarine, vitamin companies also sold about $5 million worth of vitamin tablets to the US government for shipment to servicemen and about $13 million worth of vitamins were distributed abroad though lend-lease and the Red Cross.[35] So, as a conservative estimate, during the war years, vitamin sales more than doubled. Clearly, in the alliteratively linking of vitamins and victory, in the creative correlation of nutritional supplements with national defence, war proved very healthy for the vitamin industry.

## References

1 'Vitaminzed cigars win US patent', *Drug Topics*, 23 September 1940, p. 14. For more on the vitaminised products, see 'Vitamin reference is prohibited for beer', *Drug Topics*, 29 April 1940, p. 13; 'Vitamins, vitamins', *The New Republic*, 11 January 1939, vol. 97, p. 272; R. D. Apple, *Vitamania: Vitamins in American culture*, New Brunswick, NJ, Rutgers University Press, 1996, esp. pp. 13–32.

2 'Vita-mints', *Tide*, 17 November 1940, vol. 14, no. 22, p. 28; 'Vitamin sweets will be given to British children', *Drug Topics*, 20 January 1941, p. 12; 'Vitamins for Britain', *Drug Topics*, 27 January 1941, p. 1; 'British abandon "vitamin sweets"', *Drug Topics*, 10 March 1941, p. 14. Each of the tablets in vitamin sweets contained 500 I.U. vitamin A, 50 I.U. vitamin $B_1$, 33 gammas riboflavin (vitamin g), 5 mg. ascorbic acid (vitamin C), 50 I.U. vitamin D and cane sugar, flavoured with cinnamon. Previous tablets lacked vitamin A because of the stability problem. Since the first decade of the century, the American Medical Association (AMA) and investigative reporters had been leading the fight to rid the pharmaceutical industry of disreputable promoters and questionable products. It was not until 1938 that the US Congress passed a revised Food, Drug, and Cosmetic Act which sought to rein in the extravagances of unsavoury drug promoters and products. The AMA

was at the forefront of the battle for its passage. For more on the history of health quackery in twentieth-century United States and the media and legislative manoeuvres behind the passage of the 1938 law, see J. H. Young, *The Medical Messiahs: A Social History of Health Quackery in Twentieth-Century America*, Princeton, NJ, Princeton University Press, 1967, p. 1992; C. O. Jackson, *Food and Drug Legislation in the New Deal*, Princeton, NJ, Princeton University Press, 1970.

3  R. D. Apple, 1996 op. cit.; S. R. White, 'Chemistry and controversy: regulating the use of chemicals in foods, 1883–1959', unpublished PhD thesis, Emory University, 1994. For a typical example of contemporary analysis, see E. M. Koch, 'Refinement of food and its effect on our diet, part I', *Hygeia*, 1940, vol. 18, pp. 620–3, 646; E. M. Koch, 'Refinement of food and its effect on our diet, II', *Hygeia*, 1940, vol. 18, pp. 703–4, 718.

4  'Scientists look at vitamins', *The New Republic*, 17 May 1939, vol. 99, p. 33.

5  For more on the programmes, and the patriotism and public acclaim they afforded participants, see White, op. cit.

6  By the late 1930s and early 1940s, scientists recognised that there was not one vitamin B, but rather a combination of micronutrients grouped together as vitamin B-complex. Yet, in much of the popular press, these various elements were frequently collapsed into one vitamin, vitamin B. Throughout this paper, I retain the names used in the original texts.

7  'British flour', *Tide*, 1940, vol. 14, no. 17, p. 26; 'Millers' decision', *Tide*, 1940, vol. 14, no. 22, pp. 17–18.

8  'Advertisement for Kix cereal: national defence begins at breakfast!', *Hygeia*, December 1940, vol. 18, back cover.

9  'Millers' decision', op. cit.

10  E. M. Koch, op. cit., pp. 703–704, 718.

11  R. M. Wilder, 'Hitler's secret weapon is depriving people of vitamin', *Science News Letter*, 12 April 1941, vol. 39, pp. 231, 237.

12  For more on the history of the B-vitamins, see K. Carpenter, 'Beriberi, white rice, and vitamin B'. I thank Professor Carpenter for allowing me to read his manuscript.

13  For more on vitamins in popular culture, see R. D. Apple, '"If I don't get my vitamins… anything can happen": nutrition in twentieth-century popular culture', *Pharmacy in History*, 1998, vol. 40, no. 4, pp. 123–31.

14  'Holds vitamin B1 increases ability in physical work', *Drug Topics*, 6 January 1941, p. 22.

15  'Vitamin conflict', *Business Week*, 9 August 1941, pp. 42–3; E. S. Banks, 'Feeding the family', *Parent's Magazine*, January 1942, vol. 17, pp. 50, 55, 57.

16  W. Kaempffert, 'What we know about vitamins', *New York Times Magazine*, May 1942, pp. 10–11, 23; R. M. Wilder, op. cit.

17  'Machine maker gives vitamins to workers', *Drug Topics*, 20 January 1941, p. 12; 'Vitamin pills cur absences at tool plant', *Drug Topics*, 23 June 1941, p. 14; K. M. Swezey, 'Industry goes in for vitamins to conserve manpower for defence work', *Popular Science Monthly*, May 1942, pp. 101–7.

18  In the late 1920s, Elton Mayo and his colleagues studied workers at the Hawthorne plant of Western Electric in Cicero, Illinois, US. In their experiments to enhance the productivity of workers, they altered the light levels and the timing of rest periods. They discovered that no matter how they changed the work environment, productivity increased. Their conclusion – that the psychological stimulus of being selected, and thus made to feel more important is what improved worker productivity – is known as the Hawthorne effect. Since then, their conclusion has been widely challenged, but the importance of psychosocial as well as economic and environmental stimuli remains an important element in the study of industrial relations.

19  'Vitamins at work', *Newsweek*, 16 March 1942, vol. 19, pp. 53–4; 'Plan provides free vitamins to defence industry workers', *Drug Topics*, 16 February 1942, p. 2.

20  'Pills in the contract', *Business Week*, 16 May 1942, pp. 52–3; a useful general discussion of US labour conditions in war-time is Robert H. Zieger, *American Workers, American Unions*, John Hopkins University Press, Baltimore, (second edition) 1994, pp. 62–99.

21 'Aircraft workers get a life from vitamins', *Business Week*, 25 August 1945, p. 108; 'Vitamins & vigor', *Time*, 21 May 1945, vol. 45, pp. 88–9.

22 Apple, 1996, op. cit.

23 Robert M. Yoder, 'Vitamania', *Hygeia*, April 1942, vol. 20, pp. 264–5.

24 'Vitamins for workers', *Science News Letter*, 31 July 1943, vol. 44, pp. 76–7.

25 Ibid.

26 Ibid.

27 'Vitamins pushed as efficiency aid for war workers', *Drug Topics*, 6 March 1944, p. 44.

28 D. Rennick, 'Vitamin volume totalled $179,850,000 in 1943', *Drug Topics*, 29 May 1944, p. 43.

29 'Coast men concerned over factory vitamin sales to worker's families', *Drug Topics*, 26 April 1943, p. 8.

30 D. Rennick, 'Vitamin volume totalled $179,850,000 in 1943', *Drug Topics*, May 29, 1944, p. 43; 'Pills in the contract', *Business Week*, 16 May 1942, pp. 52–3.

31 'Pills in the contract', op. cit.; D. Rennick, 'Pharmacy gets bigger share of vitamin volume', *Drug Topics*, 9 July 1945, p. 55.

32 These advertising campaigns are documented in the numerous descriptive articles published in the leading retail drug store periodical, *Drug Topics*. See, for example, 'Ad on vitamins declares they're vital to defence', *Drug Topics*, 4 August 1941, p 29; 'For defence', *Drug Topics*, 8 December 1941, p. 5; 'The IVC victory deal will pay off in folding money to the nation's druggists', *Drug Topics*, 26 January 1942, p. 34; 'Vitamin ad urges civilians to 'keep well for victory', *Drug Topics*, 5 October 1942, p. 43; 'Ties vitamins to war', *Drug Topics*, 15 February 1943, p. 35; 'Abbott Laboratories announce new Victory Vitamin Capsule [advertisement]', *Drug Topics*, 2 March 1942, p. 17; 'Abbott presents your new 'home from' window display [advertisement]', *Drug Topics*, 7 Septemeber 1942, p. 13; 'Vitamins for victory', *Drug Topics*, 7 September 1942, p. 15; 'Keeping well can help win the war, Schlegel's ad on vitamins declare', *Drug Topics*, 8 March 1943, p. 48; 'Take Vitamins to speed your efforts in winning war', *Drug Topics*, 10 May 1943, p. 40.

33 A. Bentley, *Eating for Victory: Food Rationing and the Politics of Domesticity*, Urbana and Chicago, University of Illinois Press, 1998, p. 61.

34 For some examples of these promotions, see 'Desire for good nutrition, despite rationing, boost vitamin sales 40%', *Drug Topics*, 17 May 1943, p. 45; D. Rennick, 'Women are vitamin conscious', *Drug Topics*, 17 May 1943, pp. 41–2; 'What you should know about vitamins under food rationing', *Drug Topics*, 17 May, 1943, p. 1; 'Urging widespread vitamin sales, Sen. Reynolds asks grocers to sell', *Drug Topics*, 1 March 1943, p. 3; 'Food rationing creates huge new market for druggists!' [advertisement], *Drug Topics*, 5 April 1943, p. 51.

35 'Vitamins go to war', Business Week Report to Executives, 10 July 1943, pp. 55–69; D. Rennick, 'But real competition is coming!', *Drug Topics*, 19 April 1943, p. 31; D. Rennick, 'Vitamin volume totalled $179,850,000 in 1943', *Drug Topics*, 29 May 1944, p. 43; D. Rennick, 'Pharmacy gets bigger share of vitamin volume', *Drug Topics*, 9 July 1945, p. 55.

# 10 The United Nations Protein Advisory Group

*Josh Ruxin*

The quest to end hunger and malnutrition, championed during the last few decades by the United Nations (UN), has followed an uneven and controversial course. Beginning in the late 1940s, observations of malnutrition in developing countries stimulated the UN's foray into protein deficiency. Between the 1950s and 1970s, a cadre of nutritionists called the Protein Advisory Group (PAG) influenced policy at three UN agencies: the Food and Agricultural Organisation (FAO), the World Health Organisation (WHO), and the United Nations Children's Fund (Unicef). This chapter examines the trajectory of PAG and explores the issues which arose when the group eventually found itself at odds with the UN.

PAG's history provides a case study of interactions between scientists and international policy-makers. The chapter begins by tracing PAG's concentration, during the 1950s and 1960s, upon devising new weaning foods for preventing clinical protein deficiency or kwashiorkor. It then turns to the late 1960s and early 1970s when PAG called for monumental efforts to increase protein production and availability to fill a much wider 'protein gap'. Finally, the chapter details how protein advocates were discredited and a new policy making hierarchy emerged, with nutritionists lower on the ladder of influence.

## Formation of the Protein Advisory Group

In the aftermath of the Second World War, the UN and its agencies were founded to replace earlier organisations, and to implement new programmes of international co-operation and development. The UN and FAO formally came into being in October 1945, while Unicef was formed in April 1946, and WHO in April 1948. These agencies employed scientists and provided opportunities for outside experts to take part in policy making and research programmes.[1] The need for co-operation between the agencies was soon evident, and in October 1949 a Joint Committee of nutrition experts and representatives of FAO and WHO met to discuss the co-ordination of their work. Among the conclusions was a proposal for a study to assess the prevalence of kwashiorkor in Africa.[2] This condition, characterised by thin limbs, a swollen belly, and reddish hair, had been identified in the Gold Coast by Cicely D. Williams in 1933 and linked to poor breastfeeding and inadequate protein consumption.[3]

J. F. Brock, professor of medicine at Cape Town University, and Marcel Autret, a staff member of FAO's nutrition division, carried out the study. They identified kwashiorkor in every nation they visited and reiterated the views of previous literature on prevention.[4] The recommended solutions involving milk as a dietary supplement appealed to UN administrators, particularly at Unicef, since it had been distributing dried milk across Europe. As far as international aid policy was concerned, the most grotesque disease of malnutrition, and solutions in the form of milk and 'energetic educational measures', had been identified.[5]

During the next few years, kwashiorkor remained a feature of Joint FAO/WHO meetings. Further surveys were carried out and Unicef experimented with providing skimmed milk to children in central Africa. Increasing attention was also given to locally made high-protein weaning foods.[6] In 1955, to reinforce policy making, WHO established a new expert group, the Protein Advisory Group (PAG), following a meeting of thirty biochemists, nutritionists, paediatricians, and scientists in Princeton, New Jersey. Participants urged the formation of a UN advisory group that would function autonomously and make recommendations about all aspects of indigenous protein sources.[7] According to one press statement, 'there was little brilliance of oratory and no world-shattering decisions', but the conference highlighted the confidence held in scientific approaches to protein malnutrition, and was trumpeted at agency headquarters as a breakthrough for nutritional work.[8]

The formation of PAG owed much to American philanthropy: the Princeton conference was sponsored by the Josiah Macy Foundation. Established in 1930 to assist research on 'fundamental aspects of health', the Foundation had supported studies of growth and development, and funded conferences encouraging 'a multi-discipline approach'. In 1953 it had sponsored a conference on protein malnutrition jointly with FAO and WHO.[9]

The role of PAG was to provide expert advice to FAO, WHO and Unicef on their 'protein-rich foods program'. It was to consist of leading clinical nutritionists and paediatricians who would meet periodically with representatives of UN agencies. A sub-group – the Committee on Protein Malnutrition – was provided with $550,000 from the Rockefeller Foundation and $300,000 from Unicef for supervising 'laboratory tests, process development, and support of acceptability trials of protein-rich foods'.[10] The US National Academy of Sciences had financial and auditing responsibility for the committee and the Academy's Food and Nutrition Board provided the secretariat. The committee used its initial funds for sixteen grants involving twenty research groups in a dozen countries.[11]

W. R. Aykroyd, director of FAO's Nutrition Division, was initially reluctant to support PAG. Aykroyd was a British nutritionist who had been involved in the Health Organisation of the League of Nations during the 1930s. He believed the UN agencies could develop new foods without outside help, and FAO was already working with Unicef on a fish flour project in Chile.[12] As a result of uncertainties over the role of PAG, FAO and Unicef posted observers at meetings, but did not become sponsors until 1960.[13]

William J. Darby, director of nutrition at Vanderbilt University, became the first co-ordinator and chair of PAG. Other members included W. Henry Sebrell, director of the US Public Health Service, L. Emmett Holt, Jr., professor of paediatrics at New York University, and Paul György, professor of paediatrics at the University of Pennsylvania. Members from beyond the US included Benjamin S. Platt, director of the human nutrition research unit of the British Medical Research Council (MRC) at the London School of Hygiene and Tropical Medicine, and Eric K. Cruick-shank, professor of medicine at University College of the West Indies.[14] They set to work convincing the UN agencies that protein should be the lynchpin of nutrition programmes and issued the first *PAG Bulletin* in January 1956, to nutrition experts employed and consulted by the agencies.[15] From 1956–60, PAG papers were produced by Darby and the FAO nutrition advisor to Unicef, with support from the nutrition units at the agencies. From 1960, the sponsors provided an annual budget for PAG activities and from 1963, PAG had an office and staff in New York and a full-time co-ordinator.[16] As PAG flourished, its major activities became annual meetings of its members and *ad hoc* technical group meetings throughout the year. PAG disseminated its work to the agencies primarily through the reports of these meetings.

Scientific findings added momentum to PAG's mission. In 1957, research by J. C. Waterlow and Nevin Scrimshaw helped consolidate the protein field by showing that kwashiorkor in Africa and Latin America were indistinguish-able.[17] Waterlow was head of the MRC Nutrition Unit in Jamaica, while Scrimshaw was founding director of the Institute of Nutrition for Central America and Panama (INCAP), in Guatemala (established 1949). Their prominent participation in meetings influenced the focus of PAG.

Fuelled by data indicating that kwashiorkor was prevalent and preventable, WHO's commitment to protein began to shape something of a priesthood of nutritionists, exercising substantial influence over policy. In 1958 WHO stated: 'Kwashiorkor is now the main nutritional disease with which the Organisation is concerned',[18] and their enthusiasm for protein would soon be shared by other agencies. PAG did not have a research programme as such, but its members wrote working papers about pertinent issues and summarised the state of research, which guided the projects that the agencies funded. Spurred on by PAG, Unicef, for example, spent between $500,000 and $800,000 on protein food development annually between 1960 and 1967.[19]

## PAG and protein-rich foods

During its first years, PAG focused on issues arising from the use of high protein seeds in formulas for infants and young children. Scrimshaw was, perhaps, the most influential person involved, and dedicated much effort to this area. He had rallied support for PAG's creation while chief of the Nutrition Section of the Pan American Sanitary Bureau (run from the WHO Regional Office for the Americas). Scrimshaw served several terms as a PAG member and was chair 1970–73. When PAG was formed, only soya had been used as a protein supplement, and PAG sponsors were concerned to develop other sources. The endeavours of PAG came to focus on specific technical problems, such as the threat of aflatoxin poisoning in ground peanut protein.[20]

Few high protein foods entered production, but one project using cottonseed flour, carried out at INCAP under Scrimshaw, enjoyed some success. Scrimshaw remarked in 1995 that his interest in developing a weaning food predated PAG and was stimulated by Frank Clements, head of nutrition at WHO. When Scrimshaw was starting INCAP Clements apparently remarked that the 'greatest contribution' Scrimshaw could make would be 'to develop a practical, low-cost weaning food'. Soon Scrimshaw and his colleagues were faced with the problem of what advice to give mothers of children with kwashiorkor. He recounted that when mothers were told to give the child milk, they often:

> … couldn't afford the milk … but would try to comply and put a teaspoon full … in a glass full of water. Then the child would come back … and the mother would say 'I did give the child milk but he got worse' – or she simply wouldn't come back either because the child died …[21]

According to Scrimshaw, he remembered Clements' words and started looking for alternative protein sources. This led to the invention of a process for removing a toxin from cottonseed flour and the development of 'Incaparina'. INCAP demonstrated that Incaparina effectively nourished children, but inspiring mothers to purchase and use it was difficult. Nevertheless, for a time Incaparina became widely available in Central America during the 1960s.

Incaparina's current availability is limited. While still in use in Guatemala, it can only be regarded as successful in comparison with other novel weaning foods developed with UN support. These used fish protein concentrate, soya, peanut, sesame, sunflower and leaf meals, algal protein, and synthetic amino acids.[22] They all suffered serious problems of production, cost and acceptability. PAG's main contribution was the condensation of knowledge regarding these protein sources and the development of guidelines and quality standards for their preparation.

By the early 1970s the view of senior staff at FAO, WHO, and Unicef was that PAG had achieved little in terms of its original remit. Regarding the development of new weaning foods Aykroyd noted in 1970 that while PAG had 'laboured on this problem for 10 years or more', practical success had been minimal.[23]

## The impending protein crisis

While the development of novel weaning foods became problematic, PAG and its associates made remarkable progress in encouraging interest in protein among policy makers and politicians. In 1963, FAO concluded from its Third World Food Survey that since in developing countries 'the level of animal protein intake is only one fifth of that in the more developed areas' world food supplies would have to rise by 50 per cent by 1975.[24] In 1964, Maurice Pate, first executive director of Unicef, praised PAG for bringing major UN conferences and committees to acknowledge the supreme importance of protein malnutrition. Pate concluded that there was a 'climate of increasing approval and encouragement ... for international effort in assisting countries suffering from under-nourishment in pioneering projects to produce more proteins ...'.[25]

The tone surrounding world food and hunger grew increasingly ominous in America during President Johnson's second term. His 1967 State of the Union message called peace and the 'race between food supply and population increase' the great challenges of the day, a comment which inspired a voluminous White House Paper, *The World Food Problem*.[26] Of particular concern was the 'protein gap', the rift between world protein requirements and supply. Beginning in 1966, the UN Advisory Committee on Science and Technology to Development (ACST) began following up a UN resolution to determine which resources were being 'directed towards the implementation of proposals designed to close the protein gap'.[27] ACST enlisted Scrimshaw in preparing a report. He made it clear that there were 'no short-cuts' to solving protein problems which were growing worse in developing countries and were exacerbated by population growth.[28] The report was provocatively entitled 'Feeding the expanding world population: international action to avert the protein crises', and stressed that expanded food production, unless directed toward the needy, would do little to alleviate the problem.[29]

In May 1968 an administrative reorganisation made FAO the supervising agency of PAG, providing it with greater control over PAG activities.[30] The new FAO Director-General, A. H. Boerma, suggested in November that PAG 'should serve as a focal point for concerted action' and contended that 'a major financial effort on the part of the United Nations family, as well as by Governments, is necessary for any substantial progress'.[31] PAG was ecstatic to receive such support, as its relations with FAO had been stormy. It soon became clear, however, that FAO's support was to be less vigorous than appeared from Boerma's remarks. FAO officials continued to think that FAO had sufficient expertise among their own ranks.[32] In March 1969, less than a year after FAO took over, E. J. R. Heyward, Unicef Deputy Director, complained that FAO was failing to give PAG anything to do.[33]

Heyward's criticisms sharpened the cleavage between PAG and FAO officials as a week later, Marcel Autret, now director of FAO's nutrition division, wrote an essay in which he outlined PAG's responsibilities and FAO's relationship with PAG. He recalled that PAG had initially worked co-operatively with FAO's nutrition division to focus attention on 'the No. 1 nutrition problem of the 20th century'. Recently, however, PAG had begun to address issues outside of its scope – such as food waste and high yielding varieties of cereals. Autret asserted that 'PAG's scope should be limited to … high protein foods of animal and vegetable origin, both from conventional or unconventional sources'. Furthermore, he asserted, FAO and not PAG should 'take the leadership on behalf of the UN system' in protein issues.[34]

## Filling the protein gap

By the late 1960s the critical issue for ACST, PAG and the UN agencies, was how to fill the 'protein gap'. The need for scientific expertise was thought to be diminishing and the need for expertise in implementation increasing. ACST therefore recommended that PAG be expanded to include agronomists, economists, food technologists, sociologists, and marketing experts, and this took place in 1968.[35] Yet PAG continued to overlook the question of whether educational and agricultural programmes would (or had) improved the protein status of the vulnerable members of the population. When fish production figures showed an increase of roughly 50 per cent from 1966–7 along the Ivory Coast, PAG excitedly noted that this would enable annual fish consumption to rise from 17 kg per person in 1960 to 20 kg in 1970. PAG logic seemed grounded in the assumption that any increase in protein production would result in an increase in individual protein consumption.[36]

The last great push for protein came in May 1971 when the UN published *Strategy statement on action to avert the protein crisis in the developing countries,* a new version of the 1967 ACST report, written by PAG members under the chairship of Scrimshaw. According to U. Thant, the UN Secretary-General, the report included 'substantive, institutional and financial steps that must be undertaken if effective action on this critical problem is to materialize'.[37] The document asserted the crisis was not 'impending', but 'real'. The committee suggested that rising cereal production through Green Revolution techniques had been accompanied by a decline in legume production: protein sources in the diets of the poor were disappearing. It recommended that governments of developing countries plan to attack protein malnutrition and that the UN create a special 'fund for averting the protein crisis'. In connection with this programme, they also suggested that PAG should be expanded to include all relevant UN agencies. Practical recommendations included the collection of a 'protein development tax' levied on items such as soft drinks, beer and wine.[38]

## PAG problems

Despite the involvement of Scrimshaw and his colleagues in the preparation of high-level policy documents, the relationship between PAG and the UN agencies was becoming increasingly problematic. As hopes for producing technologically-designed high-protein foods were dashed, PAG's advice was less valued. In February 1971, Scrimshaw expressed concern that a rival advisory body might emerge. However, at around the same time, PAG's financial base expanded after Boerma sought support from the World Bank. Robert McNamara, head of the Bank, agreed to sponsor PAG with a first-year contribution of $25,000 and stated that his agency was 'interested in measures to close the protein gap in developing countries'. He hoped to further this goal through association with PAG. Unfortunately, this success was accompanied by renewed conflict between the sponsoring agencies, because Boerma had approached the Bank at his own initiative. The Bank's interactions with PAG proved as problematic as those between PAG and FAO. In one incident, the PAG secretary was castigated for overstepping his powers and giving 'orders' to the Bank. Concern was also expressed about PAG's ability to keep documents confidential, and as word of such conflicts spread, esteem for the group plummeted.[39]

In an attempt to regain leverage within the UN, PAG consistently attempted to expand its terms of reference along the lines of the 1971 *Strategy Statement*, but this brought it into further conflict with FAO. In October 1973, PAG circulated a document calling for it to be given a general advisory role in nutrition policy and planning. Indicative of shifting interest away from protein at this time, the document also recommended the name of PAG be changed to the 'Protein-Calorie Advisory Group of the United Nations System'.[40] In response, Boerma expressed concern that with an elevated position and wider remit PAG might publish advice that 'may diverge from the instructions and guidance which we receive from our governing bodies'.[41] He feared UN agencies might consult PAG on nutritional questions before consulting FAO, and that it would become necessary to 'explain to governments the existence of uncoordinated advice'. Finally, he noted that there was no historical precedent that could forecast success for PAG 'in a broader policy-related role'. At Unicef, Heyward's main concern was that PAG's technical *ad hoc* meetings produced reports that had no impact on policy or programmes. As a result of this impotence, PAG's supporting agencies sent more and more junior people to the annual PAG meetings.[42]

In 1972 and 1973, toward the end of Scrimshaw's term as chair, fundamental policy divisions began to break out. For Scrimshaw, these developments centred around the decreased attention protein was receiving from PAG-advised agencies and even PAG members. FAO in 1972 conveyed its wavering support for the term 'protein gap' because FAO surveys were showing that, per capita, there was 70 per cent more protein in the world than was required to meet basic human needs. FAO was beginning to see the problem as maldistribution of the protein available rather than an absolute shortage of protein.[43] In the midst of the debate Scrimshaw began to be seen by some colleagues as over-enthusiastic in his promotion of the magnitude of the protein gap and crisis. Moisés Béhar, a friend of Scrimshaw who had worked at INCAP in the 1950s, believed that Scrimshaw had become 'obsessed'. In journals and at conferences, he appeared as an orthodox nutritionist, clinging to a concept, the empirical underpinnings of which were beginning to be cast into doubt.[44]

While the validity of the 'protein gap' was under attack, perhaps the greatest force pushing administrators away from protein enthusiasm in the early 1970s, was the growing concern that a more general world food crisis was approaching. In 1972, severe droughts in the Soviet Union, India, South-East Asia, Australia, Central and South America, and the Sahel region of Africa combined with el Niño caused food production to dip for the first time since World War Two. The demand for imports was elevated and food stocks were depleted.[45] With disaster looming, the UN organised a World Food Conference. Protein and kwashiorkor were terms conspicuously neglected in the proceedings, and PAG members were astonished to learn they had not been consulted.[46]

## New directions for PAG?

Scrimshaw's departure from the chair of PAG held the faint promise of improved PAG status. However, from the beginning of his tenure as chair in 1974, Joaquín Cravioto, a nutritionist from the Mexican Institute for Child Welfare, found himself constantly defending the integrity and author-ity of the group. PAG's near exclusion from the World Food Conference served as Cravioto's welcome to the harsh realities facing the group. In a discussion of this issue with Boerma, Cravioto suggested that the role of PAG should be 'to assess the philosophy, policy, programmes and action in the field of nutrition carried out by the UN agencies'.[47] After some prodding from other agency heads, Boerma agreed to changes in PAG's remit and in the summer of 1974, PAG became the Protein-Calorie Advisory Group of the United Nations System. Its advisory role was expanded to include socio-economic issues, trends in global food supply and consumption, and policy formulation.[48]

At around this time Donald McLaren, a nutritionist well-known for his work on nutritional marasmus in infants and on keratomalcia, a debilitating eye condition caused by vitamin A deficiency, was conducting nutritional research at the American University in Beirut.[49] For years McLaren had argued that too much emphasis had been placed upon protein deficiency and kwashiokor, and that really there was a range of gross nutritional defi-ciencies in which lack of energy rather than protein was often most important. By 1970, this view was beginning to influence mainstream opinion. Aykroyd, for example, commented in that year:

> In any country where protein-calorie malnutrition exists, the whole spectrum will be found. Certain forms may, however, predominate. In tropical Africa, for example, kwashiorkor … is particularly common and has attracted the special attention of doctors in that region. In the developing countries generally, however, forms in which marasmus is the most prominent clinical feature occur more frequently than kwashiorkor.[50]

These remarks provide evidence that a shift in thinking about nutritional disease was beginning, precisely at the time when the clamour over protein was reaching its height.

McLaren published a stinging condemnation of protein policies in *The Lancet* entitled 'The Great Protein Fiasco' in 1974. He argued that there was no 'protein gap' and that PAG had been perpetuating a myth. As a result of decades of protein obsession, McLaren declared, 'The price that has had to be paid for these mistakes is only beginning to be realised'.[51] He made it clear that among those guilty of misleading the flock were Autret and Scrimshaw. McLaren's paper symbolised the turning of the tide against protein. He had published such criticisms before, but now they received widespread support. Cicely Williams, for example, regretted that scientists had made 'lamentable errors and wasted so much time, money, and personnel'.[52]

In 1974, the World Food Crisis eclipsed concerns over the protein gap, and propelled food production and hunger rather than specific nutritional deficiencies to the forefront of discussions. As in the immediate aftermath of World War Two, when John Boyd Orr, as first Director-General of FAO produced a 'World Food Plan', food, not nutrition, was on the agenda. The effects would reshape the course of nutrition policy.

## PAG: modified or dissolved?

Concerns about global food supplies induced a critical evaluation of the cornerstones of nutrition policy. The murky results highlighted a troubling paradox: on the one hand, it was agreed that nutrition was of great importance in economic development; on the other hand, there were few widely accepted ideas regarding what to do about it. In the minds of many policy makers, the nutritionists had been unable to guide or create successful projects. Knowledge of the complexities of good nutritional status was increasing, but there was a feeling that past results of nutrition programmes had not fulfilled expectations. On protein, policy makers felt misled. After decades of hearing that protein malnutrition was the most important problem, the true problem now appeared to be more related to food quantity than quality.

Even Waterlow, a former proponent of the protein gap, announced in 1975 that the nutrition problem was really a food or energy gap.[53] The background to this shift in views included reconsideration of estimates of protein requirements, which were being revised downwards at this time.[54] Word about the exacerbation of nutrition problems due to commercialisation, urbanisation and the population explosion further obfuscated possible actions. Furthermore, in the wake of the 1974 World Food Conference, which resulted in the creation of the World Food Council, it was difficult to determine what should be done about nutrition. The Conference requested that FAO, WHO, and Unicef unite to produce an 'internationally co-ordinated programme in applied nutritional research' and to expand and rectify nutrition intervention programmes.[55] In response, between 1975 and 1978 the agencies explored and implemented structural changes in the hope of ensuring effective nutrition policies in the future.

In 1975, during the twenty-third annual session of PAG (now the Protein-Calorie Advisory Group), the sponsoring agencies intimated that the performance of the group, especially since its terms of reference had been altered, had been unsatisfactory.[56] However, PAG decided to immediately present itself to the World Food Council (WFC) as the advisory group to UN agencies on nutrition. Cravioto wrote to the heads of the agencies requesting that they recommend to the WFC that PAG should be 'the Nutrition Committee' to the Council, or should serve as the advisory body to such a committee. The accompanying rhetoric implied that PAG would be a key player in WFC's recently announced scheme for the eradication of hunger and malnutrition within a decade.[57]

In previous years, PAG had managed to extract reluctant promises of support for its expansion from the UN and sponsors, but now PAG's heady attitudes and calls for a expanded scope disturbed the agency heads. The intra-agency correspondence illuminates the depth of concern about the future course of nutrition. Halfdan Mahler, WHO's director-general, told Béhar, head of WHO's nutrition section, that while many agencies within and outside the UN were interested in developing programmes in nutrition, there was no 'mutual agreement on the basic principles'. In these circumstances there was a danger that:

> ... the present efforts may once more discredit international work in this field instead of taking advantage of the present concern and interest in the field of nutrition problems in order to institute more rational action.[58]

Mahler further noted that the increase in the World Bank's interest generated by the World Food Conference presented new opportunities for nutritional progress, but given past shortcomings, it might be most appropriate to decommission PAG. WHO, it seems, was preparing itself to pull out of PAG sponsorship.

The agencies were alarmed that PAG was trying to become an independent agency rather then an advisory group. At a meeting of agency representatives in July 1975, when Mahler expressed the view that the group had become useless and suggested that it be disbanded, the other representatives agreed.[59] Discussion began about a possible successor to PAG, which could be a functional committee of the Advisory Committee on Co-ordination (ACC), which was responsible for co-ordinating UN work and eliminating duplication. The administrators looked forward to a group consisting of 'senior officers' who would develop common nutritional approaches for the agencies. Most importantly, outside experts would only be involved on an *ad hoc* basis to solve particular problems.

In October 1975 an ACC preparatory committee met to consider nutrition. The first item was to determine why, 'despite overwhelming moral imperatives', governments and the UN had not produced a reasonable strategy for the elimination of hunger and malnutrition.[60] Three reasons were provided. Firstly, only recently had it been acknowledged that protein had been over-emphasised to the detriment of the 'real' problem, food supply. Secondly, efforts had been stymied by the complexity of the solutions required. Since the primary cause of malnutrition was poverty, only raising income could provide a permanent solution. Thirdly, governments had failed to set national nutrition targets. The elusive solution could only be found, according to the committee, 'through an integrated, interdisciplinary inter-agency approach'. The role of PAG in such efforts was highly questionable. The committee agreed that PAG might continue with limited terms of reference or could be expanded to include all branches of nutritional expertise. The lack of interest in either of these avenues suggested the elimination of PAG would be the favoured option.

Throughout 1976, it became clear to PAG that the perpetuation of the group would not be supported. In the spring, ACC presented a report to the UN Economic and Social Council regarding future arrangements for nutrition. This was tacitly recognised as the final word on PAG. The recommendations reflected an optimistic tone regarding future projects, and the knowledge in hand. According to ACC, the World Food Conference had 'crystallized the thinking about nutrition specialists and administrators, and provided an over-all framework for action in priority areas ... to promote a durable solution'.[61] The key was government nutrition and food policies designed in partnership with UN agencies. The report recommended the formation of a sub-committee on nutrition (SCN) of the ACC which would 'harmonize assistance' through strong agency representation and consultations with member governments. The SCN was envisaged as the place where agencies would present their tactics on nutrition in order to foster 'compatible decisions'. The ACC suggested that a 'nutrition advisory panel' would succeed PAG and provide advice, when requested, to the SCN.

Cravioto and others at PAG were furious. Cravioto wrote to the heads of the sponsoring agencies asserting the recommendations were 'ill-considered and potentially harmful to the cause of eradicating hunger and malnutrition in the world'.[62] They provided the illusion that great progress could rapidly be made to banish malnutrition and was in fact being made. He was livid that PAG had not been consulted and claimed the new arrangements represented a 'backward step'. The development that most angered Cravioto was the new manner in which nutrition experts would interact with the UN agencies. Whereas PAG could communicate directly with agency heads, under the new arrangements, nutritionists would be several steps removed from the programmes and policies they wished to sway.

In September 1976 at the annual PAG meeting, Cravioto announced his resignation. According to the restrained minutes he expressed 'dissatisfaction' with the turn of events during the previous year and blamed the sponsoring agencies for not requesting advice from the group.[63] FAO and WHO representatives mentioned they had been dissatisfied with PAG for several years but were willing to fund it through 1977 in an attempt to resolve their problems.

## Emergence of the SCN

In April 1977, the ACC provided the UN Economic and Social Council with a supplement to its early recommendations. This stated unequivocally that PAG would cease at the end of 1977 and that an Advisory Group on Nutrition (AGN), of five or six members, would replace it.[64] AGN was expected to respond to requests for advice from the ACC's SCN, bring issues to SCN's attention, help carry out SCN's programme, and maintain contacts with scientists outside the UN agencies.[65] SCN would direct requests at individuals or groups within AGN as required; the whole AGN was not expected to consider every request. If needed, outside consultants would be enlisted to respond to specific problems outside the scope of AGN's competence. Many scientists, among them Waterlow, contended that AGN experts should be full members of SCN in order to maintain their influence.[66]

There would, in the future, be no question about who was holding the reins: SCN would set up AGN meetings, appoint members, and service the meetings. AGN would, in essence, be a 'problem-solving group', with the capability of independently bringing certain matters to the attention of SCN.[67] SCN would be accountable to ACC and expected to gather twice per year and 'to keep under review the over-all direction, scale, coherence and impact' of the UN system's response to nutritional problems.[68] The creators of SCN intended that it should be the 'point of convergence' for attempts to co-ordinate nutrition initiatives. The UN Economic and Social Council approved these proposals in August 1977 and SCN had its first meeting in September. A dozen UN agencies attended the early meetings late in 1977.[69] As was the case with PAG, sponsoring agencies with serious interests in nutrition funded SCN and AGN at the level of the last PAG budget: $300,000.[70] FAO in Rome was appointed the seat of SCN and mid-way through 1978, SCN secretariat began its functions.

Heyward, the first chairman of SCN, commented in retrospect on the motives for replacing PAG:

… the fundamental thing was to reverse this relationship [between experts and policy makers] ... instead of the agencies sitting around listening to these scientists it was the agency people responsible for nutrition in their various agencies who were the main committee, the SCN ... was the agency people in the top position rather than in a listening position.[71]

At least initially, SCN breathed new life into inter-agency nutrition discourse as personnel had the opportunity to speak about nutrition rather than the usual 'turf and procedures'. Whereas Heyward had felt that most agencies had ignored the analyses and recommendations of PAG, he found that SCN was regarded much more highly from the start, no doubt due in part to the position of senior policy makers like himself.[72]

Within a year of its establishment, SCN assumed a practical outlook on nutrition problems. In 1978 they noted that in nutrition the role of the UN system role had 'largely been one of exhortation' of member countries. Governments had been urged to adopt food and nutrition priorities in their national development plans, commit themselves to major improvements, and display political resolve in taking action. At the same time, in the view of SCN members, the UN itself had failed to prioritise nutrition in a like manner.[73] Thus, SCN saw its primary role not as a technical agency, but in boosting the position of nutrition across the agencies, while remaining, itself, practically invisible.[74] Since Heyward was closely tied to all the major UN agencies, his leadership of SCN at least temporarily enhanced the importance of nutritional action. This may in part account for the low level of protest heard during SCN's formation; nutrition was not over, and there was an opportunity for at least some of the nutritionists to switch teams.[75]

## On experts and policy makers

Through a study of the rise and fall of PAG, this chapter has chronicled at a broad level the evolving position of nutrition experts in international policy making. Through the 1950s and early 1960s, PAG consisted mainly of experts with extensive knowledge of protein. In the early years, before the expansion of the UN agencies' bureaucracies, the outside experts were closely aligned with nutrition policy at FAO, WHO, and Unicef. In spite of some tensions, experts like Scrimshaw had tight and often informal relationships with officials that enabled them to guide the course of policy and research more than documentation can possibly reflect. The interplay between the nutrition experts, the division heads and directors-general had a pronounced impact on the trajectory of nutrition at the agencies. From the late 1950s to the early 1970s the UN system's attention was focussed principally on protein deficits as the major world-wide nutritional problem.

By the 1970s, PAG had grown from a group whose role was essentially technical to one that was more programme- and policy-oriented. Economists, agriculturists, and planners were increasingly involved in PAG. However, taking on this broader role strained the relationships between the agencies

53  J. C. Waterlow and P. R. Payne, 'The protein gap', *Nature*, 1975, vol. 258, pp. 113–17, at p. 117.

54  For a discussion of this dimension of the debate see Carpenter, op. cit., pp. 189–98.

55  'Interagency meeting on applied nutrition research', Rome, 16–17 October 1975, WHO Archives (hereafter WHO) box A.1162, folder 2, pp. 1–2.

56  M. Béhar to Mahler, 17 June 1975, WHO box A.1162, folder 1.

57  J. Cravioto, letter to Mahler and others, 11 June 1975, FAOA, box 1, Organisational PAG membership, 1/4.

58  M. Béhar to Mahler, 17 June 1975, WHO, box A.1162, folder 1.

59  M. R. Sacks, 'Note for the record', summary of meeting on 3 July 1975, WHO, box A.1162, folder 1.

60  'Institutional arrangements relating to nutrition', 13 October 1975, Unicef, CF-NYHQ-05ANS-002, p. 1.

61  'Food problems, institutional arrangements relating to nutrition: statement of the Administrative Committee on Co-ordination', 28 April 1976, UN Economic and Social Council Publications, UNL, E/5805, paragraph 11.

62  J. Cravioto, to Sponsoring agency, 7 June 1976, FAOA, box 1, Organisational PAG membership 1/4.

63  'PAG intersecretariat meeting, New York, 28 and 30 September 1976, confidential draft minutes', 18 October 1976, FAOA, NU 13/3–13/4.

64  'Institutional arrangements relating to nutrition, supplementary statement by the Administrative Committee on Co-ordination', 26 April 1977, E/5968, in *PAG Bulletin*, September–December 1977, VIII(3–4), pp. 17–20, on p. 17.

65  'Report on the new institutional arrangements in the UN system for nutrition, Second Session of the Ad hoc Committee on Food and Nutrition Policies, Rome, 6–10 March 1978', January 1978, Scrimshaw personal collection, Document ESN: FNP/78/7, p. 3.

66  J. C. Waterlow, interview, London, 22 June 1995.

67  'Unicef Information Bulletin', July 1978, Unicef, CF-NYHQ-05ANS-002, p. 3.

68  'Report on the new institutional arrangements in the UN system for nutrition, Second Session of the Ad hoc Committee on Food and Nutrition Policies, Rome, 6–10 March 1978', January 1978, Scrimshaw personal collection, Document ESN: FNP/78/7, p. 1.

69  'Report on the new institutional arrangements in the UN system for nutrition, Second Session of the Ad hoc Committee on Food and Nutrition Policies, Rome, 6–10 March 1978', January 1978, Scrimshaw personal collection, Document ESN: FNP/78/7, pp. 1–2.

70  'Institutional arrangements relating to nutrition, supplementary statement by the Administrative Committee on Co-ordination', 26 April 1977, E/5968, in *PAG Bulletin*, September–December 1977, VIII(3–4), pp. 17–20, p. 19.

71  E. J. R. Heyward, interview, 14 September 1995.

72  A. Berg, telephone interview, 12 June 1996.

73  'Harmonized policies of United Nations agencies for collaborating with developing countries in improving the state of nutrition', proposed draft report from ACC to ECOSOC (ECOSOC Res 2107(LX111)), 12 October 1978, FAOA, LL-011, p. 2.

74  L. Burgess, telephone interview, 29 May 1996.

75  Some continuity between PAG and AGN was maintained. Sol Chafkin, the last chairman of PAG served as the first chairman of AGN. A. Berg, telephone interview, 12 June 1996.

# 11 Food standards in the United States: the case of the peanut butter and jelly sandwich

*Suzanne White Junod*

Britain's 1875 and 1899 Sale of Food and Drugs Acts were similar in intent to the 1906 US Pure Food and Drugs Act, as Mike French and Jim Phillips have shown. Both statutes defined food adulterations as a danger to health and as consumer fraud. In Britain, the laws were interpreted and enforced by the Local Government Board and then, from its establishment in 1919, by the Ministry of Health. Issues of health rather than economics, therefore, dominated Britain's regulatory focus. The US Congress, in contrast, rather than assigning enforcement of the 1906 Act to the Public Health Service, or to the Department of Commerce, as some had advocated, charged an originally obscure scientific bureau in the Department of Agriculture with enforcement of its 1906 statute. In the heyday of analytical chemistry, and in the midst of the bacteriological revolution, Congress transformed the Bureau of Chemistry into a regulatory agency, fully expecting that science would be the arbiter of both health and commercial issues. Led by 'crusading chemist' Harvey Washington Wiley, the predecessor of the modern Food and Drug Administration (FDA) initiated food regulatory policies that were more interventionist than in Britain from their inception. In 1927, the regulatory part of the Bureau of Chemistry became the Food, Drug, Insecticide Administration, renamed the Food and Drug Administration in 1930.[1]

Debates about the effects of federal regulation on the US economy have been fierce, with economists and historians on both sides of the issue generating a rich literature. In general, however, the weight of evidence supports the conclusion that business itself benefited from the trials and tribulations of early federal regulation.[2] Eliminating spoilage and waste, while gaining the confidence and good will of consumers, also proved good for business.[3] During World War One, and then amidst the Great Depression, however, this early lesson was revisited. In this setting, it is a uniquely American creation, the peanut butter and jelly sandwich (white bread, jelly and peanut butter) that both illustrates and contains the basic ingredients of the United States' subsequent food standards programme.

Not a Preserve'.[20] Wiley's successor, Carl Alsberg, reconstituted a Joint Committee on Definitions and Standards in 1914.[21] The Committee's new standards were published between 1913 and 1938 in *Service and Regulatory Announcements (SRA)* as a guide to enforcement actions.[22] For jams and preserves, the Joint Committee adopted a standard specifying not less than 45 lb. of fruit to each 55 lb. of sugar. In 1917, in anticipation of World War One, *SRA 20* allowed for the addition of pectin to fruits with too little pectin 'as long as it did not disguise damage or inferiority and the presence of the added pectin was noted on the label'.[23] The war created a marked expansion in the jam, jelly, and preserve industry to supply US and allied troops. Afterwards, the industry was overbuilt and sought volume sales with low prices. By 1919, Robert Douglas had patented a process for producing refined pectin, making it possible to make better preserves without using green fruit, but also making it possible to make a jelly without using fruit at all. Regulators, concerned that pectin was being used to cheapen jams, convened a trade hearing on 16 April 1924.

In June 1924 the Supreme Court issued a landmark ruling against deceptive apple cider vinegar. Regulators were optimistic when the judges stated unequivocally that 'the statute is plain and direct. Its comprehensive terms condemn every statement, design, and device which may mislead or deceive', and admonished that 'it is not difficult to choose statements, designs, and devices which will not deceive'.[24] Commissioner Charles A. Browne, taking the justices at their word, promptly notified preservers that no action would be taken against products with 25–45 lb. of fruit for every 55 lb. of sugar, and containing pectin, if they bore a compound label. Officials illustrated just

*Figure 11.1*   Proposed label for 'compound product'. © US Food and Drug Administration.

how such a compound product should appear in comparison with a jar of pure strawberry jam. With such an austere label, they felt consumers would not be likely to confuse the two products (Figure 11.1).

Not surprisingly, manufacturers of the compound jams were less enthusiastic. Meanwhile, the Food and Drugs Administration (FDA) continued to fight off amendments by proponents of corn syrup which would have allowed the use of cheaper corn sugar in place of expensive cane sugar without declaring it on the label.[25] Rejecting the government's compound label, many companies became even more bold and inventive in creating 'distinctive names' for their products, including one company that created an entire line of low fruit products coloured and flavoured to resemble preserves. Packaged in expensive glass jars and given the fanciful and 'distinctive' yet meaningless name, BRED-SPRED [sic], it quickly became a regulatory target for both state and federal officials. Bred-Spred typified the kind of inferior product that had begun to compete with the products of traditional jam and jelly manufacturers after the war, but its attractive packaging and aggressive advertising lent an appeal that previous compound products had lacked. Both in 1927 and again in 1931, the government lost in court. The courts were not persuaded by the government's argument that the product was adulterated because pectin had lowered its quality and concealed inferiority, or that it was misbranded because it was an imitation of jam with deceptive 'pictorial designs' of fruit on the label. The Department of Justice refused to refer the case to the Supreme Court, leaving the Bureau of Chemistry to lament the 'untold difficulty' caused by the distinctive name proviso and taking the

*Figure 11.2* Inferior products marketed under 'distinctive names'. © US Food and Drug Administration.

unusual step of recommending its repeal.[26] Similarly, 'Salad Bouquet', weak vinegar promoted for use 'like vinegar', and 'Peanut Spred', with a low proportion of peanuts, were also marketed under 'distinctive' names (Figure 11.2).

Meanwhile, pressure was mounting on the Department of Agriculture to adopt quality grade labelling for canned foods. Women's groups and home economists were strong advocates for such standards.[27] The majority of the canning industry and the National Canners' Association, however, opposed quality grade labelling, believing that housewives would buy only high quality products. Nonetheless, concerned about competition with truly low-grade, branded products, they persuaded Congress to pass the McNary-Mapes amendment to the 1906 Act in 1930.[28]

The amendment authorised standards of quality, condition, and/or fill-of-container for most heat-sterilised, hermetically sealed canned foods. It did not authorise definitions and standards of identity, and without funding, the initial work was done only on peaches, apricots, cherries, pears, tomatoes and peas (Figure 11.3). Substandard products had to display a so-called 'crepe label': 'below US standard, low quality but not illegal'.[29]

Preservers tried to get their standards included under this law, but the Secretary of Agriculture refused to extend the statute to jarred products.[30] FDA also supported the industry's unsuccessful efforts to get Congress to enact legal standards for jams and jellies.[31] In 1933, however, as part of President Franklin Roosevelt's 'New Deal', the National Industrial Recovery

*Figure 11.3*  Consumers judging peas following the McNary-Mapes amendment. © US Food and Drug Administration.

Act was passed, which included provision for the establishment of Codes of Fair Practice to be enforced by a new agency, the National Recovery Administration (NRA). Preservers adopted one of the earliest codes containing quality standards. In contrast, the canned food industry, with support from grocery manufacturers, adamantly opposed the inclusion of any quality food provision in the Canners' Code. Still convinced that consumers preferred brands to any system of quality designations, the industry prevailed. Nevertheless, they were surprised when, contrary to their wishes, an Executive Order was issued requiring the industry to formulate quality standards for eventual incorporation into the canned food code.[32]

The NRA scheme was short lived, its Blue Eagle symbol of compliance brought down by the US Supreme Court in the infamous 'sick chicken' case. In 1935, a poultry producer challenged the authority of the NRA to enforce the industry code forbidding transport of allegedly ill or unfit chickens. The Court unanimously ruled that a federal agency such as NRA had no jurisdiction over interstate commerce.[33] Although historians generally consider the NRA a failure, some enduring successes, such as eliminating child labour in textile factories, did demonstrate the merits of many policies promoted by trade associations.[34] The National Preservers' Association enlisted the aid of the Federal Trade Commission (FTC) in 1936, which did issue 'cease and desist' orders against violators, but on a case by case basis.[35]

FDA experts testified at the FTC preserve hearings, but the agency's attention was focused, beginning in 1933, on drafting and passing a new federal food and drug act to replace the 1906 'Wiley' Act. The economic depression had left the food field in a 'jam'; pesticides were increasingly problematic; misleading drug advertisements and drug prosecutions were on the upswing; and cosmetics with dangerous ingredients remained unregulated. New Deal Secretary of Agriculture, Rexford Tugwell, secured permission from President Roosevelt to begin drafting a new food and drug bill.[36] The initial 'Tugwell' bill drew such a hostile response from industry that Senator Royal Copeland took up the cause for a new act.[37] Weak standards modelled on McNary-Mapes were expanded to all foods in his initial revision of the food and drug bill, but Copeland was soon persuaded by women's organisations at the first hearings on the bill in 1934, that the standards provisions should be strengthened. Alice Edwards conveyed the personal support of the President's wife, Eleanor Roosevelt, for quality grade labelling at the hearings. Representing the American Home Economics Association, Edwards testified that such standards were 'highly desirable from the point of view of the consumer, for the good of the industry itself, and for the building of consumer confidence in the advertising of these products'.[38] Women's groups also championed value for the consumer. Citing current economic hardships, Edwards advocated standards to fight against 'economic injustices', noting that 'if the commodity is one that does not give the consumer value for his money he should have an opportunity to know this even if the commodity is not so inferior as to injure health'.[39]

Harvey Wiley's widow also appeared in support of a revised bill, even though it would replace her husband's chief legacy. She complained that of nearly nine hours of hearings, only twenty-five minutes had been devoted to views of consumers, and made it clear that, in her view, food standards had the firm support of consumers.[40] Apart from the jam industry, women remained almost exclusively the ones championing food standards for the new law. Historian Charles Jackson notes that 'what distinguished them [women's groups] from militant bodies such as Consumers' Research was that failure to get all they wanted had little effect on their zeal'.[41]

## The American Chamber of Horrors

Consumers' Research, a pioneer in US consumer advocacy, launched the opening volley in the consumer war with publication in 1933 of

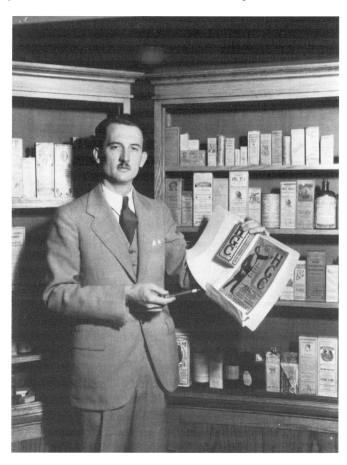

*Figure 11.4*   Commissioner Larrick explaining the 'Chamber of Horrors' exhibit. © US Food and Drug Administration.

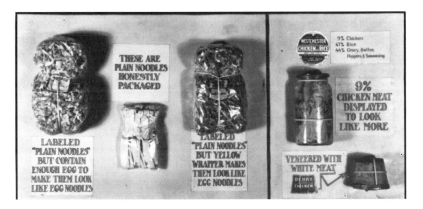

*Figure 11.5* Deceptive packaging: egg noodles. © US Food and Drug Administration.

*100,000,000 Guinea Pigs* by Arthur Kallet and Frederick Schlink.[42] To illustrate the need for a new law, FDA officials had assembled a collection of problem products. Initially merely an exhibit for Congress, publication of Kallet and Schlink's book elevated the collection into a public relations tool, particularly when Eleanor Roosevelt, a tireless advocate of causes, toured the exhibit.[43] A reporter accompanying her in 1933 dubbed it 'The American Chamber of Horrors' (Figure 11.4).

Even by the standards of the day, the 'Chamber of Horrors' was not an exciting exhibit. It was, however, both truthful and provocative, persuading

*Figure 11.6* Deceptive packaging: jarred chicken, dark meat hidden under the label. © US Food and Drug Administration.

*Figure 11.7*   Exhibit illustrating the need for compositional standards. © US Food and Drug Administration.

many companies to change their ways just to secure removal from the exhibit. A major part of the food portion of the exhibit was devoted to explaining the need for various kinds of food standards. Products such as malted milk, egg noodles (Figure 11.5), and jarred chicken products (Figures 11.6 and 11.7) all required standards of identity in order for consumers to know what they were buying, since neither price nor packaging were reliable guides.

One of the most problematic products for advocates of food standards was ice cream. Fat was considered the most valuable ingredient, and this ingredient was widely variable. Before home freezers were available, most ice cream was locally produced and consumers were often loyal to the ice cream to which they were accustomed, regardless of its fat content. Regulators believed labelling the cream content was the best way to insure that the consumer got what was expected.

Several panels of the exhibit explained both the McNary-Mapes amendment and the need to expand its provisions to other foods such as tomato paste (Figure 11.8). The 'distinctive name proviso' had created immense confusion over the labelling and adulteration of maple syrup under the 1906 Act. In one panel, regulators tried to show that the 'descriptive labelling' advocated by some manufacturers as a model for the new statute, would still not correct basic deception in the marketing of maple flavoured syrups (Figure 11.8).

Finally, the Chamber of Horrors dramatically illustrated the use of deceptive containers. McNary-Mapes had eliminated some deceptive packaging in the canned foods industry (Figures 11.9 and 11.10), but deceptively large boxes, some with false bottoms (Figure 11.11), and bottles clearly designed to deceive (Figure 11.12), remained an important problem. Fill of container was an important economic issue. Expensive flavouring extracts and teas were easy targets.

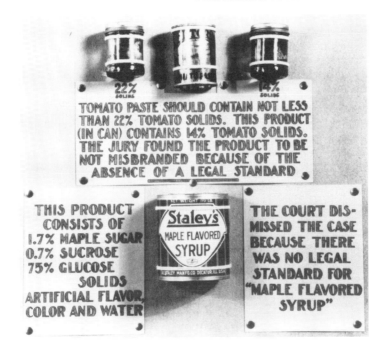

*Figure 11.8* No legal standard for tomato paste or for maple flavoured syrup. © US Food and Drug Administration.

*Figure 11.9* Grated cheese packaging before and after the McNary-Mapes amendment. © US Food and Drug Administration.

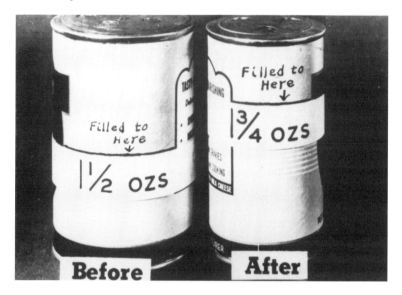

*Figure 11.10* Grated cheese packaging before and after the McNary-Mapes amendment. © US Food and Drug Administration.

The Chamber of Horrors was visually persuasive, illustrating vividly the old clichés about the worth of a picture and the one bad apple that spoils the barrel. The food industry, its trade associations and its lawyers, could and did argue that these examples were unusual, even rare, but the fact that such products existed and were easily recognised by consumers accustomed to trusting brand names made the case for regulation all the more compelling. Consumers, moreover, were more likely to accept the need for all standards proposed in the exhibit than to quibble over the merits of quality standards as opposed to standards of identity and fill of container.

The popular exhibit was displayed at the White House and the Chicago World's Fair, inspiring FDA's Chief Educational Officer, Ruth deForest Lamb, to employ a leave of absence to write a book by the same title. Where Kallet and Schlink simply condemned governmental inaction, Lamb exposed the legal weaknesses in the 1906 Act that frustrated government efforts. She also documented the less than forthright tactics employed by many industries, advertisers, trade associations, and lawyers to thwart enactment of effective regulation. Lamb was hardly a disinterested observer, but she also advocated a different kind of consumerism. Kallet and Schlink portrayed consumers as rather hapless victims, but she cleverly dedicated her book to the host of women's organisations that were actively and effectively sponsoring the new law being debated in Congress. In the *American Chamber of Horrors,* her chapter on food standards was apparently persuasive. Lamb herself was pleased at the book's reception remarking that:

*Figure 11.11*   Vanilla extract packaging before and after the McNary-Mapes amendment.
© US Food and Drug Administration.

… the only thing that makes me apprehensive is the number of endorsements from the trade press … When the 'American Grocer' appears to endorse my chapter on standards I am inclined to think there is something wrong with the chapter.[44]

Late nineteenth century reform journalists known as muckrakers had been influential in persuading the public to support the 1906 Act. Likewise, consumer advocates such as Lamb, Kallet and Schlink proved equally influential in the legislative battle to enact a new food and drug law and were soon nicknamed 'guinea pig muckrakers'.

## The 1938 Food, Drug, and Cosmetic Act

More consumer-oriented than its predecessor, the 1938 Food, Drug, and

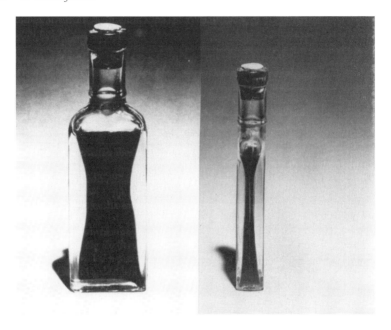

*Figure 11.12* Deceptive bottles used for marketing flavourings. © US Food and Drug Administration.

Cosmetic Act was a watershed in US food policy. In contrast to the limited health-based standards that the Ministry of Health proposed in Britain during the Depression, the US, largely through the efforts of women's groups, pioneered policies designed to protect the pocketbooks of consumers, and food standards were enacted to ensure the 'value expected' by consumers.[45] The 1938 Act eliminated the 'distinctive name proviso' and required instead that the label of a food 'bear its common or usual name'. The food would be misbranded if it represented itself as a standardised food unless it conformed to that standard. The law provided for three kinds of food standards: (1) standards (definitions) of identity, (2) standards of quality, and (3) standards regulating the fill of container. Regulators had the discretionary authority to set standards 'whenever in the judgement of the Secretary such action will promote honesty and fair dealing in the interests of consumers'.[46]

## Food standards under the 1938 Food, Drug, and Cosmetic Act: bread and jam

But what was a food standard to look like? Congress thought that standards of identity would resemble a 'recipe'.[47] Foods would be defined in terms of home recipes for goods consumers could readily identify and one would find in any well-stocked pantry. FDA supported the 'recipe' concept because it was considered a legally sound interpretation of the law's food standard provisions that also simplified enforcement. Lawyers, major food companies, and ingredient manufacturers had few objections because in many cases the standards recognised and even promoted the use of certain products and ingredients. Competitors met on a level playing field encompassing both foreign and domestic food manufacturers.[48]

The first standards issued were for tomato products, settling a long-standing dispute over the use of benzoate of soda as a preservative.[49] The standard did not recognise benzoate of soda as an ingredient, either mandatory or optional, in ketchup.[50] The second set of standards was for jams and jellies. It was a relatively easy standard to establish, since cookbooks over two hundred years old all agreed that jellies should be about half fruit or juice and half sugar, but its symbolic value was high. In a crushing blow, however, the Supreme Court ruled that a product labelled 'Delicious Brand Imitation Jam' with only 25 per cent fruit, instead of the 45 per cent required under the standard, could be marketed conspicuously labelled as an 'imitation'.[51] FDA had argued that Congress had not intended that such a product be marketed at all, since it did not meet the standard, and was marketed in competition with standardised products. In practice, the word 'imitation' did not prove commercially popular and was rarely used.

The recipe approach worked well with simple recipes during the 1940s and early 1950s and was upheld by the courts.[52] Recipe standards for enriched foods helped eliminate a number of nutritional deficiency diseases in the post-war era, particularly in southern states.[53] When challenged, the Supreme Court upheld the government's approach, ruling that manufacturers had to adhere to the mandated formula in the standards or cease to enrich their foods altogether.[54] By 1957, standards had been set for many varieties of chocolate, flour, cereals and cereal grains, macaroni products, bakery products, milk and cream, cheese, butter, non-fat milk solids, dressings (mayonnaise), canned fruits, juices, preserves and jellies, shellfish, canned tuna, eggs, margarine, and canned vegetables.

In 1954, hearing procedures were modified to waive hearings in undisputed cases. The amendment, however, also allowed 'any interested person' to initiate the standard-setting process. These procedural changes made the hearing process unwieldy, undermining FDA's own food agenda, and creating an open forum for trade wars.[55] What Congress had intended to be a fact-finding process began to resemble a trial between adversaries. The hearings to set standards for enriched white bread best illustrates the new complexities in the food standards process by the mid-twentieth century.[56]

FDA officials had a saying based on years of regulatory work that anyone with a new food additive or ingredient tried it first in bread.[57] With little information about the safety of some of these proposed new ingredients, FDA turned to the standards hearings as one way to limit the introduction of new chemicals into the food supply. In the earliest bread hearings, begun in 1941, there had been minor disputes over the suitability of several new ingredients including mono and di-glycerides, hydrogenated shortening, soy lecithin, and some so-called dough 'conditioners'. The final standards allowed most of the former ingredients, but disallowed some of the dough conditioners. World War Two then intervened and these standards were put on hold. During the war, bread was subject to a war food order mandating enrichment. After the war, when the bread hearings were re-opened, FDA elected not to mandate enrichment, but rather to write separate standards for enriched and for non-enriched products. The hearings, however, quickly began to revolve around the admission as optional ingredients in standardised bread of a new class of additives, known as polyoxyethylene monostearates (POEMS). These substances were variously described as emulsifiers, 'crumb softeners', 'staling retardants', and additives 'to prolong palatability and softness'. Had the manufacturer limited its petition to a few products from this new line of chemical additives, observers felt that they might have been successful. It was painfully clear to everyone at the hearings, however, that all twenty-seven emulsifiers had not been subjected to the same level of scientific scrutiny for either safety or suitability for use in bread. Of course, the Institute of Shortening Manufacturers and Edible Oils opposed the inclusion of this new class of competitive ingredients in the standards for white bread, and ably represented by a future Supreme Court Justice, Potter Stewart, they successfully converted the hearings into a full-fledged trade war.

The government, in a thankless attempt to locate more neutral grounds for debate, could not simply express its concerns about the safety of the new emulsifiers and the adequacy of their testing. Instead, under the law, the government had to show that the new ingredients would not promote 'honesty and fair dealing in the interests of consumers'. FDA, therefore, began to build its case trying to show that the softeners deceived customers as to the freshness of a loaf of bread. It was this issue, more than any other, that led the hearings into absurdity. Consumers, it was universally acknowledged, tested bread by squeezing the loaf. The question in dispute, therefore, became 'Did consumers conclude from squeezing, that a softer loaf was a fresher loaf?' All the tools of modern psychology and social science were brought to bear on the task of dissociating softness and freshness. In a supervised taste test, women were simply asked to indicate a preference for one of two slices of bread, and to choose which one seemed fresher. Straightforwardly, it was reported that four of five women chose the bread with the softener as the fresher loaf. A statistician giving evidence for the defence, however, insisted that the more accurate conclusion was that '1,100 consumers preferred soft bread and those who preferred soft bread preferred the bread made with the softener. Those who preferred firm bread, however, had noticed no differences between the control bread and the test bread'. Finally, the statistician testified that 'for those who prefer the soft bread, the test bread is preferred both for its softness and for the factors other than softness (presumably taste, texture, grain, etc.) while the control bread is preferred for its firmness'. This profound conclusion so confounded lawyers and listeners alike that the statistician was held over for cross-examination the next day. And so it went for day after day of the bread hearings. It was not until 1950 that a *Federal Register* notice formally announced the exclusion of POEMS from the standards of identity for white bread.[58]

Meanwhile, Congress appointed a Select Committee to Investigate the Use of Chemicals in Food Products.[59] This Committee's work led to the passage of the 1958 Food Additives Amendment which established a pre-market approval process for new food additives similar to that applied to new drugs, requiring new food additives to be shown safe and suitable before they were allowed in food products.[60] A similar Color Additives Amendment was enacted in 1960.[61] Scientific petitions on food safety replaced pitched battles over food standards. Although the new amendments removed additive safety debates from the standards process, they did not noticeably speed up the process, and it still took over a decade to issue standards for peanut butter.

## Food standard innovations: peanut butter's sticky standard

By 1958, new food products, and a newly competitive refrigerated and frozen goods industry that developed after the Second World War, had redefined the household pantry fundamentally. With more new processed and fabricated foods, less time could be devoted to issuing refined standards for variations on traditional foods such as raisin bread and egg bread. More time had to be spent establishing new standards for products such as frozen orange juice, frozen 'TV' dinners, frozen breaded shrimp, freeze dried coffee, and 'instant chocolate drinks'. The recipe concept proved ill suited to such widespread innovation in the food industry. Moreover, it did nothing to inform consumers about the composition of standardised foods.[62] Standardised foods had to list only the ingredients that were listed as optional in the food standard for that product on the product label, rather than listing all the mandated ingredients in the food standard. Ironically, consumers knew less about the contents of standardised foods than about foods for which there were no standards. Non-standardised foods had to list all of their ingredients on the food label.

Following enactment of the Food Additives amendment, FDA began to experiment with less restrictive food standards. In 1961, FDA first deviated from the recipe approach when it issued standards for 'frozen raw breaded shrimp' which simply provided for the use of 'safe and suitable' batter and breading ingredients, rather than listing all optional ingredients individually.[63] A legal definition of 'safe and suitable' was later codified and used to allow 'safe and suitable preservatives' or 'safe and suitable emulsifiers'.[64]

The peanut butter hearings were launched before this period of regulatory innovation and relaxation of standards. In 1940, peanut butter manufacturers had inquired about the addition of glycerin to peanut butter to prevent oil separation. FDA's response was ambivalent: if glycerin could be added without rendering the food adulterated, its addition would have to be set forth prominently on the product label. The term 'peanut butter', wrote the agency, 'is generally understood ... to mean a product consisting solely of ground roasted peanuts, with or without a small quantity of added salt'.[65] Perhaps fearing another bread battle over ingredients, FDA waited until after the Food Additives amendment was passed to launch its assault on inferior peanut butters. A 1959 press release explained that a survey had shown that products labelled 'peanut butter' had reduced their peanut content as much as 20 per cent, by substituting cheaper hydrogenated or vegetable oils for expensive peanuts and peanut oil. FDA proposed a standard for peanut butter consisting of 95 per cent peanuts and 5 per cent optional ingredients including salt, sugar, dextrose, honey, or hydrogenated or partially hydrogenated peanut oil.[66] Although regulators considered this an adulteration issue, it was clear that consumers often preferred peanut butter that spread more easily as well as peanut butter that had some sweetening. In 1961, therefore, FDA proposed a standard recognising 90 per cent peanuts as well as some additional sweeteners. Three competitive brands of peanut butter then entered the standards battle: Skippy, Jif, and Peter Pan. The public evidentiary hearing alone, a small fragment in the decade long process, took twenty weeks and produced a transcript of nearly 8,000 pages. A prominent attorney on the case wryly observed that the peanut butter standards 'put many lawyers' children through college'. Participants began to feel that they were close to arguing about the number of angels dancing on the head of a pin when it became clear that the disagreement between the industrial protagonists was over a mere 3 per cent difference in proposed peanut content. In the end, the government did prevail as the US Appeals Court affirmed the FDA order setting standards for peanut butter at no less than 90 per cent for peanuts and no more than 55 per cent fat. The court found the Commissioner's findings to be based upon substantial evidence and the promulgation of such standards within his authority. It was not a sweet victory, however. The peanut butter standards had merely underscored growing concerns that the food standards programme in the US had outgrown its usefulness.[67] As the standards setting process had grown increasingly complex and time-consuming, it was the peanut butter hearings that made it clear that strict standards were not only a waste of time and money, but actually and ultimately worked to the detriment of both business and consumers.

Experimentation and innovation in the food standards process, first apparent in 1961 in the frozen shrimp standards, were propelled forward in 1969 following the White House Conference on Food, Nutrition, and Health convened by President Richard Nixon. An era of regulatory reform followed which transformed and modernised the food standards program with a new emphasis on food labels and nutrition. Law professor Richard Merrill expressed the new consensus: 'we conclude that regulation should

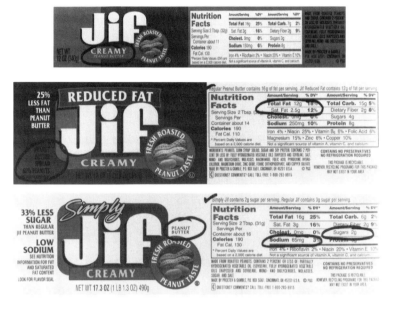

*Figure 11.13*   Modern peanut butter and peanut spread labels. © US Food and Drug Administration.

shift away from controlling food composition and focus on providing consumers with more complete information about foods'.[68] FDA, led by an innovative General Counsel, Peter Hutt, took steps to insure that regulatory practices did not stand in the way of innovative food products, provided new products were safe and informatively labelled. Freed from formulas, the ideals of a free food marketplace were close to being met during the 1970s. The agency encouraged more extensive ingredient labelling in general, and amended food standards to require the labelling of non-mandatory ingredients. A substitute food was designated 'imitation' only if it was nutritionally inferior to the original product. In the case of jams and jellies, this opened up the market for 'fruit spreds' which had less sugar and more fruit – a far cry from the era of BRED-SPRED. Non-standardised products were authorised to state exactly what the product was, so that a food standard would be unnecessary. For example, 'SEAFOOD COCKTAIL: contains X% seafood'.

Increased industry and consumer concerns about healthy diets led to the 1978 regulations on the labelling of reduced calorie and low-calorie foods.[69] In 1994, when Skippy, Jif, and Peter Pan all developed lower-fat peanut butters, FDA agreed with competitors that the product did not meet FDA's hard fought standards. The agency notified the makers that the new products could be called 'spreads' and compared with regular peanut butter on the label, or they could petition FDA to change the standard definition.[70] In an era of affluence accompanied by increased concerns about the relation between nutrition and health, the reduced fat peanut spreads have found a steady market and the standard has remained intact. Basic foods are still wholesome. They are competitive, now, however, not by strictly regulating every ingredient, optional and otherwise in the finished product, but through the standard format of mandatory nutritional food labels (Figure 11.13).[71]

Expansive labelling addresses many concerns over food composition. It allows the consumer to evaluate differences between branded and non-branded (generic) products, as well as to weigh the virtue of a modified food (low-fat, low-sodium, low calorie, etc.) against an unmodified product. The label reveals all food ingredients including food additives and food fortifications. It also offers nutritional profiles as a guide to achieving a more balanced diet. Fat, fibre, sugar, and sodium specifications have made this label the most widely read standard in American history.

## References

1 Comprehensive documentation on the history of the FDA is maintained in the FDA History Office, Rockville, MD.
2 J. H. Young, *Pure Food*, Princeton, NJ, Princeton University Press, 1989, pp. 273–91.
3 *Federal Food, Drug, and Cosmetic Law Administrative Reports*, 1908–1949, New York, Commerce Clearing House, 1951, p. 355. Hereafter cited as *Annual Reports*.
4 See Chapter 2 for details concerning the development of British regulations.
5 P. B. Hutt and P. B. Hutt II, 'A history of government regulation of adulteration and misbranding of food', *Food, Drug, and Cosmetic Law Journal*, 1984, vol. 39, pp. 2–73.
6 29 Stat 604 (March 2, 1897); S. White Junod, 'Tempest in the teapot', *FDLI Update*, 1996, vol. 2, issues 2 and 3, p. 6.
7 US Department of Agriculture, Office of the Secretary, *Standards of Purity for Food Products*, Circular 10, Washington, 1903 (also Circulars 13, 17, and 19).
8 *William J. Buttfield v. Nevada N. Stranahan*, 1904, 192 US 470.
9 O. Anderson, *The Health of A Nation*, Chicago, University of Chicago Press, 1958, pp. 153–4; Young, op. cit., pp. 161, 162, 264, 265.
10 H. W. Wiley to William Frear, 25 May 1906, FDA History Office, Rockville, MD (hereafter FDAHO) file, 'Letters showing history and growth of food standards'.
11 L. M. Friedman, *A History of American Law*, New York, Simon and Schuster, 1973, p. 586.
12 B. Gutterman and T. Bellis, 'Food standards – a brief history', unpublished ms., 1965, FDAHO, Food Standards file.
13 *Savage v. Jones*, 1912, 225 US 501.
14 42 Stat. 1500 (1923).
15 34 Stat. 669, 674 (1906), Section 8.
16 M. White and O. Gates, *Decisions of Courts in Cases Under the Federal Food and Drugs Act*, Washington, DC, GPO, 1934, p. 39.
17 Ibid., p. 40.
18 Ibid., p. 741.
19 Ibid., p. 1204.
20 W. Janssen, 'A case history on food standards', speech delivered to the Annual Convention

of the National Preservers Association, Chicago, IL, 3 March 1952, p. 3, FDAHO, Food Standards file.

21 'Food Standards Committee of the Food and Drug Administration', *Science*, 1938, vol. 88, p. 234–5.

22 H. Lepper, 'The evolution of food standards and the role of the A.O.A.C.', *Food, Drug, and Cosmetic Law Journal*, 1953, vol. 8, pp. 133–89, at p. 146.

23 *Service and Regulatory Announcements, Food Inspection Decision* 221, July 2, 1917.

24 *US v. Ninety Five Barrels, More or Less, Alleged Apple Cider Vinegar*, 1924, 265 US 438; 1931 *Annual Reports*, p. 741. White and Gates, op. cit., pp. 1118–21.

25 F. Linton, 'Leaders in Food and Drug Law Part Four', *Food and Drug Law Journal 50th Anniversary Special Edition*, 1995, pp. 39–47, at pp. 44–7. R. Lamb, *American Chamber of Horrors*, New York, Farrar & Rinehart, 1936, p. 171.

26 *Annual Reports*, p. 742.

27 Ruth Lamb cites as supporters: 'American Home Economics Association, National League of Women Voters, General Federation of Women's Clubs, National Council of Women, American Association of University Women, American Federation of Labor, Consumers' Research and every Government agency that was by way of knowing anything about the subject'. Lamb, op. cit., p. 183.

28 46 Stat. 1019 (1930).

29 *Annual Reports*, p. 746; *Service and Regulatory Announcements, FD no. 4, rev. 2* revised labeling requirements for substandard goods. The original crepe label was retained for vegetables, but for fruits the new crepe label read: 'Below US Standard, Good Food, Not High Grade', *Annual Reports*, p. 1781.

30 Janssen, op. cit., p. 4.

31 Hearings Before the Committee on Agriculture and Forestry, US Senate, 71st Cong., 2d Sess., April 16 and 24, 1930, Washington, DC, GPO, 1930.

32 R. Lamb op. cit., pp. 183–4. Lamb credits connections to Eleanor Roosevelt with the surprise Executive Order.

33 R. Grover, *An American History*, Reading, PA, Addison and Wesley, 1976, p. 843.

34 G. Tindall, *America: A Narrative History*, New York, Norton, 1984, pp. 1074–5.

35 'Preserve Standards Now before Federal Trade Commission', *The Glass Packer*, 1936, vol. 15, pp. 429–30; D. Forbes, 'Enforceable standards for food products', *The Glass Packer*, 1938, vol. 17, pp. 163–4.

36 P. Dunbar, 'Memories of early days of federal food and drug law enforcement', *Food, Drug, and Cosmetic Law Journal*, 1959, vol. 14, p. 134.

37 'Over the bumps with the "Tugwell" Bill', *Food Industries*, 1934, vol. 6, pp. 23–5.

38 *Legislative History of the 1938 Act*, 1974, vol. 2, p. 95.

39 Ibid.

40 Ibid., p. 170.

41 C. Jackson, *Food and Drug Legislation in the New Deal*, Princeton, NJ, Princeton University Press, 1970, p. 66.

42 A. Kallet and F. Schlink, *100,000,000 Guinea Pigs: Dangers in Everyday Foods, Drugs, and Cosmetics*, New York, Vanguard Press, 1933.

43 Lamb claims the exhibit was first assembled in 1912 for hearings on the Sherley Amendment. Lamb, op. cit., p. 133.

44 R. Lamb to W. Wharton, Frontispiece of presentation copy of *American Chamber of Horrors*, n.d., FDAHO.

45 *Legislative History*, vol. 2, p. 93.

46 Pub. L. No. 75-717, 52 Stat. 1040 (1938).

47 R. Merrill and E. Collier, 'Like mother used to make', *Columbia Law Review*, 1974, vol. 74, p. 567.

48 S. R. White [Junod], 'Chemistry and controversy, regulating the use of chemicals in foods, 1883–1959', unpublished PhD thesis, 1994, Emory University, pp. 259–63.

49  Ibid., pp. 46–95; A. Smith, *Pure Ketchup*, Columbia, SC, University of South Carolina Press, 1996, pp. 77–118.

50  The courts upheld the standard's prohibition of benzoate of soda in *Libby, McNeill & Libby v. United States*, 148 f.2d 71(2d Cir. 1945).

51  *62 Cases of Jam v United States*, 1951, 340 US 593.

52  Merrill correctly views the 1940s and 1950s as a period of enthusiasm for increasingly narrow standards, but this judgement has the benefit of hindsight. R. Merrill and E. Collier, 'Like mother used to make', p. 576. Also, H. Austern, 'The F-O-R-M-U-L-A-T-I-O-N of Mandatory Food Standards', *Food, Drug, and Cosmetic Law Quarterly*, 1947, vol. 2, p. 532.

53  Federal standards combined with state statutes, for example, helped eliminate pellegra and beriberi in the US. D. Roe, *A Plague of Corn*, Ithaca, NY, Cornell University Press, 1973, pp. 132–3.

54  *Federal Security Administrator v. Quaker Oats*, 1943, 318 US 218; S. White Junod, 'Whose Standards Should Prevail?: Quaker Oats' Battle Over Bottled Sunshine', *FDLI Update*, 1999, vol. 5, no. 2, p. 12; R. Apple, 'Patenting University Research: Harry Steenbock and the Wisconsin Alumni Research Foundation', *Isis*, 1989, vol. 80, pp. 375–94.

55  68 Stat. 54 (1954).

56  This account of the bread hearings is summarized from S. White, op. cit., pp. 254–308.

57  M. Markel, 'Baking industry progress', *Food, Drug, and Cosmetic Law Journal*, 1951, vol. 6, p. 782.

58  17 *Federal Register*, 15 May 1952, p. 4453.

59  *Hearings Before the House Select Committee to Investigate the Use of Chemicals in Food Products*, 81st Cong., 2d Ses., 1950.

60  72 Stat. 1748 (1958).

61  74 Stat. 397 (1960).

62  Merrill and Collier, op. cit.

63  30 *Federal Register*, 5 March 1965, p. 2860.

64  39 *Federal Register*, 15 May 1974, p. 17304.

65  *Trade Correspondence, March 15, 1940*, FDA Precedent File, F-341(1)54.

66  'Peanut butter – a new food standard proposed by FDA', FDA Press Release, 2 July 1959.

67  Merrill and Collier, op. cit.

68  Ibid., p. 562.

69  42 *Federal Register*, 19 July 1977, p. 37166; 43 *Federal Register*, 22 September 1978, p. 43248.

70  'Can you trim much of the fat and still have peanut butter'?, *USA Today,* 6 April 1994, p. 6D.

71  Pub. L. No. 103-417, 108 Stat 4325 (1994).

# 12 Departmental, professional, and political agendas in the implementation of the recommendations of a food crisis enquiry: the Milne report and inspection of overseas meat plants

*Lesley Diack, T. Hugh Pennington, Elizabeth Russell and David F. Smith*

By the 1960s, the threat of typhoid as an epidemic disease was considered minimal in the western world. It was worrying, therefore, when typhoid was discovered in Aberdeen in May 1964 and within a few days the outbreak was growing rapidly. Over five hundred people were admitted to hospital from late May to early July. By 26 May, just a week after the first case was definitely diagnosed, the medical officer of health for Aberdeen announced that the cause was probably 'a tin of corned beef imported to Britain'.[1] The scale of the outbreak caused the government to announce the establishment of an official committee of enquiry to investigate the source of the outbreak. The committee, consisting of a group of experts from outside government departments, chaired by a retired civil servant of the Scottish Office, Sir David Milne, was established at the height of the outbreak in early June and reported before the end of 1964.[2]

This chapter is the first published product of a three-year research project on the history of the Aberdeen typhoid outbreak, and considers only one aspect of the affair, the recommendations of the committee of enquiry. More specifically, the analysis focuses upon reactions to only one of the recommendations. This concerned the possibility that inspections of overseas meat plants by veterinary personnel of the Ministry of Agriculture, Fisheries and Food (MAFF) might be enhanced by the involvement of medical personnel. This may seem a relatively minor matter. Nevertheless, the analysis presented provides a useful case study. It casts light upon the factors likely to be at work in the implementation of the recommendations of official enquiries concerning food crises. There is strong resonance between this analysis and other case studies in this volume, and the chapter connects with Peter Koolmees' study, in Chapter 4, of the role of the veterinary profession in meat hygiene.

## Background to the certification and inspection of overseas meat plants

From 1908, Britain instituted a system for certification of imported fresh pig meat. Imported meat needed an official certificate provided by a competent authority of the country of origin, usually the country's central veterinary service. The certificate was to show ante- and post-mortem inspections of animals had been carried out, and the meat was prepared under hygienic conditions. This system was later extended to cover all meat and meat products.[3] The Public Health (Imported Food) Regulations of 1937 placed responsibility for recognising certificates upon the Ministry of Health, and certificates were recognised for plants in many countries without any extensive checks. During the Second World War, the Ministry of Food assumed responsibility for managing the nation's food supply and the new Ministry established a Meat Inspection Advisory Service to oversee slaughterhouse hygiene in Britain. Under the Imported Food Regulations of 1948 the recognition of overseas certificates also became the responsibility of the Ministry of Food. It became usual practice for officers from the Meat Inspection Advisory Service to inspect foreign meat plants supplying Britain. In 1951, in accordance with a report of an Interdepartmental Committee on Meat Inspection, a firm policy was established whereby new certificates were recognised only after a visit to the country concerned by a veterinary officer of the Ministry of Food. This arrangement continued after the Ministries of Food and Agriculture merged in 1955 to form MAFF.[4] Until the 1960s, the veterinary officers concerned were L. B. A. Grace and R. V. Blamire and in 1964, as Chief Technical Adviser on Meat Inspection, Grace was the senior officer. Their work came under the Meat Hygiene and Slaughterhouse Branch of the Food Standards, Hygiene and Slaughterhouse Policy Division of MAFF. Both Grace and Blamire were former inspectors at London markets. Grace had worked at Smithfield, while Blamire had worked at Islington, and both held the Diploma in Veterinary State Medicine.[5] They were members of MAFF's State Veterinary Service, which was responsible to the Chief Veterinary Officer and associated with the work of various MAFF divisions.

Peter Koolmees and others have explored some aspects of the long-term struggle of the veterinary profession to establish and maintain their role in public health.[6] The analysis presented in this chapter may be regarded as part of this history. The debate about the Milne recommendation on the inspection of overseas meat plants highlights the limited role in public health that had been assigned to the British veterinary profession. Turn of the century disputes about the respective competencies in meat inspection of the medical and veterinary professions had been settled in favour of the latter in most other European countries. In Britain, the outcome from the point of view of the veterinary profession, had been an unsatisfactory stalemate. Consideration of the Milne Report and other policy initiatives in the mid 1960s re-opened the issue. The hopes of MAFF veterinarians for improving their position had already been raised by a working party considering the creation of a nationalised veterinary service, reporting in March 1963, and a comprehensive review of recruitment for the veterinary profession completed in June 1964.[7] The general election victory of the Labour Party in October 1964, with an explicitly technocratic manifesto, and the appointment of a reforming Minister of Agriculture, Fred Peart, provided further encouragement. However, it was not until thirty years later, as part of the response to the BSE crisis, that a meat inspection service was established in Britain under veterinary control along the lines of services in existence elsewhere in Europe.[8]

British veterinarians envied the prestige and employment opportunities in veterinary public health enjoyed by their colleagues in many other countries. They harboured ambitions to expand their responsibilities and jealously guarded their own limited positions in the field. There is evidence that before the Aberdeen outbreak, Grace was determined to protect the specialised niche that he occupied on behalf of the veterinary profession from alternative claims to expertise. Following three small typhoid outbreaks during 1963 – in Harlow, South Shields and Bedford – it was decided to send him to Argentina to investigate the factory which seemed to be the source of the corned beef common to all three outbreaks, and to check conditions at other establishments in South America.[9] During the preparations for the trip, it was suggested that a canning expert should accompany Grace to South America. However, in response Grace remarked to G. O. Lace, Assistant Secretary of the Food Standards Division of MAFF, that while he could not claim to be an expert on canning

> ... after a long experience of meat plants and canneries in the important meat exporting countries I might, possibly ... be considered at least knowledgeable in what constitutes good canning practice ... one might make out an equally good case for attaching an expert bacteriologist to an advisory team. My opinion is that neither is necessary and that the suggestion is impractical.[10]

Grace made the trip to South America alone, but during the Milne Enquiry, questions were asked as to why no canning expert had been involved.[11] However, as has been indicated, the main threat to veterinary authority in the Milne Report came not from canning experts, but from their longer-term rivals: the medical profession.

## Background to debate about the division of departmental responsibilities

Besides the Milne Enquiry, three policy review exercises dealing with aspects of meat hygiene were completed during 1964. Two of these, in particular, raised questions concerning divisions of responsibility between the Ministry of Health and MAFF, which conditioned reactions to the Milne recommendations. The first was the Committee of Enquiry into Fatstock and Carcass Meat Marketing and Distribution, which reported in February 1964. This

Committee, chaired by Sir William Verdon-Smith, consisted mainly of businessmen and academic economists and recommended the establishment of a Fatstock Meat Authority with a wide range of functions.[12] These functions were to include the development and operation of a central meat inspection service that would carry out ante- and post-mortem inspections throughout the country. This was intended to improve standards in England and Wales in particular, where there was little ante-mortem inspection, and some meat escaped post-mortem inspection. In October 1963 new regulations had already been introduced in England and Wales regarding post-mortem inspection, which were intended to secure 100 per cent inspection by the local authorities within two years.[13]

The other two exercises consisted of internal working parties of civil servants. One was formed at about the time the Aberdeen outbreak began. This was the Lees working party, appointed by the Treasury, and chaired by Stanley Lees, director of organisation and methods at that department. It was to investigate the division of responsibilities regarding food hygiene under the Imported Food Regulations, the Food and Drugs Act (1955), and other legislation, with the aim of making the division of responsibilities more logical and economical. Efforts to rationalise government were not unusual and since 1946 shifts in remits between departments were often made by 'Transfer of Function' orders. Richard Rose shows that 322 such orders were made from 1946–83. Of twenty-two departments, agriculture and health were third and seventh most prone to transfers during that period.[14] But the Lees working party was part of a special review by the Conservative administration which, after being in power since 1951, aimed to reinvigorate government in advance of an imminent general election.[15]

In connection with the Lees working party, during June 1964 the Meat Hygiene and Slaughterhouse Branch of the Food Standards Division prepared a memorandum arguing that overseas meat inspection should remain the responsibility of MAFF.[16] This was not the view of the senior MAFF staff. Sir John Winnifrith, the permanent secretary, perhaps with the problems caused by the recent typhoid outbreaks in mind, thought that MAFF

> ... should agree that responsibility for the hygiene of imported meat and meat products should go back to the Ministry of Health, with such veterinary assistance and advice as the Ministry of Health need being provided by our veterinary establishment.[17]

Nevertheless, as regards home-killed meat, Winnifrith wanted to reserve judgement in view of the decision making required following the Verdon-Smith recommendation for a central meat inspection service. He remarked:

> So long as there is any possibility of such an organisation with a strong element of vets supervising ... it would be madness to transfer responsibility to the Ministry

of Health. The fact is that this department alone has the necessary nucleus of full-time and part-time staff up and down the country.[18]

In August, the report of the Lees working party recommended that the inspection of overseas meat plants should be the responsibility of the Ministry of Health, but carried out on their behalf by MAFF veterinary officers. But it went on to state that the final decision should be deferred until policy regarding the inspection of home-killed meat was settled. Both the Ministry of Health and MAFF were making strong bids for the control of the proposed centralised service at this time.[19]

The establishment of the third review, a working party on food safety, resulted from discussion between the Minister of Health and the Minister of Agriculture, Fisheries and Food.[20] The initiative, it was suggested, would allow the claim that the issues raised by Aberdeen were in hand before the outbreak. Yet, as the discussion took place towards the end of June, any such statement would have been false. John Pater, director of establishments and organisation at the Ministry of Health, chaired the committee. The members were all civil servants from MAFF, the Ministry of Health, and the Scottish Office, and the report was not published. The Ministry of Health proposed a broad remit, covering all aspects of food hygiene.[21] MAFF, however, objected to the inclusion of meat inspection and slaughterhouse hygiene, because they would shortly be assessing the effects of the October 1963 regulations.[22] These matters were therefore dropped, and the working party avoided the most contentious questions of division of ministerial responsibilities.[23] On the question of overseas meat plants, the report merely made the uncontroversial proposal that a letter should be prepared for overseas governments, specifying the standards required in meat production for export to Britain.[24] This recommendation also appeared in the Milne Report, and had been implemented by the time it was published.

## The Milne Enquiry

The intention to form a committee of enquiry to investigate the Aberdeen outbreak was announced by Michael Noble, Secretary of State for Scotland, at the beginning of June 1964.[25] The terms of reference were to 'investigate the cause of the primary infection in the recent outbreak of typhoid fever in Aberdeen and the means by which it was disseminated'.[26] The committee consisted of J. W. Howie, director of the Public Health Laboratory Service in England and Wales, and A. B. Semple, medical officer of health and port medical officer for Liverpool, along with a meat producer and a representative from the Women's Institute. According to the committee's secretary, Alex. Stephen, an official of the Scottish Home and Health Department, the timing of the announcement was crucial. Noble acted quickly to prevent government departments in Whitehall from taking control. He also favoured Howie and Semple because of their Scottish backgrounds. They were medical graduates of Aberdeen and Glasgow Universities, respectively, and Howie was former professor of bacteriology at Glasgow.[27] Later, however, the initiative for dealing with the recommendations shifted from Scotland, the main departments concerned being MAFF and the Ministry of Health.

By September, the committee had received oral and written evidence from 104 witnesses. Drafts of the report were sent to government departments for comments in October and November. There was considerable discussion as to how and when to release the report and who should announce it. It was eventually decided to present the report to the House of Commons just before the Christmas recess. This timing would hopefully exert a 'deflationary effect' and minimise comment.[28] Since the general election in October had brought in Harold Wilson's Labour government, the task fell to a new Secretary of State for Scotland, Willie Ross. On 17 December, the day of publication of the report, Ross told the House of Commons:

> The Committee make a number of detailed recommendations, some of which have already been acted upon. Overseas suppliers have been provided with a detailed statement of our hygiene requirements for the production of meat and meat products and the staff engaged on the overseas inspection of meat production establishments has been augmented. These are two of the things that the Committee recommended should be done.[29]

## The recommendation for medical participation in overseas inspections

The recommendation concerning inspection teams to which Ross referred stated that

> ... the personnel presently employed in the inspection of canning establishments abroad should be augmented and that any inspection team, particularly at the time of the first visit, should also include a medical officer.[30]

The aim was to make good the deficiencies that the committee perceived to exist in the overseas inspection system. In the report the committee remarked that it was 'with some surprise' that they had learnt that inspections covering 'all countries exporting meat and meat products to us' were 'discharged by only two senior veterinary officers'.[31] By December 1964, two additional veterinary officers had already been assigned to the overseas work formerly undertaken by Grace and Blamire alone. The second part of the recommendation, concerning the addition of a medical officer, was still the subject of discussion between MAFF and Ministry of Health, and consensus had not yet emerged.

None of the individuals or organisations listed in the report seems likely to have made the suggestion for medical involvement. No associations representing the medical profession gave evidence, for example. Since, as will be seen, the original rationale for the recommendation concerned alleged weaknesses in veterinary knowledge of bacteriology, and the effect of implementation would be to enhance the role of the medical profession, it is possible that Semple and/or Howie were responsible. However, the recommendation was already in place in draft form by early October, when Animal Health Division II of MAFF was considering their attitude towards it:

> If the Ministry of Health are in favour of implementing this recommendation, as they can be expected to be, it would be impossible to oppose it, since even the most stringent precautions cannot be entirely secure for all time and failure to take the Committee's recommendation would leave the Minister without defence, if despite sound precautions, a further connection between imported canned meat and disease should be established in the future.[32]

The view that it would be necessary to implement the recommendation, if only from the point of view of public relations, and because of the political risks of rejecting it, set the tone for much of the subsequent discussion. At the beginning of November, the chief medical officer at the Ministry of Health, Sir George Godber, dictated some comments on a draft of the report. These display ambivalence about what might be achieved by overseas inspections. He remarked that the passage on this matter had been written as if such inspections were 'a real insurance against unhygienic methods'. In Godber's view they could only provide a 'commentary on the way in which the inspectors of the country of origin do their work'.[33]

MAFF now made representations to the committee about the recommendation, and some alterations were agreed. The draft report pointed out that while the primary concern of veterinary officers was to prevent the importation of animal diseases, 'an equal if not greater regard must be paid to the human health aspects', and went on to suggest the future involvement of medical officers:

> It appears to us ... that in the field of hygiene, requiring as it does a comprehensive knowledge of bacteriology and having its basis in preventative medicine, someone with a medical training is required to oversee this part of the inspecting team's duties.[34]

These sentences expressed the view that the main role of the veterinarians was confined to animal diseases, hardly recognising the role of the profession in meat inspection, let alone any broader public health function. The redraft, which appeared in the published report, also emphasised the continuing importance of protection against animal diseases, before stating: 'in the light of recent experience there is now a need for intensifying measures to safeguard human health'. In contrast to the earlier draft, the new one went on to refer positively to the qualifications of veterinarians, before a much weaker and barely logical comment about possible medical involvement:

> ... the course for the Diploma in Veterinary State Medicine, which the Minister's Advisers hold  ... [provides] a full grounding in Bacteriology, particularly in

relation to food hygiene, similar to the specialised instruction which a medical graduate undergoes if he takes the Diploma in Public Health. We think nevertheless that there might be an advantage in medical participation in the duties of the inspection team.[35]

MAFF had successfully defended their veterinary staff against the most derogatory remarks in the draft report. During the final preparations for publication, MAFF commented to the Ministry of Health that since the notion that veterinarians were not so well trained as doctors had been taken out, there was now no supporting argument for medical participation. MAFF would therefore have to consider the matter carefully.[36]

On 10 December, at an interdepartmental meeting to prepare advice to Ministers as to how to respond to the report, there was no agreement as to whether it was desirable for a medical officer to join overseas inspections. It was decided to advise Ministers to state merely that the recommendation was under consideration.[37] This was the line adopted. The briefing paper agreed by the departments, also stated, along the lines of Godber's view, that the Committee had failed to take on board the point that overseas inspections could not offer a complete safeguard. The document told ministers that the inspections were 'in the first instance to explain our hygienic requirements and thereafter  ... check on the standard of inspection carried out in the country of origin'.[38]

## Reaction of the medical and veterinary professions

The government's strategy of publishing the report just before Christmas appears to have worked and the response in the national press was muted. National coverage consisted largely of factual summaries of the report. The initial response of the medical press was similar: the *British Medical Journal*, in its Boxing Day issue, simply printed a long synopsis. *The Lancet* was rather more critical, describing the report, on 2 January 1965, as 'an account of a dangerous situation, created by Ministerial inaction and by the seeming indifference of the meat-importing trade'. But while *The Lancet*'s leading article pointed to the failure of past overseas inspections, there was no reinforcement of the suggestion of future medical involvement. It appears then, as far as the wider medical profession was concerned, there was no particular interest in pursuing this recommendation.[39]

In contrast, there were immediate signs of resistance from the veterinary profession to the suggestion that doctors might encroach upon their responsibilities. The President of the British Veterinary Association, D. F. Oliver, wrote to *The Times* about the matter.[40] During his trip to South America in early 1964, Grace had discovered and reported a factory using unchlorinated river water for cooling purposes. This plant produced the corned beef that was later responsible for the Aberdeen outbreak. Oliver commented that the Milne Committee had failed to accord sufficient credit for this achievement.

He further argued that the number of veterinary inspectors should be increased since they were 'the best qualified to safeguard our imported meat supplies' and because they had the necessary 'long experience and specialised knowledge'. The argument continued in an editorial in *The Veterinary Record* in early January 1965:

> What must be criticised is the system under which the inspection of meat and meat products remains – in this country almost alone in the western world – primarily a medical and not a veterinary matter. The minds of successive Governments have remained obstinately closed on the subject, and here it appears again as misconceived as ever. In making its recommendation about the inclusion of a medical officer in future overseas inspection teams the Report gives no reason; it does not suggest what part the medical officer could usefully play, nor how the Chief Adviser's survey could have been improved by medical advice.[41]

Meat inspection was 'primarily a medical matter' in England and Wales, in the sense that health departments of local authorities were responsible for enforcing regulations. These remarks suggest the attitude of the veterinary profession to the Milne recommendation was closely connected with its hopes that these arrangements would be changed by the establishment of a centralised meat inspection service in Britain under veterinary control.

## Inter-departmental negotiations

Despite their earlier ambivalence, Godber and his colleagues at the Ministry of Health began to see the attractions of participating in overseas inspections, or at least of pressing the point upon MAFF. A draft letter even suggested that, in view of medical officers' routine duties in monitoring water quality, it was possible that 'if a medical officer had joined the inspectorate earlier certain defects at canning establishments might automatically have come to light'. Perhaps the four recent typhoid outbreaks might even have been avoided.[42] The final version was more subtle, and while referring to the medical officer's expertise concerning water, emphasised more the political dimension:

> Although inspection from this country can never be a safeguard in itself ... if we had another major outbreak ... the Government's inspection arrangements would be almost bound to come under fire (however unjustified) ... If it then transpired that one of the recommendations of ... [the Milne] report had been rejected, against the advice of the C. M. O., I feel sure that both your department and mine would find themselves in difficulty.[43]

MAFF was reluctant to accept these arguments. In the published report it was merely stated that it would be a 'good idea' for a doctor to be involved in inspections. And while the point about medical officers' knowledge of water hygiene was superficially attractive, the principles applying in canning establishments were specialised matters of which Ministry of Health doctors were likely to have little experience. In considering the response to be made to the Ministry of Health, Mr Lace, assistant secretary of the Food Standards Division of MAFF, commented to his colleagues:

> A further point which ought to be made although it may strike at the pride of the medical profession is that throughout the world outside this country and a few Commonwealth territories who march in step with us, these matters are universally under the control of veterinary services and the intrusion of medical men into an already delicate field of extra-territorial enforcement of our standards would only serve to make for bad feeling and poorer efficiency.[44]

Negotiations concerning the implementation of the recommendation on meat inspection of the Verdon-Smith Report, and the proposals of the Lees working party on division of responsibilities were underway at this time. MAFF was about to tell the Ministry of Health that it considered that a centralised meat inspection in Britain should be established, under the control of veterinarians. Conceding the Milne recommendation on overseas inspection of canneries would weaken their case.[45]

By mid-January 1965, Godber's position was firmly in favour of medical involvement in overseas inspections. In a conversation with Sir John Ritchie, Chief Veterinary Officer, he suggested an additional advantage. The medical officer would be able to consult with local health authorities regarding health conditions surrounding the establishment under inspection. But Ritchie told his colleagues that he was convinced this was 'nothing but setting up a front'. Nevertheless, he could see 'considerable difficulties' with the Ministry of Health if implementation of the recommendation was opposed by MAFF.[46]

Lace, at MAFF, now raised the questions of costs, administrative difficulties, and the objections of the veterinary officers. Concerning the notion that the medical officer might check on local health conditions, he thought this would introduce a whole new set of criteria for assessing imported foods. The purpose of recent efforts regarding the quality of cooling water had been to ensure that food was safe even when imported from countries like Argentina, where diseases such as typhoid were endemic. Finally, he intimated that his feeling was that Ministry of Health officials were 'embarrassed by the recommendation, but are playing safe in supporting it'.[47] In early March a meeting of under-secretaries took place. Afterwards, John Hensley, under-secretary for MAFF, advised his colleagues that although the Ministry of Health did not contend that medical participation in overseas inspections had great merit, it was difficult to reject.[48] They would have to accept a form of words saying there should be greater co-operation and that medical participation would be considered in cases where there were special problems.

By this time MAFF's proposals for a centralised meat inspection service were well advanced. Fred Peart, the minister, had rejected the idea that the service would be under the control of the Meat Commission envisaged by

Verdon-Smith, and favoured the establishment of a service under MAFF. Since the preparation of the Lees Report, Ministry of Health officials, despite continued scepticism, had also shifted their position. MAFF officials now believed that their counterparts would not advise their minister to oppose the proposal, and thought a joint approach could be made to the Treasury.[49] MAFF was apparently winning the argument for the veterinary control of meat hygiene. In this context, the earlier willingness of senior MAFF staff to give away overseas meat inspection appears to have faded. Hensley saw the situation in the same way as MAFF's veterinary staff. He suggested that a suitable agreement with the Ministry of Health on overseas inspections

> ... should maintain the principle that veterinarians were in charge of the job and were qualified to do it, and avoid any unjustified contention that they could not do it without medical advisers breathing down their necks.[50]

MAFF drafted a formula that it hoped would satisfy the Ministry of Health while 'not weakening the position of our veterinary staff'.[51] The MAFF formula stated that '... if special circumstances were thought to warrant it the need for medical participation in an overseas visit would be considered'.[52] The Ministry of Health countered with a sentence in which 'will be arranged' was substituted for 'would be considered', also asserting that the agreement should be supported with an 'actual joint visit in the near future'.[53] Lace advised Hensley that this placed the onus on MAFF to suggest when a joint visit would be appropriate. He commented, 'this will make it easier for us to operate the procedure and to avoid our officers being saddled with medical companions in circumstances of particular embarrassment to them'.[54] The Ministry of Health's formula formed the basis of an agreement. However, Hensley made it clear to his opposite number that, on any joint visits, the medical officer would not be allowed to interfere with work of the veterinary officer, who would be in charge.[55]

## A package deal

No immediate progress could be made as Grace was in Australia, from where he returned at the end of June 1965, then going to the USA before anything was settled.[56] In August, Lace pressed Grace to suggest a suitable visit. He told Grace that 'the hard fact is that Ministers are being advised to announce some measure of acceptance of this bit of Milne, and that it will have to be seen to have been accepted'.[57] Grace repeated the now familiar objections to the participation of medical officers and added that he could identify no past situation in which a medical officer would have been useful. He further commented that the Milne committee produced 'no evidence that I or my colleagues have failed in any aspect of our investigations in the past'.[58] Nevertheless, Grace suggested a medical officer might be invited to a forthcoming visit to Yugoslavia, as information about deficiencies of Yugoslavian pasteurised canned meat had been received by the Ministry of Health from local health authorities and forwarded to MAFF.

By this time, the Treasury's disappointing negative response to the proposals for a centralised meat inspection service had been made. Against the background of the serious economic difficulties that the Labour government had encountered, it was now clear that the aspirations for a new veterinary-led central meat inspection service under MAFF were over-ambitious.[59] A much cheaper and less challenging programme was under discussion with the Ministry of Health, involving controlling the hours of slaughter, leaving the supervision of meat inspection in the hands of local health authorities, and modestly expanding the existing advisory role of MAFF veterinary officers with regard to meat inspection.[60]

As part of this 'package deal' agreed with the Ministry of Health, Hensley, the under-secretary, advised Peter Humphreys-Davies, deputy secretary at MAFF, that while no one thought much of the idea of medical participation in overseas visits, the matter would have to be settled.[61] Humphreys-Davies subsequently told the permanent secretary, Sir John Winnifrith, that it was proposed to offer the Yugoslavia visit 'by way of a gesture, and to anticipate more embarrassing demands'.[62] Winnifrith agreed the 'gesture would do no harm'. A medical officer could accompany Blamire, Grace's deputy, to Yugoslavia, but Blamire would be in charge.[63]

On 25 August, the permanent secretary of the Ministry of Health, pressed MAFF to push ahead with organising a joint inspection. He told Winnifrith that 'the participation of our medical staff in the overseas work should be put into actual effect on at least one occasion soon, and should not be left simply as an agreement on paper. Otherwise I fear we may incur criticism'.[64] A joint visit to Yugoslavia was quickly arranged.

## An expedition to Yugoslavia

On 6 September 1965 MAFF sent an official invitation to the Ministry of Health for a medical officer to join the visit to Yugoslavia,[65] but negotiations about the trip were already underway. John Ross, the medical officer who would be involved, was unhappy about the proposal. He felt it was not the sort of visit that had been envisaged as a joint venture, but realised that the Ministry of Health would have to be represented. Otherwise MAFF might claim 'that we rejected their first request for a medical officer to join their veterinary inspector'.[66] He complained to Godber about the short notice and told Godber that there would be a clash with an important meeting. This was the first meeting of a committee established to implement another of the Milne recommendations: the Panel on the Microbial Hazards in Food of the Committee on Medical Aspects of Food Policy. Ross suggested it would be undiplomatic to send someone to Yugoslavia until the panel had given their advice on the inadequacies of Yugoslavian canned meat. With these considerations in mind, the departure date was delayed until 11 October 1965.[67] The administrators of the Ministry of Health who had been involved in the negotiations saw the trip more positively. One expressed satisfaction that 'We have at last succeeded in persuading MAFF ... that a medical officer should accompany veterinary staff in the inspection of overseas meat establishments'.[68]

During the two-week visit, Ross and Blamire inspected twenty establishments and the central control laboratory, and held discussions with the Yugoslav authorities. Their collaboration appears to have been unproblematic, but tensions between MAFF and the Ministry of Health re-surfaced during the production of a report. While Ross was able to comment on a draft,[69] Blamire alone signed the report. Ross commented to a colleague 'since "we" is used throughout the report "we" should have signed it'.[70] However, Ross sympathised with MAFF's 'desire to maintain procedures'[71] and felt that now that the 'ice has been broken' similar proposals in the future should not cause any 'heart-burning'.[72] Ross and Blamire collaborated on a number of inspections over the next few years, visiting Ethiopia, Eritrea, Argentina, and Uruguay in the late 1960s. This represented a small proportion of the 10–15 overseas trips annually, and the reports show little evidence of specific contributions from the medical officer.[73] The participation of a medical officer in overseas visits is mentioned in the Chief Veterinary Officer's annual reports for 1965 and 1966. The reports for 1967 and from 1970 refer to visits by 'veterinary staff' only, while those for 1968–9 mention the Ministry's 'technical advisers'.[74] Clearly, the implementation of the recommendation that has been discussed in this chapter, was, as MAFF officials termed it, never much more than a 'gesture'.

## Conclusions

This analysis has provided a number of insights into the factors that conditioned the process of implementation of one recommendation of the enquiry into the Aberdeen typhoid outbreak. It seems worth commenting firstly that since the original rationale for the recommendation in the draft report was so easily challenged by MAFF, there was a significant element of chance at play in its inclusion in the report. More generally, it might be suggested that the nature of the recommendations that appear in the reports of investigations into food crises, may be partly determined by the haste in which investigations are sometimes conducted and reports are written.

Secondly, as has been seen, the fate of the recommendation under examination became closely connected with inter-departmental politics and ongoing departmental negotiations. Specifically, considerations concerning the proposals to create a new system for organising meat inspection in Britain, conditioned the departments' responses. In other words, it seems that existing processes of policy development and the inter-departmental tensions involved must be taken into account when considering the process of implementation of recommendations.

Thirdly, an essential factor in determining the course of events was the determination of the veterinary profession to maintain and expand its responsibilities in public health. This was reinforced by the backing which members of the State Veterinary Service within MAFF received by representatives of the wider profession. Therefore, it may be suggested that besides departmental agendas, long-term professional agendas may also be expected to play an important role in responses to food crises.

Fourthly, the civil servants saw the implementation of the recommendation as essential, mainly because they would stand accused of negligence if it were rejected and then another incident occurred. It is clear, however, that neither the Ministry of Health nor MAFF saw any great merit in the recommendation, and the implementation amounted to little more than a token effort in the interests of good inter-departmental and public relations. Similarly, the politicians' main concern appears to have been being able to claim that they had implemented the recommendation. In effect, whatever the technical arguments for or against recommendations of enquiries into food crises, wider political considerations may assume greater importance in determining whether or not they are accepted.

Finally, it is worth noting that with this particular recommendation, business interests were of little direct relevance – except in connection with the wider issue of the arrangements for meat inspection in Britain, where the matter of who should pay for the proposed centralised service was important.[75] This contrasts with some of the other recommendations of the Milne Committee. For example, the Committee stated that the corned beef withheld after the 1963 and Aberdeen outbreaks could be safely reprocessed and sold for human consumption. This led to months of lobbying by the traders affected, who wanted to implement the recommendation as quickly as possible. However, this procedure was not implemented because of the criticism of the government expressed by the public, politicians and in the press, and the intervention of the Prime Minister, Harold Wilson.[76] Such controversy was dangerous to the Labour government, which was clinging on to power at this time with only a very slim majority. As in the case of the recommendation discussed in this chapter, political considerations were very important, or even decisive in the decision-making process.

Analysis of the fate of more of the fourteen Milne Report recommendations remains to be completed. It is expected that, based on this analysis, it will be possible to construct a model of policy making and implementation that may be compared with other enquiries following other food crises. It may be anticipated, however, that the factors in play in the episode discussed in chapter, are likely to be important in many other policy making and implementation processes.

## Acknowledgements

The authors wish to thank the Wellcome Trust for the financial support of the research upon which this chapter is based, and also Mark Bufton, Jim Phillips, Virginia Berridge, Richard Perren, Bernard Harris and especially Peter Koolmees for their comments on earlier versions of this chapter.

# References

1 W. Beattie, 'The typhoid source – a tin of beef', *Scottish Daily Express*, 27 May 1964.
2 Scottish Home and Health Department (SSHD), *The Aberdeen Typhoid Outbreak 1964*, Edinburgh, HMSO, 1964.
3 R. V. Blamire, 'Meat hygiene: the changing years', *Journal of the Royal Society of Health*, 1984, vol. 5, pp. 180–5; for background to the early British developments see M. French and J. Phillips, *Cheated not Poisoned*, Manchester, Manchester University Press, 2000, pp. 78–95.
4 K. A. Bird, 'Imported meat and meat products', 16 June 1964, Public Record Office (hereafter PRO) MAF 282/90; Blamire, 1984, op. cit.
5 Oral evidence, R. V. Blamire, 12 January 2000. Tape reference, Aberdeen Typhoid Outbreak project, (hereafter ATO)/37. All oral evidence referred to in these endnotes consists of interviews conducted by L. Diack.
6 P. A. Koolmees, 'The development of veterinary public health in Western Europe, 1850–1940, *Sartoniana*, 1999, vol. 12, pp. 153–79; P. A. Koolmees, J. R. Fisher and R. Perren, 'The traditional responsibility of veterinarians in meat production and meat inspection', in F. J. M. Smulders (ed.), *Veterinary Aspects of Meat Production, Processing and Inspection. An Update of Recent Developments in Europe*, Utrecht, ECCEAMST, 1999, pp. 7–31; C. W. Schwabe, *Veterinary Medicine and Human Health*, Baltimore, Williams and Wilkinson, 1984 (third edition); J. Swabe, *Animals, Disease and Human Society: Human-Animal Relations and the Rise of Veterinary Medicine*, London, Routledge, 1999.
7 For files relating to these enquiries see PRO MAF 287/102 and 219.
8 Blamire, 1984, op. cit.
9 For details of the 1963 outbreaks and responses to them see PRO MAF 282/75.
10 L. B. A. Grace to G. O. Lace, 17 December 1963, PRO MAF 282/75.
11 Note from A. J. D. Winnifrith, 3 June 1964, PRO MAF 282/87.
12 Ministry of Agriculture Fisheries and Food, *Report of the Committee of Enquiry into Fatstock and Carcass Meat Marketing and Distribution*, London, HMSO, 1964.
13 The Meat Inspection Regulations 1963, S.I. No. 1229.
14 R. Rose, *Ministers and Ministries. A Functional Analysis*, Oxford, Clarendon, 1987, pp. 45–52.
15 For files relating to this review see PRO CAB 21/5081–2 and T 277/1371–4.
16 'Meat hygiene and slaughterhouse policy branch', June 1964, PRO MAF 260/256.
17 A. J. D. Winnifrith to P. Humphreys-Davies, 21 July 1964, PRO MAF 260/356.
18 Ibid.
19 'Report of the Working Party on departmental responsibility for food hygiene and related matters', 25 August 1964, PRO MAF 260/356.
20 M. D. M. Franklin to J. P. Cashman, 4 June 1964, PRO MH 148/252.
21 J. H. Hauff to M. Pearson, 25 June 1964, PRO MH 148/252.
22 J. Hensley to J. E. Pater, 1 July 1964, PRO MH 148/252.
23 A. W. France to Winnifrith, 1 September 1964, PRO MH 148/254.
24 'Report of the Pater Working Party on food safety and hygiene', August 1964, PRO MH 148/252.
25 M. Noble, 'Aberdeen typhoid outbreak', *Parliamentary Debates (Commons)*, 1964–5, vol. 695, cols. 925–6.
26 SHHD, op. cit.
27 Oral evidence, A. Stephen, 17 June 1999, ATO/18.

# 13  Post-war nutrition science and policy making in Britain c. 1945–1994: the case of diet and heart disease

*Mark W. Bufton and Virginia Berridge*

Comparative international statistics indicate that until very recently the UK has had one of the highest rates of premature mortality from coronary heart disease.[1] Journalist-turned food researcher, Geoffrey Cannon, views this situation as indicative of a comparatively slow and lagging policy response to the problem. According to Cannon, scientific consensus on the cause of heart disease has been partially ignored on the one hand, and certain policy actors have attempted to block or undermine the evidence on the other. In his view, the UK authorities were slow to recognise the dangers to health of diets high in saturated fat and sugar. Cannon has remarked – typically from the journalist's 'heroes and villains' perspective – that Britain was 'the last country in the Western world officially to concede that fats and saturated fats, in the quantities typically present in Western food, are a cause of heart attacks'.[2]

This alleged delay in policy response appears unwise in the light of Cannon's analyses of 100 scientific reports on diet and health produced by expert committees between 1961 and 1991, nearly all of which advocated reducing saturated fat intake. Cannon's study appears to indicate that scientific opinion on the causes of heart disease and the appropriate action that follows has converged during the post-war period.[3] Cannon has also argued that the recommendations of inter-war British nutritionists – such as those embodied in the BMA's 1933 report on nutrition – encouraged the consumption of foods high in animal protein and fat. The increasing consumption of meat, milk, eggs, and dairy products, helped to establish eating habits in the UK inimical to the maintenance of a healthy heart.[4]

In stark contrast to the arguments of Cannon are those of James Le Fanu. Le Fanu, a general practitioner and medical journalist, has argued that the recommendations of British inter-war nutritionists, though not scientifically sound, were not harmful to cardiovascular health. Le Fanu further asserts that the epidemiological bases of the diet-heart disease and other diet-disease hypotheses are fundamentally flawed. From his perspective, epidemiological sophistry has become embodied in the expert committees that have recommended that people should change their dietary habits. Le Fanu argues that the long-term and world-wide trends of premature mortality from heart disease are more consistent with those of a disease caused by an infectious agent, although its impact may be accentuated by dietary factors.[5]

Clearly, on one interpretation, Le Fanu and Cannon can be seen at either end of a spectrum, where on one side policy has been culpably slow to respond to the emerging scientific consensus – Cannon. On the other side the policy response was uncalled for and the scientific evidence was anything but conclusive – Le Fanu. Nevertheless, for both Cannon and Le Fanu, expert committees and their recommendations have played a fundamental role. Cannon and Le Fanu also present their differing arguments in similar style and rhetoric, each seeing the issues as relatively clear-cut.

In this chapter, we will consider the role of the most important expert advisory committee in the Britain with regard to food and health, the Committee on Medical Aspects of Food Policy (commonly referred to as COMA). We shall also look at the wider policy environment in which COMA functioned. We will analyse some of the complex factors that mediate the science and policy interrelationship and in so doing will show that the issues are not as simple as Cannon and Le Fanu indicate.

## The emerging diet and heart disease thesis in the 1950s and 1960s

The Ministries of Food and Health won the prestigious Lasker Award from the American Public Health Association for their contribution to public health during World War Two. But the long-term effects of government policy during this era have been criticised. Cannon, for example, acknowledges that British food and nutrition policy during the war 'worked', but also claims that it reinforced consumption trends for foods not wholly conducive to health and that by the 1950s, British food was mostly fatty and sugary. The academic sociologist Alan Warde, drawing on data from the National Food Survey, has made a differing observation. Warde notes that abrupt changes in food consumption trends occurred in the early 1950s when rationing came to an end and the consumption of meat, white bread, and butter all rapidly increased.[6] During the late 1940s and early 1950s foods and other goods were slowly de-rationed, although bread and potatoes were rationed for the first time in 1946–8.[7] As the free play of markets returned, people could again choose what they wanted to purchase and eat and pre-war food consumption trends were either accentuated or significantly changed. Either way the shift in preferences seems clear. People began to eat significantly more sugar and fatty foods.

The Annual Report of the Chief Medical Officer (CMO) of the Ministry of Health for 1954 indicated that the authorities were aware of the revived trends in fat and sugar consumption. Before the Second World War consumption of fat, per head per day, measured in grams from all sources, was 130; this fell to 119 from 1940–44 and 114 in 1945–49 before rising to 127 in 1950–3 and 139 in 1954. Sugar consumption, measured in pounds per head per day, was 109 before the war, falling to 69 in 1940–4, before increasing to 86 in 1945–9, 96 in 1950–3, and 114 in 1954.[8] A second emerging trend was the rise in ischaemic heart disease, which had become by the 1950s the major cause of premature death. The death rate of men from this cause continuously rose until it peaked in the 1970s.[9]

Officials already linked these consumption trends with the growing rates of heart disease as the report commented:

> ... there are certain degenerative diseases to which Western populations are at greater risk in times of plenty than in hardship. There is much evidence relating atherosclerosis with fat intake, and, like fat intake, deaths from arteriosclerotic heart disease show post-war increases. It is noteworthy, however, that when pre-war death rates and fat consumption levels are related, this association breaks down, fat consumption levels being high, whereas arteriosclerotic heart deaths were less than half what they are today.[10]

Behind the scenes, pressure was being applied too. In 1955, Horace Joules, the Medical Superintendent at the Central Middlesex Hospital wrote to the government's Standing Advisory Medical Committee, part of the Ministry of Health. Joules, who had been pressing the government on the issue of smoking and health said, 'The work of Ancel Keys and others, together with increasing clinical observation, suggests that there is a relationship between excessive intake of fat in adult life and the occurrence of atheromatous lesions, resulting especially in coronary thrombosis'.[11]

The above quotes indicate that officials and the authorities knew of a possible relationship between diet and heart disease. Stewart Truswell, professor of human nutrition at the University of Sydney, has remarked that during the 1950s there was '... a slow realization that the major degenerative diseases of older life might at least be partly determined by something as humble, as domestic, as enjoyable as the foods we eat habitually'.[12]

Certainly the CMO's views seem to reflect this, but his remarks also throw into focus a curious anomaly. Prior to the war fat consumption seems to have been similar to that after the war, but death from heart disease was lower. Mel Bartley has argued that the apparent increase in the incidence of heart disease was more apparent than real. In her view, heart disease has been the leading cause of death in middle age for men and women since at least the 1840s. Changes in the classification of deaths have been largely responsible for the increase in incidence during the twentieth century.[13] These developments may partly account for the apparent trend causing the CMO's anxiety during the 1950s. Others have argued that the issues of classification above cannot entirely account for the rise in premature mortality from heart disease. Therefore even taking account of Bartley's point, we still need explanations of why deaths from heart disease increased in the post-war period.

Explanations for the rise, whether real or apparent, began to focus on diet. The explanation which was to emerge as dominant, was that dietary fat, and saturated fat in particular, was a central cause. This first emerged in the early 1950s through the work of Ancel Keys. Keys was a renowned epidemiologist who in 1952 offered the first instalment of the dietary explanation as to why heart disease was apparently increasing. He had led the seminal Minnesota studies on semi-starvation and it is from his work that much modern research into the nutritional basis of adult chronic disease stems.[14] Keys' explanation was to form the core of the scientific consensus concerning the nutritional causes of heart disease. In a paper published in *The Lancet* in 1952, Keys linked the age-related increase in the incidence of coronary heart disease in American males with increasing serum cholesterol levels. He compared his study to another undertaken in Italy, which found that serum cholesterol levels rose in Neapolitans until they were thirty but then levelled off. Keys reasoned that this was due to the low-fat diet consumed by the Neapolitans, and from this concluded that dietary fat was responsible for increases in total serum cholesterol.[15] Five years later Keys and two co-workers went into detail about what types of fat might produce relatively high serum cholesterol levels. They suggested that by substituting vegetable oils for common animal fats in high fat diets might reduce high serum cholesterol levels.[16] In 1952 Keys also began his seven countries study (Japan, Finland, Greece, Yugoslavia, Italy, USA, Netherlands) which took inspiration from the Framingham heart study began in 1948 in Boston, USA.[17]

Keys' research was influential in an emergent international consensus. During the 1960s, a number of western governments commissioned expert committees to investigate the causes of coronary heart disease. During the decade four important official or professional medical association expert committee reports were released; in 1961 (American), 1963 (Norwegian), 1965 (Swedish) and in 1968 a tripartite Scandinavian report.[18] Most advocated that individuals should lower their sugar and saturated fat intake and increase their polyunsaturated fat intake and it was a Scandinavian report which helped to trigger developments in the UK. The diet and heart disease thesis gained scientific credibility.

How did this emergent scientific fact filter into the arena of policy? Here the role of an expert committee was important. The UK's expert committee on food and health, the Standing Committee on Nutritional and Medical Problems, which had lain moribund for some years, was revived and renamed in 1957 because of the increased interest in diet and heart disease.[19] In its new form as the Committee on Medical and Nutritional Aspects of Food Policy (COMA), the Ministry of Health looked to this committee for advice on health matters relating to diet.[20] COMA was chaired by the CMO, and its official role was to advise the government on 'medical and scientific aspects of policy in relation to nutrition'. It consisted of individuals considered of 'standing' in the field of nutrition and science, together with representatives from government departments,[21] Notably, John Charles, Chief Medical Officer at the Ministry of Health, J. Barnes, the Director of the Toxicology Unit of the Medical Research Council and Norman Wright, the Chief Scientific Adviser to MAFF.[22]

In 1959 COMA was asked to investigate the fat content of milk in relation to coronary heart disease. In response, COMA appointed a panel to consider the role of milk fats and fats used in milk substitutes in the diet. COMA's response was part of a more general investigation it was beginning into the role of fats and fatty acids. The initial report of this panel showed an equivocal response to the fat heart disease thesis. At the very outset they reported that the dietary importance of milk fat should not be considered in isolation, but in the context of the fat content of the diet as a whole. The report stated, 'We have reviewed much evidence, published and unpublished, on the possible relationship of dietary fat to coronary disease. Some of it is conflicting and none of it conclusively proves that one is causally related to the other'.[23] Clearly the UK's expert committee remained to be convinced. There was concern within the health administration about the nature of the British diet, but there was an absence of conclusive evidence to compel decisive action.

## COMA and the diet and heart disease thesis: the 1974 report

In the 1960s COMA began to take a different stance. In 1965, it was reconstituted and the word 'Nutritional' dropped from its title. The Committee was now dealing with a wider range of issues including the toxicological, carcinogenic, and bacterial hazards of food consumption. As before, the Committee was chaired by the CMO, and consisted mainly of hospital, university, and government scientists.[24] At the January 1969 meeting, the agenda included, at the CMO's request, a discussion of a Scandinavian paper entitled 'Unsaturated fats in relation to heart disease'. While one member of the committee thought the document very sensible, another asserted that opinions among Scandinavian experts were really much less clear cut than the paper suggested. It was agreed that COMA could not endorse the paper without examining the problem further. Godber therefore suggested a panel should be appointed to investigate the matter, led by Professor Frank Young, an endocrinologist from the department of biochemistry at Cambridge University. The membership included Dr Reginald Passmore, a physiologist from Edinburgh University and author of the standard nutrition textbook in Britain,[25] and John Yudkin, professor of nutrition at Queen Elizabeth College, London.[26]

The COMA panel on diet and heart disease was established in 1970. Its terms of reference stated that it was to advise COMA on 'the significance of any relation between nutrition and cerebro-vascular and cardio-vascular disease, and on any indications for future action'.[27] Its first report, *Diet and Coronary Heart Disease,* released in 1974,[28] was not, however, the outcome of wholly unified scientific advice. Minutes of COMA meetings show that there was widespread disagreement on all but the most basic of issues. Young reported that the progress made by the panel was slow and it was difficult to reach any conclusions. In June 1973 he remarked that the draft report, which was the result of three years' work, could be described as the 'lowest common multiple (or highest common factor) of agreement which it was possible for the Panel to reach'.[29] This was because the subject 'was proving to be complex; research on the many aspects of the problem being continuous and relevant literature seemingly endless'.[30] Indeed in 1976 Frank Young remarked that only a bare majority of members of the panel subscribed to the Report's recommendation that people should lower the amount of fat, especially saturated fat, that they ate.[31] One scientist strongly disagreed. John Yudkin wrote a note of reservation which appeared in the published report. Yudkin claimed that his colleagues had 'exaggerated the possible role of dietary fat' in causing heart disease and had minimized the possible role of dietary sucrose.[32] Yudkin's view was that high sugar rather than high fat consumption was responsible for high rates of heart disease. In promoting this position, he displayed the flair for media advocacy of science which was to become characteristic of the public health field more generally in the 1980s and 1990s. His arguments appeared in the popular press over a long period, and received particularly widespread attention when he published a best selling book, *Pure, White and Deadly*, in 1972.[33]

While the COMA panel was deliberating, interest in diet and health was also developing elsewhere in government. In 1973, Sir Keith Joseph, Secretary of State for Social Services, set up a working party to look at the matter, because of the growing public confusion that was said to exist.[34] But the British government took little public health action to promote the findings of the 1974 COMA report. Ten years later, David Ennals, the Labour minister responsible for the Department of Health and Social Security (DHSS) between 1976 and 1979, was asked why. He replied:

> ... it was frankly impossible to get an agreed conclusion from the panel of the Committee on Medical Aspects of Food ... they simply did not agree. It was not through any lack of trying on behalf of successive Secretaries of State, and certainly no layman can say, 'This is what ought to be done: this is what the experts say' when the experts say different things.[35]

Clearly, the lack of consensus on the COMA panel had an effect. The main impact of its report seems to have been on advertising. Here it was used as a reference point. If a proposed advertisement made health claims, unsupported by the conclusions of the COMA report, then it was turned down.[36] But the lack of policy outcome of the 1974 COMA report also raises an additional question: what in the policy domain is enough evidence to constitute proof that can then be used as a spur to action? When we come to consider later events, it soon becomes clear that the answer is not fixed, but rather changes over time, and here too, the media have a role to play.

## Public health advocacy and the diet and heart disease consensus

The environment within which the diet and heart disease arguments and COMA were operating began to change in the 1970s. That decade saw the emergence of a new lifestyle risk-focused public health and the establishment of public health advocacy organisations to promote its case. In addition, new consumerist organisations were taking an interest in dietary issues. For example, in 1974 the pressure group 'Technology Assessment Consumerism Centre' attacked the nutritional value of the white loaf. John Burnett cites this attack as the beginning of a growing impetus for change in the UK diet.[37]

At the same time, British medical professionals began to argue for more emphasis to be put upon preventative measures that would reduce the rates of heart disease. Keith Ball, a physician at the Central Middlesex Hospital, argued in *The Lancet* in 1971 for such a preventative approach, and later became co-founder, in 1979, of the Coronary Prevention Group.[38] In 1976, the Royal College of Physicians published a report on diet and cardiovascular disease, which again recommended that people should lower their saturated fat intakes.[39] In the view of Phillip James, director of the Rowett Research Institute at Aberdeen, this report was important in encouraging further consensus and action.[40] In the same year, the DHSS released *Prevention and Health: Everybody's Business* (1976) and *Prevention and Health: Eating for Health* appeared two years later.[41] The first document, according to many commentators, symbolised a turning point towards more interventionist policies, increasingly focused upon changing lifestyles.[42] Similar events were occurring across the Atlantic Ocean. The McGovern Committee of the US Senate, chaired by Senator Edward McGovern, produced *Dietary Goals for the United States* in 1977, which called for large reductions in the consumption of meat and dairy products.[43] One former member of COMA cited this as a highly influential report, which provided further impetus to those pushing the case for dietary change in the UK.[44]

## NACNE 1983 and COMA 1984

As the shift towards 'health promotion' gathered pace, a new expert committee on diet and heart disease was convened. The National Advisory Committee on Nutrition Education (NACNE) was established in 1979 by the Health Education Council and the British Nutrition Foundation (BNF), a food industry-funded body. The NACNE report on diet and health appeared in 1983 and made extensive recommendations for dietary change.[45] The NACNE report drawn up by an *ad hoc* working group of NACNE (which included amongst others nutritionists such as Derek Miller and Jim Mann and the food campaigner Caroline Walker) was led by NACNE's Vice-Chairman, Professor Philip James. The NACNE report recommended that individuals reduce their average total fat intake by 10 per cent, their average saturated fatty acid intake by 15 per cent, and their intake of sugar, alcohol, and salt.[46] The DHSS greeted the report with hostility and told members of the committee that they had gone well beyond their original remit.[47] Cannon, in the *Sunday Times*, exposed the hostile reaction of the DHSS and the BNF to the report and how they proposed to join Philip James in re-drafting the report.[48] *The Lancet's* accusation that government ministers had obstructed the NACNE report and restricted its circulation received widespread media attention.[49]

The NACNE report stimulated reaction from not only the BNF but also the industry-funded Butter Information Council and food producing firms. Food manufacturers objected to the NACNE report for obvious commercial reasons, as one former COMA member pointed out, taking the recommendation on salt as an example:

> If your advice is a thirty odd per cent reduction in salt intake you can imagine a salt company would be a bit worried, wouldn't you? If all of a sudden I said ... I am going to go and reduce your salary by thirty per cent, you'd be worried wouldn't you?[50]

In response to NACNE, industry public relations and research organisations like the Butter Information Council publicised the work and views of those scientists who disagreed with the prevailing consensus of scientific advice.[51] The producers of the 'unhealthy' foods attempted to undermine the growing tide of advice, while the companies making the foods that were deemed healthier saw a market opportunity and took it. Unilever, the manufacturers of Flora margarine, set up the 'Flora Heart Project', aimed at making people more aware of 'healthy eating', and promoting the consumption of Flora margarine, a food high in polyunsaturated fatty acids.[52] Christina Hardyment captured the paradoxical situation nicely when she wrote, 'The food manufacturers hastened both to defend themselves and to supply new products that met all the new criteria of health'.[53]

In June 1980, a year after the foundation of NACNE, members of COMA agreed that it was advisable, and the time appropriate, to set up an expert panel to update the findings of the 1974 report, although it is unclear why. At a further meeting in December it was recorded that ministers had given approval to the proposal.[54] It appears from the evidence that it was the initiative of members of COMA that drove the setting up of the new panel. Philip James, vice-chairman of NACNE, has been reported, however, as asserting that the panel was established in order to allow the government a mechanism whereby it could distance itself from new policy statements, while it considered its own. James also claimed that the COMA panel felt under pressure to produce a report acceptable to the government.[55]

Whatever the process by which the 1984 COMA recommendations were arrived at, they were similar to those of the NACNE report. The main difference was that COMA had virtually nothing to say about alcohol consumption, and there was little on salt intake.[56] The absence of alcohol may have been connected with the parallel reports on alcohol from the Cabinet Office Central Policy Review Staff in 1982, *Alcohol Policies in the UK* and the Department of Health and Social Security's *Drinking Sensibly* in 1981.[57] According to one account, salt was neglected in the report because the panel could not agree on what level of intake they should recommend.[58] In addition, despite the similarities of the COMA and NACNE recommen-

dations, the COMA panel report concluded that the evidence against saturated fats fell short of proof. One member of the COMA panel, Professor J.
R. A. Mitchell of Nottingham University, strongly disagreed with the asser-
tion that there was a high probability of a causal link between saturated fatty
acid intake and the risk of coronary heart disease.[59] He felt that scientists were
damaging their reputation by asserting that diet was a significant cause of
heart disease without sufficient evidence.[60] One year before the publication of
the 1984 COMA report, a member of the panel, Professor Michael Oliver of
the Cardiovascular Research Unit of Edinburgh University, had also questioned the prevailing tide of opinion. He cast doubt on the view that whole
populations should be advised to change their diets in order to lessen rates of
heart disease.[61]

Other scientists, including former COMA member Reginald Passmore
were also sceptical about the claims of NACNE and COMA. Passmore
referred to many of those involved as the 'New Puritans' and stated that
much more 'hard scientific evidence' was needed before their claims should
be heard. Sceptical articles appeared in the popular 'conservative' press. One,
in *The Spectator* by the well-known social commentator Digby Anderson,
Director of the Social Affairs Unit, branded the recommendations of
NACNE and COMA as extreme and the views of 'food Leninists'.[62] Two
years later Le Fanu published *Eat your Heart Out*, which amounted to a
thoroughgoing critique of the diet-heart disease thesis.[63]

Compared with the situation in 1974, however, the report did lead to
limited action. For example there was the Health Education Council's 'Look
after your Heart Campaign', a national 'umbrella' initiative for many local
projects designed to increase the awareness of heart disease and how suscept-
ibility to it could be reduced. This campaign, piloted in 1984–5 as the
'Heartbeat Wales Campaign', was launched nationally in April 1987. Its
objective was to promote lifestyle changes in individuals – particularly
those from the lower social economic groups who were seen as being most
at risk from coronary heart disease.[64]

What led to this greater degree of policy acceptance? Clearly both specific
and more general changes in public health policy were involved. Specifically,
there was the role of key individual scientists. The chair of the COMA panel,
Philip Randle, professor of clinical biochemistry at Oxford University, was
subsequently chairman of an ongoing body concerned with the implementation of the 1984 COMA recommendations.[65] One former member of both
the 1974 and 1984 COMA panels recalled that: 'Randle was very determined
that it [the 1984 report] should have some national impact'. Other panel
members also wanted to see the report make an impact, and so did the main
COMA committee.[66] One member of the 1984 COMA panel referred to a
fellow panel member as 'fanatical' about the dietary fat-heart disease thesis.[67]
Clearly the individual scientific commitment to policy implementation was
greater during the period following the 1984 report.

A second issue was the role of the media. As other interviewees noted, the publicity the media had given to the unequivocal recommendations of the NACNE report 'made it easier' for the COMA report to gain acceptance.[68] BBC and Channel 4 programmes were made, which featured 1982–4 COMA panel members such as Geoffrey Rose, professor of epidemiology at the London School of Hygiene and Tropical Medicine, and Philip James. These programmes claimed that if the British public changed its dietary habits cardiovascular health would improve.[69] Although some members of the COMA panel condemned the 'exaggerated rhetoric and sensationalist symbolism' deployed, they clearly had an impact.[70] Just as the press had exposed the efforts to suppress the NACNE report, attempts to stifle a document produced by the Joint Advisory Committee on Nutrition Education (JACNE, in effect a restructured NACNE) were made public in 1985. The DHSS had commissioned JACNE to prepare a booklet for the public based upon the recommendations of the 1984 COMA report. The press, however, revealed that this report had been interfered with by the government, and quoted James saying, 'The government is attempting to impose censorship because of short-term political aims … It is outrageous that people will continue to die of heart attacks because of government interference'.[71] Thirdly, the report's implications fitted the new emphasis on health promotion in primary care. The 1984 report was also taken seriously by many general practitioners. One member of the 1984 panel commented: '… my wife was concerned with community medicine in Slough and a lot of the GPs around her seemed to take note of it and advise their patients on the basis of what was said in the report'.[72]

But, action on the NACNE and COMA reports during the 1980s may also be seen as an aspect of longer term-trends. Alan Beardsworth and Teresa Keil have remarked that, 'In the post-war period an increasing emphasis has been placed upon the individual's responsibility to protect his or her own health through adopting the eating patterns and dietary choices congruent with current scientific orthodoxies concerning the links between diet and health'.[73] The diet and heart disease consensus was also part of a wider public health consensus established in these years round the role of individual lifestyle and the need for population-based policy interventions.[74] Policy based on such an approach rather than attempts by government to regulate food consumption more directly, is also likely to be less threatening for the food industry, and may even create new opportunities. The 'current scientific orthodoxy' to which Beardsworth and Keil refer has been long in the making in connection with diet and heart disease. The general background to which they refer may, however, have been another important factor in encouraging scientific consensus, policy making and action during the 1980s.

The most recent COMA report on diet and heart disease, published in 1994, makes similar recommendations to those made in 1984.[75] However, this time there were no dissenters on the COMA panel, and this may be a reflection of the now greater scientific consensus that now exists on the diet-heart disease relationship. This is the view of Michael Oliver.[76] As a reflection of this, Oliver gave the example of the many voluntary action groups on diet and health that could not agree on exactly what advice should be given to the public in the 1980s. By 1998, the British Cardiac Society, British Hyperlipidaemia Association, British Hypertension Society, and British Diabetic Association, all subscribed to a common set of recommendations.[77] Michael Marmot chaired the 1994 COMA panel and bemoaned the hostile press coverage that the report received in the media. However, as we have seen, the press can help the scientist disseminate his message, as with the case of John Yudkin.[78]

## Conclusion

This inquiry into the science-policy interrelationship surrounding diet and heart disease began by counterposing two different positions on the subject. On the one hand, there were the arguments of Cannon, who was quite clear in his view that the overall consensus of expert committees pointed to the conclusion that fatty diets helped to cause heart disease. In this light, the policy response of the UK government had been sluggish. In contrast, Le Fanu was equally convinced that the epidemiology was fundamentally flawed. The British government's policy responses were therefore based on little more than fashion and were likely to be a waste of money, futile, and unnecessary.

Both positions assume the role of science as some type of absolute truth rather than the product of historical contingency. Cannon writes that '... thanks to the work of scientists beginning in the 1950s, new food and agricultural polices designed to improve public health can be based on a firm foundation: for on the issue of food and health, the experts agree'.[79] But this survey of post war events shows a far from linear picture of scientific progress. Little public health action was undertaken following the 1974 COMA report in contrast to the response to the 1984 report. The nature of these responses is not just a matter of 'delay' in responding to scientific 'truth' but rather a complex process in which the role of individuals, of the media and of changes more generally in public health policy and public culture have been inextricably involved.

## Acknowledgements

The authors thank the Wellcome Trust for funding the 'Science speaks to policy' programme at LSHTM of which this research is part. We thank David Smith for helpful comments and criticisms.

## References

1 M. Rayner, C. Mockford and A. Boaz, *Coronary Heart Disease Statistics*, London, British Heart Foundation, 1998, pp. 19–20.

2 G. Cannon, *The Politics of Food*, London, Century Hutchinson, 1987, pp. 324–5.

3 G. Cannon, *Food and Health: the experts agree: an analysis of one hundred authoritative scientific reports on food, nutrition and public health*, London, Consumers' Association, 1992.

4 G. Cannon, 'The new public health', *British Food Journal*, 1993, vol. 95, pp. 4–11, p. 5; British Medical Association, *Report of Committee on Nutrition*, London, BMA, 1933.

5 J. Le Fanu, *Eat your Heart Out: The Fallacy of the Healthy Diet*, London, Macmillan, 1987. See also idem, *The Rise and Fall of Modern Medicine*, London, Little, Brown, 1999, pp. 322–50.

6 A. Warde, *Consumption, Food and Taste: Culinary Antinomies and Commodity Culture*, London, Sage Publications, 1997, pp. 164–5.

7 D. Hollingsworth, 'Rationing and economic constraints on food consumption in Britain since the second world war', in D. Oddy and D. S. Miller (eds), *Diet and Health in Modern Britain*, London, Croom Helm, 1985; I. Zweiniger-Bargielowska, 'Bread rationing in Britain, July 1946–July 1948', *Twentieth Century British History*, 1993, vol. 4, pp. 57–85.

8 The figures for 1954 are provisional; *Report of the Ministry of Health for the Year ended 31 December 1954: Part II: on the State of the Public Health. Being the Annual Report of the Chief Medical Officer for the Year 1954*, London, HMSO, 1955, p. 128.

9 For a good set of statistical information on mortality from ischeamic heart disease refer to J. Charlton and M. Murphy (eds), *The Health of Adult Britain 1841–1994*: volume 2, decennial supplement, no. 13, London, HMSO, 1997, ch. 18.

10 Ministry of Health, *Annual Report of the Chief Medical Officer for 1953*, London, HMSO, 1954, p. 128.

11 Public Record Office (hereafter PRO) MH133/197, Letter to Secretary, Standing Medical Advisory Committee, from Horace Joules, 16 February 1955.

12 A. S. Truswell, 'The evolution of diets for western diseases', in D. Harriss-White and R. Hoffenberg (eds), *Food: Multidisciplinary Perspectives*, Oxford, Blackwell, 1994.

13 M. Bartley, "Coronary' heart disease – a disease of affluence or a disease of industry?', in P. Weindling (ed.), *The Social History of Occupational Health*, London, Croom Helm, 1985.

14 W. P. T. James, 'The evolution of nutrition research in Britain and other European countries', in K. K. Carroll (ed.), *Current Perspectives on Nutrition and Health*, London, McGill–Queen's University Press, 1998, pp. 10–11.

15 A. Keys, 'The trend of serum–cholesterol', *The Lancet*, 1952, vol. 2, pp. 209–11.

16 A. Keys, J. T. Anderson and F. Grande, 'Prediction of serum–cholesterol responses of man to changes in fats in the diet', *The Lancet*, 1957, vol. 2, pp. 959–65.

17 A. Keys, *Seven Countries: a Multivariate Analysis of Death and Coronary Heart Disease*, London, Harvard University Press, 1980; D. Kromhout, A. Menotti and H. Blackburn, (eds), *The Seven Countries Study: A Scientific Adventure in Cardiovascular Disease Epidemiology*, London, n.p., 1994.

18 Cannon, 1992, op. cit., pp. 22–7.

19 See Chapter 7.

20 PRO MH56/442, 'Mr Sinson', 30 September 1961.

21 Ministry of Health, *Annual Report of the Chief Medical Officer for 1957*, London, HMSO, 1958, p. 171.

22 PRO MAF260/1, 'Terms of reference and membership of the committee on the medical and nutritional aspects of food policy', n.d.

23 PRO MH56/489, 'Draft: report of the panel on milk fat with reference to the possible relationship between milk fat and coronary disease', December 1958.

24 PRO MAF282/97, 'Committee on medical and nutritional aspects of food policy: reconstruction of the committee under revised terms of reference', n.d., Mrs M. A. J. Pearson to Mr Hensley, 24 March 1965.

25 This textbook has passed through many editions since it was first published in 1959: S. Davidson, A. P. Meiklejohn and R. Passmore, *Human Nutrition and Dietetics*, Edinburgh, Livingstone, 1959.

26 National Cataloguing Unit for the Archives of Contemporary Scientists, University of Bath (hereafter NCUACS), Frank Young papers, file 'Current appointments to COMA and minutes', COMA Minutes, 10 December 1969.

27 DHSS, *Annual Report of the Chief Medical for 1970*, London, HMSO, 1971, p. 115.

28 DHSS, *Diet and Coronary Heart Disease*, London, HMSO, 1974.

29 NCUACS, Young papers, file 'Current appointments to COMA and minutes', COMA Minutes, 8 June 1973.

30 Ibid. COMA Minutes, 9 December 1971.

31 Ibid. 'Comments by F. G. Young on "Prevention of Coronary Heart Disease"', 26 May 1976, p. 2.

32 DHSS, 1974, op. cit., p. 35.

33 O. Franklin, 'The Prof. fills me with doubt... ABOUT DIET', *Daily Mail*, 5 May 1958; H. McLeave, 'Why a sweet tooth is under suspicion', *Daily Mail*, 10 January 1967; J. Yudkin, *Pure, White and Deadly*, Harmondsworth, Penguin, rev. and exp. ed., 1988; J. Yudkin, 'Why suspicion falls on sugar as a major cause of heart disease', *The Times*, 11 July 1974. For a biographical overview of Yudkin see D.F. Smith, 'Nutrition in Britain in the Twentieth Century', unpublished PhD thesis, University of Edinburgh, 1986, ch. 5.

34 C. Walker and G. Cannon, *The Food Scandal: What's wrong with the British Diet and how to put it right*, London, Century, 1984, pp. viii–xvii; C. Leverkus, I. Cole-Hamilton, K. Gunner, J. Starr, with A. Stanway, *The Great British Diet: Dieticians and their families test a recipe for healthy eating*, London, Century, 1985, pp. 7–11.

35 Lord Ennals, 'Heart disease', *Parliamentary Debates* (Lords) 5 series, vol. CDLV, 13 vol. of session 1983–4, 23 July–19 October 1984, vol. 455. col. 381, 25 July 1984.

36 Interview, 25 June 1999. As with all subsequent interviews referred to in these footnotes, MB conducted the interview and the interviewee was a scientist and a former member of COMA or a COMA panel. The interviews were conducted on the basis that quotations would be cited anonymously.

37 J. Burnett, *Plenty and Want: A Social History of Food in England from 1815 to the Present Day* (3rd ed.), London, Routledge, 1989, p. 326; also see T. Lang, 'Going public: food campaigns during the 1980s and early 1990s', in D.F. Smith, (ed.), *Nutrition in Britain: Science, Scientists and Politics in the Twentieth Century*, London, Routledge, 1997 for an overview of pressure group developments.

38 R. Turner and K. Ball, 'Prevention of coronary heart disease: a counterblast to present inactivity', *The Lancet*, 1973, vol. 2, pp. 1137–40.

39 Joint Working Party of the Royal College of Physicians of London and the British Cardiac Society, *Prevention of Coronary Heart Disease*, London, RCPL, 1976.

40 Philip James commenting upon an earlier spoken version of this chapter, 10 April 1999.

41 DHSS, *Prevention and Health: Everybody's business: a reassessment of public and personal health*, London, HMSO, 1976; DHSS, *Prevention and Health: Eating for health*, London, HMSO, 1978.

42 V. Berridge, *Health and Society in Britain since 1939*, Cambridge, Cambridge University Press, 1999, p. 88; C. Webster, *The National Health Service: A political history*, Oxford, Oxford University Press, 1998, pp.137–8.

43 Select Committee on Nutrition and Human Needs, *Dietary Goals for the United States*, Washington, USA Government Printing Office, 1977; see also Burnett, op. cit., pp. 326–7.

44 Interview, 17 March 1999.

45 W. P. T. James, *A discussion paper on proposals for national guidelines for health education in Britain, prepared for the NACNE by an ad hoc working party under the chairmanship of Professor Philip James*, London, Health Education Council, 1983.

46 Ibid. pp. 33–5.

47 M. Mills, 'Expert policy advice to the British government on diet and heart disease', in B. G. Peters and A. Barker (eds), *The Politics of Expert Advice: Creating, using and manipulating scientific knowledge for public policy*, Edinburgh, Edinburgh University Press, 1993; M.

Mills, 'The case of food and health and the use of network analysis', in D. Marsh and R. W. A. Rhodes (eds), *Policy Networks in British Government*, Oxford, Clarendon, 1992, p.156.

48 G. Cannon, 'Battle for the British diet', *Sunday Times*, 8 July 1983.

49 'Britain needs a food and health policy: the government must face its duty' (Editorial), *The Lancet*, 1986, vol. 2, pp. 434–6; T. Prentice, 'Ministers accused of failing in fight against bad-diet deaths', *The Times*, 25 August 1986.

50 Interview, 17 March 1999.

51 In the early 1980s the Butter Information Council began to publish the series *Fats & Health* which became *Diet & Health* in 1983. These publications contained many commentaries questioning the prevailing tide of opinion.

52 Le Fanu, 1987, op. cit., pp. 144–7.

53 C. Hardyment, *Slice of Life: The British way of eating since 1945*, London, BBC Books, 1995, p. 173.

54 NCUACS, Young papers, file 'COMA 5.12.80', COMA Minutes, 6 June 1980; file 'Appointments to COMA and Minutes', COMA Minutes, 5 December 1980.

55 Mills, 1992, op. cit., pp. 148–66.

56 DHSS, *Diet and Cardiovascular Disease: Committee on Medical Aspects of Food Policy: report of the panel on Diet in Relation to Cardiovascular Disease*, London, HMSO, 1984.

57 B. Thom, *Dealing with Drink, Alcohol and Social Policy: From Treatment to Management*, London, Free Association Books, 1999.

58 Interview, 16 June 1999.

59 DHSS, 1984, op. cit., p. 22; Interviews, 7, 16, 25 June 1999.

60 J. R. Mitchell, 'What constitutes evidence in the dietary prevention of coronary heart disease – cosy beliefs or harsh facts?', *International Journal of Cardiology*, March 1984, vol. 3, pp. 287–98.

61 M. Oliver, 'Should we not forget about mass control of coronary risk factors?', *The Lancet*, 1983, vol. 2, p. 37.

62 D. Anderson, 'The men who march on our stomachs', *The Spectator*, 17 August 1985, pp. 8–9.

63 Le Fanu, 1987, op. cit.

64 Department of Health, *Annual Report of the Chief Medical Officer for 1988*, London, HMSO, 1989, pp. 43, 49–53, 64. Interviews, 16, 25 June 1999.

65 Interview, 10 June 1999. This ongoing review was carried out through a small panel which monitored developments in scientific research. See P. Randle, 'Beyond COMA 1984', in R. Cottrell (ed.), *Food and Health: Now and the Future*, Carnforth, Parthenon, 1987, p. 14.

66 Interview, 25 June 1999.

67 Interview, 16 June 1999.

68 Interviews, 17 March, 25 June 1999.

69 Le Fanu, 1987, op. cit., pp. 19, 170 endnote 16.

70 Interview, 7 June 1999.

71 O. Gillie, 'Guide to healthy eating blocked', *Sunday Times*, 4 August 1985.

72 Interview, 16 June 1999.

73 A. Beardsworth and T. Keil, *Sociology on the Menu: An Invitation to the Study of Food and Society*, London, Routledge, 1997, p. 135.

74 G. Rose, 'Strategies of prevention: the individual and the population', in M. Marmot and P. Elliott (eds), *Coronary Heart Disease Epidemiology: From Aetiology to Public Health*, New York, Oxford University Press, 1992; G. Rose, *The Strategy of Preventive Medicine*, New York, Oxford University Press, 1992, pp. 23–4, 36–8, 39–41, 49–50, 77–8, 112–113.

75 Department of Health, *Nutritional Aspects of Cardiovascular Disease: Report of the cardio-vascular review group: Committee on Medical Aspects of Food Policy*, London, HMSO, 1994.

76 In the mid-1980s Oliver explicitly questioned the idea that there was a consensus on the

issues. M. Oliver, 'Consensus or non-sensus conference on coronary heart disease', *The Lancet*, 1985, vol. 1, p. 1087. Interview, 7 June 1999.

77 D. Wood, 'Joint British recommendations on prevention of coronary heart disease in clinical practice', *Heart*, 1998, vol. 80, supplement 2, pp. S1–S29.

78 M. G. Marmot, 'Diet and disease, and Durkheim and Dasgupta, and Deuteronomy', *Epidemiology*, 1988, vol. 9, pp. 676–80.

79 Cannon, 1992, op. cit., p. 193.

# 14 Recent experiences in food poisoning: science and policy, science and the media

*T. Hugh Pennington*

There is little doubt that concern in the UK about the relationship between science and food policy has never been greater than at the present time. Questions about the handling of this interface in the cases of BSE, recurrent food scares following food poisoning outbreaks, and genetically modified foods, have played and are playing major roles in driving this interest. As a contribution to this debate, I present descriptions and analyses of two areas of interaction between science and policy. In one area, concerning the work of expert advisory committees, the relationship is relatively direct. In the other, covering the role of science in the media, the connection with policy is more indirect. These analyses focus on the microbiological safety of food and are mostly based on personal experience. The section on expert committees comments primarily on the working of the Pennington Group enquiry into the 1996 central Scotland *E. coli* O157 outbreak. It should be read in conjunction with the Group's final report.[1] Both sections draw occasionally on the enormously rich resource that the BSE inquiry has provided.[2]

## Expert advisory committees

A summary of the UK Government's advisory structure for the microbial safety of food appears in a memorandum submitted to the House of Commons Agriculture Committee in November 1997. This was prepared by the Ministry of Agriculture, Fisheries and Food (MAFF), the Department of Health of England and Wales, and the Scottish, Welsh and Northern Ireland Offices, as part of their response to the committee's enquiry into food safety. Under the heading 'The Role of Expert Advisory Committees', the memorandum states:

> In order to assist it in policy development, the Government seeks the advice of independent expert committees. In 1989 the previous Government established the Richmond Committee to advise on matters related to the microbiological safety of food. One of its recommendations was to establish a committee which could provide advice in this area on a continuous basis. Consequently, the Advisory Committee on the Microbiological Safety of Food (ACMSF) was established in

ACSMF option was eschewed. The location of the Group in Scotland turned out to be important, as a second *E. coli* O157 outbreak occurred while it was sitting and the Secretary of State sought advice during one of the meetings. There are other factors that have to be considered as possible reasons favouring the establishment of a Scottish group, apart from the desire of the Scottish Office to retain control of a problem in its patch. These include residual tensions between the Scottish Office and MAFF stemming from a vigorous debate in 1995. This concerned the closure of the MAFF-funded Food Science Laboratory at Torry in Aberdeen, a proposal driven by MAFF's wish to centralise such research at a new laboratory near York. Furthermore, the presence of a new Scottish Chief Medical Officer, whose background was as an academic surgeon, may have played a part. He had only taken up his post six weeks previously and so the outbreak forced him to ascend a very steep learning curve while simultaneously – in his own words – 'undergoing a baptism of fire'. The establishment of the Group was not, neither did it become, a party political issue.

The only regular attendees from outside Scotland at the meetings of the Group were observers from MAFF and the Department of Health for England and Wales (DH). They were invited only after a debate at the Group's second meeting. It was felt that although the Group was large enough and had sufficient experience and expertise, the benefit in facilitating liaison might help to fast-track consideration of issues 'of common interest or debate'. The Group took written and oral evidence from a wide range of interested parties. The earliest meetings focused on the outbreak itself. The Group met Mr Barr, the butcher at the centre of the outbreak, visited his premises, and interviewed the outbreak control teams. At this time it also considered papers from members on the microbiology of *E. coli* O157 and public health issues raised by the outbreak. It met with senior Scottish environmental health officers, experts from Veterinary Laboratory Agency, and senior staff from the Meat Hygiene Service and the Meat and Livestock Commission. The Group heard about previous *E. coli* O157 outbreaks from the outbreak control teams that had investigated them. It even reviewed the recommendations of the enquiry into the 1964 Aberdeen typhoid outbreak.[6]

The experience and backgrounds of its members were, of course, very influential in shaping the Group's deliberations. Also influential were the circumstances of its establishment. These compounded to give the Group the expectation – which was realised – that a window of opportunity had arisen to drive forward food safety policies that would have a good chance of acceptance by the Government. It was hoped it would be possible to introduce policies that had been proposed before but rejected because of objections from interested parties. Similarly, there was a chance to introduce policies which clashed with the deregulatory ethos that had dominated the Government's thinking for more than a decade. An iterative process, mediated by Scottish Office officials observing and participating in the Group's work, meant the Group could be reasonably confident in receiving

*Figure 14.2* Cartoon by G. High (with permission). Published in *The Scotsman*, January 1997.

political support for its recommendations. Strong public and media interest, and the Group's high expectations of firm action were important in influencing it to consider radical recommendations (Figure 14.2).

Counter to the radical intentions of the Group, however, was the influence of the MAFF and DH observers, and ACMSF. Group members met with the latter body twice, which had set up its own subcommittee to re-investigate *E. coli* O157. In general, the position taken by ACMSF and the London observers was that existing arrangements would probably suffice, if properly implemented, to contain *E. coli* O157. The first meeting that the observers from London attended was after the Group's interim report had been published in mid-January 1997. They made it clear from the start that licensing of butchers, recommended in the interim report, had not been favoured by Ministers when the Food Safety Act had been going through Parliament in 1990. After 'a spirited debate', the Group held its ground because of the need for urgent enforceable action. The DH observer urged that the problem of unsafe butchers could be solved through industry guides – documents endorsed by Government ministers but carrying no legal sanction. The Group rejected this view.

The atmosphere at the meetings with ACMSF was frosty. The Group did not accept ACMSF's recommendations, in its 1995 report on *E. coli* O157, that the avoidance of cross-contamination from raw meat to ready-to-eat products could be achieved by separation in time and space. Resolution of these disputes was important because the Group's recommendations were intended to have force across the UK. They would also influence the inter-are to be done and *how much* effort or money is to be spent on them. But these are the controlling decisions, the decisions that must be made in the upper levels of the hierarchy if a government is to have any unity of purpose and action. This necessity, too, leads the higher officials to deal with the less scientific aspects of their major problems.[11]

## Science and the media

My last job as chair of the Pennington Group was to appear at a press conference on 8 April 1997 with the Secretary of State to describe the main points of the final Report and field questions. The large numbers of media personnel present, including science and environment correspondents from the national TV news services (BBC, Independent Television and Channel 4 News), their Scottish equivalents, and radio reporters, indicated the high degree of interest. It is a reasonable assumption that this level of media activity reflected in large part the long-established strength of food safety stories for the media. Jacquie Reilly and David Miller have pointed out that it is accepted that the role of the media as a communicator about risk has important effects on industry, government, pressure groups, and many other organisations. They have gone so far as to claim that that the Food Safety Act 1990 was probably born partly out of media coverage of *Salmonella* and *Listeria*.[12]

I have described in detail elsewhere the levels of media activity during the Pennington Group's existence, using the number of telephone enquiries from media organisations to my office as a measure.[13] In summary, calls between 28 November 1996 and 8 April 1997 numbered 477. On nine occasions, they peaked at ten or more per day. The first peak reflected media activity on the day of the announcement of the expert group. One peak coincided with the meeting at the Scottish Office at which the composition of the group was decided and five occurred on the day before meetings of the group. Media pressure was particularly sustained just before and on the day of the meeting at which the Report was finalised. The largest peak, thirty-six enquiries on 6 March 1997, was linked to the leaking of the first draft of the Swann report, a review by the Meat Hygiene Service of abattoir hygiene practice conducted in 1995. Highly critical of aspects of abattoir practice, the report underwent significant drafting changes and was eventually put into the public domain in a low-key way in June 1996.[14] Much of the press coverage on and following 6 March focused on the actions of the Meat Hygiene Service, Government departments, and Ministers. My input started with a call from the 'Today' programme at about 7.20 am as to whether I knew about the report, in any of its versions. My comment that 'I hadn't been shown any of them, and that I was not pleased', became part of the story.

The high profile resulting from these activities has resulted in a continued high level of enquiries to my office from many sources. In 1998, we logged

*Table 14.1* Number of telephone enquiries from media outlets to the author's office logged in 1998

| | |
|---|---|
| January | 81 |
| February | 18 |
| March | 19 |
| April | 41 |
| May | 15 |
| June | 5 |
| July | 13 |
| August | 31 |
| September | 10 |
| October | 13 |
| November | 34 |
| December | 5 |

283 enquiries and their distribution throughout the year is shown in Table 14.1. Some months were much busier than others but no single 'food scare' accounted for this unevenness. In fact, 1998 was a relatively quiet year in the UK for outbreaks of food poisoning caused by microbes, with no major incidents. With the exception of *Campylobacter*, a general decline in the number of human infections was reported.[15]

Above average numbers of enquiries were made in January, April, August, and November. In all four months, the single largest reason was the publication of a document with important policy implications, or an announcement of Government plans. In January, the Food Standards Agency white paper was published while in April the report of the Agriculture Committee's enquiry into food safety appeared. August coincided with the Sheriff's determination into the fatal accident enquiry into the 1996 Central Scotland *E. coli* O157 outbreak, while November was the month of delivery of the Queen's Speech. Other questions were also important in January. Comments were asked for on issues involving contaminated meat, the disposal of slurries and abattoir waste, abattoir league tables, green top (unpasteurised) milk, and *E. coli* O157. Several outlets, including *La Aciona* in Argentina, made enquiries about the possibility that *E. coli* O157 had originated in that country. This illustrates two common features in the evolution of media stories: an incubation period, and a subsequent period of growth when different media outlets infect and feed on each other.[16] The story started on 15 December 1997 when I gave a presentation to the Parliamentary and Scientific Committee. A *New Scientist* reporter heard me say the haemolytic uraemic syndrome, a well-known complication of infection with *E. coli* O157, had been a common cause of renal failure in Argentinean children for many years. This raises the question of whether *E. coli* O157 could also have been present in Argentina before its appearance in North America and Europe. An article about this in *New Scientist* engendered media enquiries about the matter in the second and third weeks in January.

The largest group of enquiries was twenty on 23 and 24 November. These concerned the omission of any reference to the proposed Food Standards Agency (FSA)[17] in the Queen's speech, which set out the government's legislative programme for the coming parliamentary session. My well-known enthusiasm for the FSA proposal probably accounts for the media interest. Critical comment was expected – a correct prediction. Most of these enquiries resulted in immediate outcomes such as interviews on electronic media or press comments. One enquiry with a more delayed effect was a call from the BBC's 'Panorama' team at the end of November, about their intention to make a programme about food poisoning. They had been considering this for some time, and were stimulated to press ahead by the omission in the Queen's speech. Filming took place in early January and the programme was transmitted at the beginning of February. Private comments I heard at this time by senior officials in the MAFF/DH Joint Food Standards and Safety Group indicated that it was watched intently by policy makers. An even longer incubation period attended the making of a similar programme on food poisoning by the BBC's 'Frontline Scotland'. This focused on chickens and was filmed and shown in December. The stimulus was the tenth anniversary of Mrs Edwina Currie's announcement 'that sadly most of British egg production is contaminated by *Salmonella*' and her subsequent resignation as Under-Secretary for Health on 16 December 1988.

All these events demonstrate not only a sustained interest by the media in food safety but the wide range of issues that act as triggers. It is probable that the media's knowledge of public attitudes and concerns plays an important role in its persistent and strong interest in the topic. Health stories in general have good viewing figures. The calculated viewing figure for the 'Panorama' programme referred to was 4.5 million, with a 23 per cent share of the audience, slightly greater than the 4.1 million achieved by one on meningitis a few weeks later. The highest viewing figure for 'Panorama' recorded so has been 4.6 million.[18]

The wide range of food safety issues which the media pursue and its propensity to feed on itself is, not surprisingly, paralleled by a large number of media outlets chasing stories. In 1998, twenty-nine different television and radio news organisations rang my office, consisting of five different Scottish BBC desks, six UK network BBC desks, eight local BBC stations, and eight commercial outlets. BBC 'producer choice' and its internal market have induced many of its news gatherers to compete for strong stories as well as duplicating them. Media news outlets were nearly always seeking live comment from me as an expert on an issue or a breaking story. Interviews were usually short. Newspaper enquiries took a different form, with the majority of reporters seeking help with writing their stories. Although attributed quotes would appear in these, newspaper interviews were always much longer, often taking the form of in-depth briefings. Most of these reporters were generalists, but a few specialists in farming and in health from BBC radio and TV and from Sunday broadsheets kept in touch regularly. A third kind of media involvement was in set-piece pre-recorded programmes. During 1998 these included 'Panorama', 'World in Action', 'Countryfile', 'Landward' (a Scottish rural affairs and farming programme), 'Frontline Scotland', and 'Food and Drink'. Participating in these was always preceded by in-depth discussion with programme makers, who always had a well-formed notion of the issues that they wished to address. Finally, a good deal of media coverage came from being a participant in public events covered by the media.

It is well known that certain 'fright factors' powerfully influence topic choice by the media when covering health risk stories. Such factors for *E. coli* O157 include its *involuntary* acquisition, for example by consuming seemingly safe but microscopically contaminated ready-to-eat cold meats. Others are its *inequitable* distribution (five times commoner in Scotland than England), and its ability to cause *irreversible* damage to kidneys and brain, particularly in *small children*, and *painful death*.[19] As Jeremy Bray, MP commented, 'As the families of too many of my constituents have discovered, dying from *E. coli* is a horrible way to die'.[20] As factors determining media interest, these are almost certainly sufficient to explain the long-term concern. However, hardly any of them seemed to play a role in determining the major fluctuations in the number of enquiries. Rather, these related mostly to political events. Other well-known media triggers map on to these circumstances. The alleged concealment of the Swann Report by the Meat Hygiene Service, Ministry of Agriculture and the Scottish Secretary provides questions of *blame, cover ups, human interest, links with high profile personalities* and *evidence of conflict.*

The analysis presented here is very incomplete. It has hardly considered media outputs, for example. It suffers from the defect that a participant in events might be deemed to lack objectivity. There is even the potential problem that by reporting on the activities of the media one might perturb relations with it – a variant of the 'media uncertainty principle' of Barbara Jasny and her colleagues.[21] Nevertheless, I believe that a personal account can provide useful information about how the media works. There is abundant evidence that policy-makers not only pay serious attention to what the media says, but are influenced in their decisions and the position they take by media action.[22] I believe that media coverage has played an important role in keeping two issues in which I have been involved before the public – the licensing of butchers and the establishment of the Food Standards Agency. The publicity has favoured the chances of implementation of these proposals. This is in accord with Dorothy Nelkin's view that 'by their selection of newsworthy events, journalists define pressing issues. By their focus on controversial problems, they stimulate demands for accountability, forcing policy makers to justify themselves to a larger public'.[23]

## Conclusion

The case analysed here has been presented as an illustration of the way science interacts with policy makers and opinion formers in Britain. However, the Pennington Group was set up by and reported directly to a cabinet minister. Inquiries of this type are rare. Instead, ever since the British government began to apply expert knowledge to policy-making in public health it has primarily used central and local 'in-house' systems. Under John Simon in the 1860s, for example, the Privy Council Medical Department hired young physicians as temporary civil servants to conduct investigations and report on outbreaks of disease, vaccination, and other issues.[24] Their work was published in Simon's annual reports, an important aim being to shame local authorities into action. The role of local government remains and in food safety it still plays a major role as inspector and enforcer. What then induces central government to intervene? What features of public health disasters cause governments to seek advice from outside experts - advice additional to that which is routinely available? How does the government go about seeking such advice, and what are its aims?

Analysis of incidents that have caused governments to set up expert groups in the twentieth century shows that a large number of deaths is not a consistent feature. For some, such as the Aberdeen typhoid outbreak, mortality was negligible.[25] Neither was size always decisive. A Committee of Inquiry into the smallpox outbreak in London in 1973 was set up after four cases, two of which were fatal.[26] Clearly, other factors are significant. Particularly important are the nature of the incident itself – the circumstances, victims, and identity of the causative agent – and the political background. The 1973 smallpox incident is illustrative. The virus infected a worker in a laboratory in central London. When in hospital her infection was transmitted to the son and daughter-in-law of the patient in the next bed, possibly *via* a newspaper. Both died. The diagnoses were made very late, so a deadly virus much feared by the public had escaped unnoticed, had not then been adequately contained, and killed two bystanders. This happened when the World Health Organisation eradication campaign was rapidly achieving its targets in the few countries left with endemic smallpox. The WHO declared London a smallpox-infected area – a major political embarrassment.

Jim Phillips and Mike French have also shown, in their study of the pure beer campaign around the beginning of the twentieth century, the importance of the political setting when considering the central government response to a public health incident.[27] For years, farmers had been agitating for tighter control of beer ingredients and much parliamentary time was taken up with the issue. Bills were introduced after an epidemic of arsenic poisoning from contaminated brewing sugar that killed at least 70 beer drinkers. The government responded by appointing a Royal Commission, chaired by Lord Kelvin, to study beer components and arsenic in food. This brought in outside experts and 'wise men', partly de-politicising the issues.

The priority given by central government at the end of the twentieth century to food safety is well illustrated by the response of Prime Minister Margaret Thatcher, to a recommendation by the Health Minister, Kenneth Clarke. On 30 January 1989, Clarke proposed the establishment of an inquiry into the microbiological safety of food. Thatcher immediately set up a Cabinet Ministerial Group on Food Safety, and the first meeting was chaired by her on 7 February 1989. It discussed a possible inquiry 'and also salmonella in eggs, a problem of enormous public importance at that time' (Edwina Currie had resigned over this issue less than two months before). The Group decided to establish the Committee on the Microbiological Safety of Food, chaired by Sir Mark Richmond, with the following remit:

> ... to advise the Secretary of State for Health, the Minister of Agriculture, and the Secretaries of State for Wales, Scotland and Northern Ireland, on matters remitted to it by Ministers relating to the microbiological safety of food and on such other matters as it considers needs investigation.[28]

Much of the Ministerial Group's subsequent business was concerned with the preparation of a Food Safety Bill which became law as the Food Safety Act in 1990, a major reform.

How does the Government seek external expert advice? The taxonomy of the bodies it sets up is complex. For BSE and CJD the titles of expert groups include the 'Working Party' on BSE (Southwood), the 'Consultative Committee' on Research, the 'Expert Group' on Animal Feedingstuffs, the Medical Research Council 'Co-ordinating Committee' on Research on the Spongiform Encephalopathies in Man, the 'Advisory Committee' on Dangerous Pathogens, and the 'Committee' on the Safety of Medicines. Some of these are statutory, some were *ad hoc*. We have also seen that governments have responded to public health disasters by setting up Royal Commissions (for arsenic in beer), Committees of Inquiry (for smallpox under the 1946 NHS Act), and Departmental Committees of Enquiry (for the Aberdeen typhoid outbreak under the Public Health (Scotland) Act 1897 and the 1936 Public Health Act). The most important members of these groups are their chairpersons. Chairs like Kelvin, Richmond and Southwood, fall into the category of the 'great and good' as well as being senior members of the scientific establishment. Southwood's expertise in BSE, for example, counted less than more generic attributes such as scientific reputation, 'breadth of vision, and skills as Chairman'.[29]

What is the relationship between government and its external expert advisors? They interact in at least three ways.[30] The expert can be 'on tap but not on top' with advice being used at the discretion of a civil servant or minister. On the other hand, people and organisations outside government may use advisory committees to influence policy: the notion that committees can be captured by vested interests is pervasive in the food safety field.[31] Lastly, those inside government may use experts for support as well as, or even instead of, sources of information. Dominique Pestre has put it nicely: 'Since science is a discourse that claims not to depend on partisan decisions, it enables one to 'technicalize' public action, or to 'de-politicize' it, to render it impersonal, to bypass the democratic rules of accountability ... it gives to political decision the force of necessity'.[32]

The setting up of a post-disaster inquiry is a political act: it demonstrates something is being done. Disasters have been defined as 'unmanaged phenomena ... the unexpected, the unprecedented ... "unscheduled events" '.[33] They do not fit at all into the normal pattern of work of the civil service, described by Don K. Price as:

> ... a profoundly conservative force – not in the sense of being opposed to left-wing economics, but in the sense of looking on the government and its program as a single coherent machine in which inconsistencies cannot be permitted. Any novel idea is an inconsistency that could cause temporary waste and disorder and inefficiency and would probably detract from the current program.[34]

An expert inquiry provides a way of bridging this difficulty of coping with the unplanned, at worst by giving policy makers a breathing space, and at best by giving high quality technical advice at speed.

The Pennington Group was typical in that it had a number of these properties. Food safety had been a major political issue for a long time. BSE and its link to CJD had caused a crisis earlier in 1996. *E. coli* O157 was becoming well known to the public as a killer 'virus', analogous in some ways to smallpox in its lethality. Something needed to be done and needed to be seen to be done, and it was clearly convenient to call on science to de-politicise an issue close to a general election. The Group provided an opportunity for individuals both inside and outside government to pursue a reforming agenda and provided experts 'on tap' during a crisis. The establishment of the Group before the outbreak peaked provided a breathing space for officials and ministers by 'technicalising' action: the 'wait for Pennington' line could be taken.

The media played a very important role, and this is nothing new. Simon's biographer commented that from 1849, his 'alliance with *The Times* ... was something of enormous consequence for (his) career'. *The Times* had a circulation treble that of the other London dailies put together and the alliance 'gave the sanitary cause a peculiar potency'.[35] More recently, the use of the media during the 1964 Aberdeen typhoid outbreak was held by the Committee of Enquiry to have exaggerated 'the outbreak and the possible dangers of its spread ... to such an extent that the incident received publicity out of all proportion to its significance'.[36]

The media also play a crucial role in publicising disagreements between scientists. Such publicity damages science's image as standing above partisan decisions and its claim to be a privileged source of information. This, in turn, makes it difficult for policy makers to de-politicise their problems by falling back on experts. The British government's problem with genetically modified foods is a good example. The enormous impact of a few words on television by Aberdeen scientist Dr Arpad Puzstai about the effect of feeding potatoes to rats confirms the massive influence of the media. It demonstrated that for this issue at least, despite the efforts of the scientific establishment through the Royal Society, opinion formers no longer accept that the scientists' recommendations carry any more weight than those of pressure groups, ethicists or journalists.[37] All this means that for historians of food, science, policy and regulation, the richness, number and importance of research topics will increase and multiply as they enter the new millennium!

# References

1 The Pennington Group, *Report on the circumstances leading to the 1996 Outbreak of Infection with E. coli O157 in Central Scotland*, Edinburgh, Stationery Office, 1997.
2 The BSE Inquiry homepage. Online. Available HTTP: http://www.bse.org.uk/ (24 March 2000).
3 Agriculture Committee (House of Commons Session 1997–8), *Fourth Report, Food Safety*, vol. 2, London, Stationery Office, 1998, paras 4.20, 4.23.
4 T. R. Southwood, BSE Inquiry/Statement No. 1. Online. Available HTTP: http://www.bse.org.uk/witness/htm/stat001.htm (24 March 2000).
5 Advisory Committee on the Microbial Safety of Food, *Report on Verocytotoxin-producing Escherichia coli*, London, HMSO, 1995.
6 Scottish Home and Health Department, *The Aberdeen Typhoid Outbreak 1964*, Edinburgh, HMSO, 1964.
7 Ministry of Agriculture, Fisheries and Food, 'Review of MAFF funded bacteria foodborne zoonoses and meat hygiene research', *Report of a meeting in London, 25–26 June 1997*, London, Stationery Office, 1997.
8 Pennington Group, op. cit., p. 39.
9 Agricultural Committee, op. cit., Memorandum C101, Annex 2, pp. 411–13.
10 Pennington Group, op. cit., pp. 12–14.
11 D. K. Price, *Government and Science*, New York, Oxford University Press, 1962, p. 166.
12 J. Reilly and D. Miller, 'Scaremonger or scapegoat? The role of the media in the emergence of food as a social issue', in P. Caplan (ed.), *Food, Identity and Health*, London, Routledge, 1997, pp. 234–50.
13 T. H. Pennington, 'The media and trust: *E. coli* and other cases', in P. Bennett and K. C. Calman (eds), *Risk Communication and Public Health*, Oxford, Oxford University Press, 1999, pp. 81–94.
14 W. J. Swann, BSE Inquiry/Statement No. 158. Online. Available HTTP: http://www.bse.org.uk/witness/htm/stat158.htm (24 March 2000).
15 'Where have all the gastrointestinal infections gone?' (Editorial), *Eurosurveillance Weekly*, 1999, vol. 4, pp. 1–2.
16 T. H. Pennington, 'Necrotizing fasciitis: quantitative characteristics of the 1994 British media outbreak', *Journal of Infection*, 1995, vol. 30, pp. 63–5.
17 Ministry of Agriculture, Fisheries and Food, *The Food Standards Agency. A Force for Change*, London, Stationery Office, 1998.
18 BBC, personal communication.
19 P. Bennett, 'Understanding responses to risk: some basic findings', in Bennett and Calman, op. cit., pp. 3–19.
20 J. Bray, '*E. coli* (Pennington Report)', *Parliamentary Debates (Commons)*, 1996–7, vol. 288, col. 330, 15 January 1997.
21 B. Jasny, R. B. Hanson and F. E. Bloom, 'A media uncertainty principle', *Science*, 1999, vol. 283, p. 1453.

22 See, for example, D. Acheson, 'BSE Inquiry Statement No. 251', paras 80–92. Online. Available HTTP: http://www.bse.org.uk/witness/htm/stat251.htm (24 March 2000).

23 D. Nelkin, *Selling Science*, New York, Freeman, 1995, p. 73.

24 R. Lambert, *Sir John Simon 1816–1904 and English Social Administration*, London, Macgibbon and Kee, 1963.

25 Scottish Home and Health Department, op. cit.

26 P. Cox, K. McCarthy, L. Millar and T. Crawley, *Report of the Committee of Inquiry into the Smallpox Outbreak in London in March and April 1973*, London, HMSO, 1974.

27 J. Phillips and M. French, 'The pure beer campaign and arsenic poisoning 1896–1903', *Rural History*, 1998, vol. 9, pp. 195–209.

28 H. M. Thatcher, BSE Inquiry/Statement No. 401. Online. Available HTTP: http://www.bse.org.uk/witness/htm/stat401.htm, 24 March 2000.

29 BSE Inquiry, 'Revised factual account 1 the Southwood Working Party', para. 18. Online. Available HTTP http://www.bse.org.uk/rfa/rfa01.pdf (24 March 2000).

30 Price, op. cit., p. 129.

31 E. Millstone, Memorandum (Appendix 51) submitted to the House of Commons Agriculture Report on Food Safety. London. The Stationery Office. II pp. 573–6.

32 D. Pestre, 'Science, political power and the state', in J. Krige and D. Pestre (eds), *Science in the Twentieth Century*, Amsterdam, Harwood, 1997, p. 65.

33 K. Hewitt, 'Excluded perspectives in the social construction of disaster', *International Journal of Mass Emergencies and Disasters*, 1995, vol. 13, pp. 317–39, at p. 332.

34 Price, op. cit., p. 188.

35 Lambert, op. cit., p. 140.

36 Scottish Home and Health Department, op. cit., p. 61.

37 E. Masood, 'Gag on food scientist is lifted as gene modification row hots up ', *Nature*, 1999, vol. 397, p. 547.

# 15 Regulating GM foods in the 1980s and 1990s

*David Barling*

Controversy has surrounded the shaping of the regulation of genetically modified (GM) foods and dates back to well before the concerns of the late 1990s. From the development of the technology in the early 1970s to its commercial mobilisation in the early 1980s, the regulatory debate has quickly expanded. Initial narrow discussion about scientific aspects of GM foods was transformed into what now amounts to a multi-dimensional and ongoing process of technology assessment. The scope, depth, and interpretation of scientific knowledge of the risks of GM in agriculture, and in food, have all been contested. Debates have encompassed the implications of GM food production for biodiversity and agriculture, animal health and welfare, human health, the economy, and society. The boundaries of risk assessment for genetically modified organisms (GMOs) and foods have been disputed, leading to controversies over whether it is the composition of the product or the production process that should be regulated. The evolution of the regulatory regimes in the United States (US) and the European Community (EC) reflects these debates.

While small-scale opposition to GM foods was a feature of the 1980s, the promotion of GM technology became a feature of high politics in the US and EC. With the large-scale entry onto the market of foods containing GM soybean and maize in the late 1990s this position changed. Consumer reaction has forced the regulation and promotion of GM onto the mainstream political agenda. Areas of debate now include the ability of consumers to make informed choices and the rules of international trade, as well as the industrialisation, concentration and control of food and agriculture. A key tension exists between regulating GM foods in the interest of human and environmental health and safety, and promoting the technology in view of potential economic gains.

This chapter focuses upon the dynamics shaping GM crop and food regulation covering the US and EC, and the international organisations and agreements that have been involved. The roles of coalitions involving scientific, economic and social interests, and different actors, departments and agencies within the US government and the EC will be examined.

The promotion of high technology industry was pursued by the Commission from the early 1980s. In 1984, round-table discussions with industrialists from high technology sectors took place, with a view to using the Commission as a platform for transnational collaboration. One outcome was a programme for information technology, but attempts to draw in biotechnology industries were less successful.

In June 1985, the European Biotechnology Co-ordination Group was set up. This involved five industrial associations representing chemicals, pharmaceuticals, food, agrochemicals and microbial food enzymes. Over the next few years further Euro-associations and national biotechnology industry associations joined the group. However, the organisation was unwieldy, lacked an executive centre, permanent base and secretariat, and collapsed in 1991.[11] The former head of CUBE has observed that the industries had indicated 'their reluctance to devote effort and resources to lobbying or representational activities on behalf of biotechnology in Europe. A vacuum had developed which others filled'.[12] The Commission's first attempt to engage industry in a network to promote biotechnology proved unstable and ineffective.

## Regulating the release of GMOs into the environment

The first major application for an experimental release of GMOs in US agriculture was made in 1982, for the 'ice-minus bacteria', designed for spraying onto strawberries to impede frost production. There were two different applications, from a group at the University of California, Berkeley, and from a commercial company, Advanced Genetic Systems. The trials attracted much publicity, as Rifkin's organisation launched legal challenges questioning the environmental impact assessments under the National Environmental Policy Act. In addition, the experiments involved local residents in debate, and opponents used the trials as a focus for protest against GM technology. The University's application, held up by the legal challenges and laboratory tests required by the regulators, did not receive approval until 1987. For Sheldon Krimsky and Alonzo Plough, the debates reflected differences in the framing of risk between molecular geneticists and ecologists. Nonetheless, both groups of scientists shared a common 'technical rationality'. More marked were the gaps between this rationality and lay perceptions of risk.[13] Such differences were to be a key dynamic in the 1990s European consumer reaction, following the entry of GM foods onto the market.

The 'Coordinated Framework', adopted by the NIH in 1986, held that biotechnology products were not fundamentally different from conventional products, and should be regulated according to their function. Consequently, existing laws and regulation were deemed adequate. The 'Framework' was a reflection of the 1980s US regulatory climate, shaped by the goals of the Reagan administration, which sought limited domestic government and to restrain the regulatory state which had developed since the 1960s.[14] The

'Framework' mapped the legislation and the responsibilities of three main agencies: the Food and Drug Administration (FDA), the US Department of Agriculture (USDA), and the Environmental Protection Agency (EPA). There were several laws relevant to the deliberate release of GMOs that were the responsibility of these agencies, which would consider applications case-by-case. A problem was the definition of terms, such as what constituted a deliberate release, and the agencies had to decide which GMOs they were each responsible for. A GMO would be considered a pest by the USDA and a pesticide by the EPA (as with the 'ice minus' bacterium) to fit under existing legislation.[15] The 'Framework' also lacked detail on how risk should be examined. The National Academy of Sciences supported the document, however, with a report concluding that GMOs posed no unique hazards to the environment. A report on the same lines by the National Research Council followed. In contrast, the National Wildlife Federation reflected environmentalists' concerns in calling for specific legislation to govern the deliberate release of GMOs.[16]

The US regulatory framework was informed by the joint efforts of the industrialised nations that sought to facilitate the application of GM technology. The Organisation of Economic Co-operation and Development (OECD) set up an expert committee to study rDNA safety, and issued a report in 1986.[17] The deliberations involved regulators from the European Commission, but the EC was to later take a different line to that of the US.

From 1989, the development of high technology industries was central to the economic strategy of the Bush presidency. As part of this policy vice president Quayle, as chair of the Council on Competitiveness, reviewed biotechnology regulation. The first generation of pathogen- and herbicide-resistant GM crop plants, was ready for full-scale testing. The existing framework for environmental release, based on a case-by-case process of small-scale trials, was seen by industry as inadequate. Inter-agency divisions were also emerging. The EPA and USDA favoured subjecting GMOs to regulations determined by the type of genetic changes; the FDA wanted to focus on how the GMO was likely to interact with the environment.[18] After a sequence of reports and statements from the President's Council, the Office of Science and Technology Policy, the 'Exercise of Federal Oversight Within Scope of Statutory Authority: Planned Introductions of Biotechnology Products into the Environment', was issued in February 1992. This affirmed 'a risk-based, scientifically sound approach that focuses on the characteristics of the biotechnology product and the environment into which it is being introduced, not the process by which it is created'. It explained that 'oversight will be exercised only where the risk posed by the introduction is unreasonable, that is, when the value of the reduction in risk obtained is greater than the cost thereby imposed'.[19] The product-based approach to GM food regulation had been confirmed, and the implication was that the regulatory burden should be light.

In the EC, Denmark and Germany took the lead in developing legislation.

Denmark's deliberate release regulations were stringent, from 1986 only allowing GMO releases in special cases after public consultation.[20] In Germany, the crossover of protest from the anti-nuclear movements was important. Organisations such as the Genethisches Netzwerk acted as extra-parliamentary foci for opposition to the development of GM technology.[21] Germany's regulations (1990) also made experimental release subject to local public consultation. Germany and Denmark drove environmental protection standards higher as the EC moved to the single market, and took a lead in the introduction of the EC's deliberate release legislation.

Within the European Commission, conflict began to appear with the development of Directives regulating GMOs. In 1985, the Biotechnology Steering Committee established the Biotechnology Regulation Inter-service Committee (BRIC) and in 1986 the Commission submitted a communication to the Council of Ministers on a framework for the regulation of biotechnology. This was produced mainly by the Environment DG working through BRIC. The Council of Ministers then assigned *chef de file* (lead role) in the preparation of the deliberate release legislation to the Environment DG.[22] This helped to shape the regulatory regime. In the European parliament the Environment Committee became the main committee concerned with the legislation; the final legislative decision passed to the Council of Environment Ministers. Furthermore, the effective management committee of the regime eventually established was based on national environment agencies. These arrangements did not guarantee a harmonious policy community in perpetuity, but did suggest an environment protection-centred rather than an industry-dominated approach.

An important debate occurred over the extent to which the Directive should cover risk assessment of GM products such as food, the responsibility of the Industry DG, and seeds, pesticides and animal feed, the responsibility of the Agriculture DG. The original proposals excluded products covered by specific legislation that included a risk assessment. The final Directive 90/220 amended this. Only products already subject to the type of environmental risk assessment laid down in the Directive would be excluded, which, in effect, placed uniform environmental standards upon future product legislation.[23] Gordon Lake has shown that the Environment Committee's scrutiny of the Directive introduced the approach of microbial ecology into the debate, which was adopted by opponents of the technology and those who advocated a precautionary stance.[24] The view of risk assessment among promoters of the technology tended to reflect the perspectives of molecular genetics. This epistemological tension has been a feature of the regulatory debates. The precautionary view was embodied in the legislation, but the criteria for environmental risk assessment were vague, making the operation of the Directive problematic.

Environmental and biodiversity implications of biotechnologies were also on the agenda of the UN Conference on Environment and Development at Rio in 1992. The resultant Convention on Biological Diversity called for consideration of a protocol for 'the safe transfer, handling and use of any living modified organisms resulting from biotechnology that might have adverse effects on the conservation and sustainable use of biological diversity'.[25] The Convention sought to protect less developed countries, and called for equitable access to the benefits from the use of their genetic resources. The US refused to sign, reportedly at the urging of the biotechnology corporations. Subsequently, the Conference of Parties agreed to seek to negotiate a protocol (the Jakarta Mandate, 1995). Despite their formal absence, the US government played a major role in later negotiations for an International Biosafety Protocol.[26]

## Regulating GM food

The development of medical biotechnology was characterised by university–industry alliances, with start-up companies emerging from universities. Agricultural biotechnology proceeded differently, as multinational companies grasped the agricultural potential of GM food before university administrators. Consequently, the main research into applications in agriculture and food production was developed by the multinationals, who raided the universities for scientists.[27] Several companies, including Monsanto, Upjohn, Cyanamid and Eli Lilly, produced different types of recombinant bovine growth hormone, or bovine somatotropin (BST), which enhances milk production by cows, and sought approval for the milk produced. The process in both the US and the EC proved lengthy and led to divergent decisions.

From 1984 in the US, approvals were requested to utilise the milk from BST trials in dairy products. The early debate appeared to provide consensus that BST milk was safe, and opposition focused on the effects on farming. BST promised economies of scale for large producers, threatening the viability of small farms. As the debate progressed, animal welfare implications were also considered. The opposition included core opponents to the technology and a coalition involving small farmers, rural interest, animal welfare, consumer, and environmental groups. The FDA gave approval to BST in 1993, but demanded labelling information on possible adverse effects on animal health. Animal health concerns included the incidence of mastitis and effects on the cow's life expectancy and reproductive capacity.[28] The FDA also allowed for voluntary labelling, such as 'rBGH free', offering a focus for consumers opposed to the technology. Fred Buttel shows that the result was a decline in sales in states that deployed the labelling option. However, he suggests that mobilisation of opposition was compromised by the farmers' suspicions of animal welfare interests.[29]

In the EC, the debate about BST also covered animal welfare and socio-economic issues. The Commission's Committee for Veterinary Medicinal Products granted approval for Monsanto's BST in 1991, after a 4-year evaluation. However, the Council of Ministers granted requests from the DG for Agriculture for delays for further evaluation. The Agriculture DG's

Scientific Veterinary Committee thought there were still doubts about animal health effects.[30] In 1988, the chair of the European parliament's Environment Committee, had also introduced the concept of a 'fourth hurdle' for regulatory approval of veterinary medicines and pharmaceuticals.[31] Approvals for pharmaceuticals were based on criteria of safety, quality and efficacy – originally proposed by the OECD. The need for a 'fourth hurdle', based on social and economic impact, gained currency in the debates over BST. The potential impacts of biotechnology on European farming had been registered by the European parliament since 1986. BST threatened aspects of the Common Agricultural Policy (CAP), such as the reduction of milk over-production. The result was that in 1994 the Council of Ministers declared a further moratorium on the commercialisation of BST, to be reviewed in 1999. While the Commission asserted the importance of the three established criteria, they reserved 'the right to take a different view in the light of its general obligation to take into account other Community policies and objectives'.[32] The priorities of the CAP, and the Agriculture DG, took precedence over the marketing of the BST.[33]

A significant step in establishing a common international framework was the OECD's *Safety Evaluation of Foods Derived by Modern Biotechnology - Concepts and Principles* (1993). The key principle was 'substantial equivalence': 'if a new food or food component is found to be substantially equivalent to an existing food or food component, it can be treated in the same manner with respect to safety'.[34] Where the food, or food component, was less well known or totally new, then the new characteristics should be the focus of further deliberations. It was felt that 'many new foods will be found to be substantially equivalent to existing products'. This approach was adopted by the US and, eventually, by the EC.

In the US, the FDA, in May 1992, responded quickly to the 'Scope' policy statement, which had endorsed their thinking. They issued a 'Statement of Policy on Foods Derived From New Plant Varieties', which provided a template for GM food regulation in the US. The policy established a voluntary process for industry to decide whether a new plant variety needed pre-market approval from the FDA, which would be necessary if the modification increased the concentration of a natural toxicant or introduced an allergen.[35] The statement opened the way for the numerous GM crops that were awaiting large-scale testing, and reflected the 1990 position paper of the International Food Biotechnology Council, a consortium of academic and private sector scientists, which included representatives of the food biotechnology corporations.[36]

While the US regulatory framework seemed to be settled by 1992, this was not so in the EC. One consequence of Directive 90/220 was a breakdown in relations between the DGs. The DGs responsible for Industry and Research and Development requested the Secretariat General, under Commission President Jacques Delors, to intervene to co-ordinate biotechnology policy. The result was the formation of the authoritative inter-service, Biotechnology

Co-ordinating Committee (BCC), based in the Secretariat General. The BCC brought together the Directors-General of the various DGs concerned with biotechnology.

In effect, the DGs for Industry and Research and Development sought a new policy domain for biotechnology, to counter the role the Environment DG had acquired. They attempted to refocus the promotion of biotechnology around a network involving the leading biotechnology industries. This aim had been revived with the creation of the Senior Advisory Group on Biotechnology (SAGB) in 1989, based on the European Chemical Industry Federation. The Group included Unilever, Hoescht, Ferruzzi, Rhone Poulenc, ICI, Sandoz, and Monsanto (US owned). It acted as policy advocate for industrial interests in the EC's policy formulation, a role welcomed by the DGs for Industry and Research and Development.

The creation of the BCC marked a step forward in the co-ordination and promotion of biotechnology policy. This was reflected in a communication drafted by the vice president of the DG for Industry, *Promoting the Competitive Environment for the Industrial activities based on Biotechnology within the Community* (1991).[37] This plan for co-ordinated action was incorporated into a larger statement entitled *European Industrial policy for the 1990s*.[38] The latter formed the basis for the section on biotechnology in Delors' *White Paper on Growth, Competitiveness and Employment* (1993).[39] The BCC then updated the 1991 communication as *Biotechnology and the White Paper on Growth, Competitiveness and Employment – Preparing the Next Stage* (1994).[40]

The BCC's original 1991 communication closely paralleled a series of papers issued by the SAGB, that met the approval of promoters of biotechnology within the Commission, while critics suggested that it reflected the Commission's corporatist ambitions.[41] They were now able to develop a stable and strong policy network as industrial interests began to contribute in a positive and organised fashion, unlike the earlier situation. This policy network was able to feed into the wider advocacy coalition surrounding industrial policy. The coalition enjoyed support from the network around the Research and Development DG, that claimed the voice of 'scientific reason', and was able to mobilise elements of the scientific community, such as the European Science Foundation, in their efforts to loosen the regulatory regime.[42] Nonetheless, despite the powerful connections of BCC, the Environment DG, the regulators of the deliberate release of GMOs, still had their own powerful network, given the provisions of Directive 90/220.

The BCC's 1994 communication reflected the view of the Commission that, 'public authorities could help stimulate competitiveness by adopting a consistent and supportive approach in relevant areas'.[43] This was to be achieved by a revision and completion of a coherent regulatory framework. The communication stressed the need for 'balanced and proportionate regulatory requirements commensurate with the identified risks' since 'the biotechnological regulatory framework is a factor impacting upon industrial competitiveness'.[44] The BCC favoured the 'one door one key' principle, meaning any product would only undergo one assessment procedure before being placed on the market. The intent was to follow the US approach, and regulate the product and not the process of production, and to reduce stigma and discrimination against the technology. To this end, the Commission sought to move towards more product-based legislation.

The Regulation on Novel Foods and Food Ingredients (258/97) was introduced by the Commission in 1992, but did not become law until early 1997. The main areas that were contested were the scope of the Regulation and the labelling provisions. Environmental risk assessment under 90/220 was retained, contrary to the 'one key' principle. However, the Regulation excluded food additives, extraction solvents and flavourings, as they fell under existing product legislation. And under the principle of 'substantial equivalence', foods and ingredients deemed to be equivalent to conventional foods were to be approved under simplified procedures.[45]

Labelling was an important area of disagreement in the European parliament and Council of Ministers. Germany, Denmark and The Netherlands opposed the Commission's industry-supported proposals for voluntary labelling. The final Regulation allowed for labelling only for live GMOs and where the composition of the final product was deemed not equivalent to an existing food or ingredient. The labelling had to indicate the characteristics or properties modified, together with the method (or process) of modification. There was provision for labelling on ethical grounds, and where ingredients had an allergy implication for a section of the population.[46] However, this did not end the labelling debate. Just as the Council of Ministers was finalising the Novel Foods Regulation, the large-scale entry of GM foods and ingredients into the European market began. At the same time, the procedures for approving GMOs under 90/220 were becoming increasingly divisive.

## GM foods enter the market: consumer reaction, regulatory quandary

The first widespread planting of GM crops began in 1996. Farmers in the US, Canada and Argentina grew an estimated 27.8 million hectares of GM crops by 1998, and 39.9 million hectares in 1999.[47] This first generation of GM crops were herbicide-tolerant or insect-resistant, properties introduced by bacterial genes. In 1996, Monsanto's 'Roundup Ready' soybean received an EC marketing licence for grain importation, storage and agricultural use. Novartis' corn borer-resistant 'Maximiser' maize was licensed in 1997. Subsequently, in 1998 some 15,000 hectares of GM maize were grown in Spain and 1,000 hectares in France.[48] The EC's approval of the Novartis maize had been extremely divisive. The presence of a 'marker gene' for resistance to the antibiotic ampicillin led several national authorities to vote against commercial approval. The stand-off was ultimately resolved by the Commission imposing approval, after receiving assurance from three of its scientific advisory committees.[49]

The boundaries for environmental risk assessment under the deliberate release Directive were continually contested as new products were put forward. The legitimacy of the regulatory regime was weakened as individual member states, such as Austria, France and Luxembourg, denied market access to some GM varieties that had been approved by the EC. The Council of Ministers announced a *de facto* moratorium upon further approvals in June 1999, until a revision of the regulatory regime had been completed.[50] This revision had been instigated by the German Presidency in the hope of reducing regulatory burdens upon German industry. The biotechnology industries, promoters of the technology within the Commission, and the US government, who all anticipated a streamlined and more benign approval process, supported it. However, the growing public concern over GM food, coupled with the member states' disagreements over risk assessment, resulted in a much stricter regime emerging from the Council of Ministers. The Common Position of the Council of Ministers suggested a more careful and specific environmental, biodiversity and agricultural risk assessment process, and provided for post-release monitoring.[51]

The first large shipment from the US of mixed GM and non-modified soybean reached Antwerp in 1996, where Greenpeace attempted to prevent its unloading, raising public awareness of GM commodities in the European food chain. The disquiet among the German public led some of the processors and distributors, including Unilever and Nestlé, to seek to remove oil from GM soybeans from their ingredients at the end of 1996.[52] Public discontent spread to other European nations, notably France and the UK, during 1998. Surveys suggested that the European public was wary of GM food, wanted clear labelling, and was concerned about environmental impacts as well as health risks. Trust in the regulators was extremely low, reflecting the lack of confidence from successive food crises, such as BSE.[53] The publicity attached to the soybean and maize imports and the increased focus on potential impacts of GM crops upon biodiversity and farming all helped to heighten public concerns. The sluggish response of the regulatory process was quickly outpaced by the commercial players as the public voiced their disquiet as consumers.

Calls from retailers and processors for the segregation of GM from non-GM soybean were met with resistance from US grain companies and the American Soybean Association.[54] A UK frozen food retailer, Iceland, responded by leading a search for non-modified sources of soya (from Canada and Brazil) for their own-brand products.[55] The major supermarkets in the UK and Northern Europe then rushed to declare they were attempting to provide GM-free foods. The major processors, under pressure from the retailers, followed suit, as did some restaurant and catering groups. In effect, a private system of market-led regulation appeared, enabled by the corporate concentration in retailing, processing and catering, and by improvements in detection technology for GM protein and DNA. The sensitivity of the European market was reflected in the case of GM tomato paste successfully launched in the Sainsbury and Safeway supermarket chains in the UK in 1996. By the end of the decade, they had withdrawn the product due to falling sales. Sainsbury responded to increased media reports about GM food in early 1999 by opening a dedicated customer call line. They received 300 calls in the first 4 hours, and reacted accordingly.[56] The US suppliers began to make more positive responses to the question of segregation of exports to Europe (and Japan) by the end of the decade, as their share in these markets declined.

The prevalence of soya derivatives in processed foods highlighted the shortcomings of the labelling provisions in the EC's Novel Foods Regulation. It was estimated that about 60 per cent of foodstuffs on sale in Europe contained GM soya derivatives, but was not labelled as such.[57] Within months of the passage of the Regulation the European commissioner for Industry admitted the labelling provisions would need revision.[58] The Commission then began a process of strengthening the GM food labelling provisions. However, the extensions of the labelling regime still focused on the composition of the final product, not upon the methods of production. Systems for traceability from seed to shelf, which might allow consumers to make a process-based choice, were not enacted in the 1990s. Nonetheless, the European Commission conceded that systems of complete traceability would be its goal, and the requirements in the Common Position on the revision of 90/220 reflected this.[59]

The market response stimulated a form of democratisation of the GM food issue in Europe, but the reaction of the regulators was mixed. The EC's confusion over labelling, and the risk assessment of GM crops, saw concessions to the public demand for transparency and traceability, and the protection of biodiversity and agricultural systems. However, the response of US regulators to the resistance of European consumers was one of recourse to high politics and international regulatory arenas. The General Agreement on Trade and Tariffs Uruguay Round agreements from 1993 had set up a rules-based regime for international trade, including food and agriculture, under the World Trade Organisation (WTO). The agreement gave the WTO governance over disputes concerning food standards, including the power to impose sanctions on member states deemed to have broken the rules. The advisory body on food safety and standards to the WTO was to be the United Nations' FAO/WHO Codex Alimentarius Commission.[60] A further agreement, on Technical Barriers to Trade, also included a rule prohibiting the imposition of labels on traded goods that discriminated against them on the basis of means of production. This offered a potential challenge to the evolving European labelling regime through WTO disputes procedures. These agreements loomed large over the increasing divergences between the US and EC on GM foods.

The US attempted to use the WTO over the refusal of the EC to accept recombinant bovine growth hormone treated meat. While the WTO disputes panel seemed to rule in favour of the US, the issue remained under diplomatic negotiation at the end of the 1990s.[61] WTO insiders feared that attempts to use the organisation to challenge the EC regulatory regime could do more harm than good. Attempts to expand the scope of the WTO at the end of 1999 in Seattle were marked by public protests and disagreements between delegations. However, the US did employ the rhetoric of potential trade war over the transatlantic disagreement about GM foods, and the Clinton administration put pressure on the UK government under Tony Blair to seek concessions from their European partners.[62]

Many of the differences between the US, EC and other nations were the subjects of negotiations within the Codex Alimentarius Commission. For example, in 1997, it was agreed that risk assessment for BST could encompass other legitimate factors, although these remained to be defined. The labelling of GM foods was also under negotiation within Codex.[63] Another result of the trade tensions was the establishment of a Codex task force on food biotechnology, which first met in early 2000 to formulate an agenda. Also, in early 2000 an International Biosafety Protocol was finally agreed, after extensive delays. The agreements reached suggested a positive way forward, but there remained differences between the WTO agreements and the Protocol. Also, the relationship between these agreements in international law remained ambiguous.[64] Finally, the largest industrial nations, the G8, announced in 1999 that they would ask the Organisation for Economic Co-operation and Development (OECD) to seek to resolve the scientific evidence over GM food safety. Under this mandate, the UK government organised a conference in early 2000, which highlighted continuing disagreements and lacunae in the scientific evidence.[65] The recourse to the OECD has become common practice over the past two decades. However, the regulatory debate, well and truly in the public domain, is now less likely to be resolved within the confines of such elite organisations.

## Conclusions

As we have seen, the initial debates surrounding GM technology were framed by molecular biologists, but the awareness of commercial applications swiftly brought in additional voices. In the case of food crops, ecologists questioned some of the assumptions of the molecular biologists, and agricultural and conservation scientists also became involved. The assessment of food products and their ingredients involved specialists in toxicology, allergenicity, physiology and veterinary medicine. The framing of the risks differed according to the scientific perspectives deployed. In addition, the commercial applications immediately broadened the debates beyond the scientific aspects, and social and economic factors also conditioned decisions. Promotion of biotechnology as a spur for industrial innovation and economic growth mobilised a powerful advocacy coalition of scientists, industrialists, civil servants and politicians. Finally, the need to regulate GM foods in the public interest brought additional social and economic dimensions to the debates.

Given the novelty of GM foods, the scientific assessment of risk was strongly framed by political management decisions. The US and the EC adopted different positions in the case of risk assessment for GM crops, but took the same approach regarding the substantial equivalence for food products and ingredients. The political decision making process was also driven by departmentalism, notably within the European Commission, challenging the Commission to find ways of policy co-ordination.

Social and economic dimensions assumed most importance in the market place, when the reaction of European consumers brought powerful economic interests near the consumption end of the food chain into the equation. Retailers, caterers and manufacturers responded to consumers by operating a *de facto* system of regulation. At the production and commodity distribution end of the chain, corporate concentration facilitated the development of biotechnology. Ironically, corporate concentration at the retail and processing end facilitated the consumers' rejection of the technology.

At the end of almost two decades of GM food regulation, conflict remains embedded in the process. The next generation of GM foods promise more tangible benefits to the consumer, in terms of enhancements of nutritional qualities. However, they will bring far more complex chemical changes, promising renewed scientific dissension, besides additional social and economic arguments. The recourse of policy makers to the arenas of international policy advice that occurred in 1999 is unlikely to placate an aroused public. To adopt a much quoted phrase, the genie is now well and truly out of the bottle.

## References

1 A. Bull, G. Holt and M. Lilley, *Biotechnology: International Trends and Perspectives*, Paris, OECD, 1982, p. 21.
2 Commission of the European Communities, *COM (93) 700 final*, Brussels, European Commission, 1993, p. 115. The definition might be technical, but it is an issue of regulatory debate. The definitions used in this chapter are not seen as absolute, but attempt to provide some clarity to the meaning of the terms.
3 For the case of the UK see D. Barling and R. Henderson, *Safety first? Public sector research in to GM food and crops in the UK*, Centre for Food Policy Discussion Paper No. 12, London, Thames Valley University, 2000.
4 P. Berg, D. Baltimore, H. Boyer, S. Cohen, R. Davis, D. Hogness, D. Nathans, R. Roblin, J. Watson, S. Weissman and N. Zinder, 'Potential biohazards of recombinant DNA molecules', *Science*, 1974, vol. 185, p. 303.
5 P. Berg, D. Baltimore, S. Brenner, R. Roblin and M. Singer, 'Summary Statement of the Asilomar Conference on Recombinant DNA Molecules', *Proceedings of the National Academy of Sciences*, 1975, vol. 72, pp. 1981–4.
6 H. Gottweis, *Governing Molecules: the Discursive Politics of Genetic Engineering in Europe and the United States*, Cambridge, MA, MIT Press, 1998, pp. 91–105.

7 E. Baark and A. Jamison, 'Biotechnology and Culture: The impact of Public Debates on Government Regulation in the United States and Denmark', *Technology in Society*, 1990, vol. 12, pp. 27–44; R. Bud, *The Uses of Life: A History of Biotechnology*, Cambridge, Cambridge University Press, 1993, pp. 178–81; M. Cantley, 'The regulation of modern Biotechnology: A Historical and European Perspective', in D. Brauer (ed.), *Biotechnology Volume 12: Legal, Economic and Ethical Dimensions*, Weinham, VCH, 1995 (second edition), pp. 505–681, at p. 566.

8 C. Plein, 'Biotechnology: Issue Development and Evolution', in D. Webber (ed), *Biotechnology: Assessing Social Impacts and Policy Implications*, New York, Greenwood Press, 1990, pp. 147–65.

9 Office of Science and Technology Policy, 'Coordinated Framework for the Regulation of Biotechnology', *Federal Register*, 1986, vol. 51, pp. 23302–93.

10 M. Cantley, 'Managing an invisible elephant', *Biotechnology Education*, 1991, vol. 2, pp. 90–7.

11 J. Greenwood and K. Ronit, 'Established and Emergent Sectors: Organised Interests at the European Level in the Pharmaceutical Industry and the New Biotechnologies', in J. Greenwood, J. Grote and K. Ronit (eds), *Organised Interests and the European Community*, London, Sage, 1992.

12 Cantley, 1995, op. cit., p. 633.

13 S. Krimsky and A. Plough, *Environmental Hazards: Communicating Risks as a Social Process*, Dover, MA, Auburn House, 1988, ch. 3.

14 L. Salamon and A. Abramson, 'Governance: the politics of retrenchment', in J. Palmer and I. Sawhill (eds), *The Reagan Record*, Cambridge, MA, Ballinger, 1984, p. 36.

15 S. Shapiro, 'Biotechnology and the design of regulation', *Ecology Law Quarterly*, 1990, vol. 17, pp. 1–90.

16 National Academy of Sciences, *Introduction of Recombinant DNA-engineered Organisms into the Environment: Key Issues*, Washington, National Academy Press, 1987; Committee on Scientific Evaluation of the Introduction of Genetically Modified Microorganisms and Plants into the Environment, *Field Testing Genetically Modified Organisms and Plants into the Environment*, Washington, National Academy Press, 1989; M. Mellon, *Biotechnology and the Environment*, Washington, National Wildlife Federation, 1988.

17 OECD, *Recombinant DNA Safety Considerations*, Paris, OECD, 1986.

18 M. Crawford, 'Biotech Companies Lobby for Federal Regulation', *Science*, 1990, vol. 248, pp. 546–7.

19 Office of Science and Technology Policy, 'Exercise of Federal Oversight Within Scope of Statutory Authority: Planned Introductions of Biotechnology Products into the Environment', *Federal Register*, 1992, vol. 57, pp. 6753–62, at p. 6753.

20 J. Toft, 'Denmark seeking a broad based consensus on gene technology', in L. Levidow and S. Carr (eds), 'Special issue on biotechnology risk regulation in Europe', *Science and Public Policy*, 1996, vol. 23, pp. 171–4.

21 Gottweiss, op. cit., pp. 266–93.

22 Commission of the European Communities, *COM (86) 573*, Brussels, European Commission, 1986.

23 *Official Journal of the European Communities*, 1990, L 117, pp. 15–27; J. Hodgson, 'Europe, Maastricht and Biotechnology', *Bio/Technology*, 1992, vol. 10, p. 1421–6.

24 G. Lake, 'Biotechnology Regulations: Scientific Uncertainty and Political Regulation', *Project Appraisal*, 1991, vol. 6, pp. 7–15.

25 Article 19 of the UNEP Convention on Biological Diversity, reprinted in S. Johnson, *The Earth Summit: The United Nations Conference on Environment and Development*, London, Graham & Trotman, 1993, p. 90.

26 'The Jakarta Ministerial Statement on the implementation of the Convention on Biological Diversity', *UNEP/CBD/COP/2/19*, 1995, pp. 37–8; Anon., 'Talks get underway on UN Biosafety Protocol', *ENDS Report*, 1996, vol. 259, pp. 35–6.

27 M. Kenny, *Biotechnology: the University-Industrial Complex*, New Haven & London, Yale University Press, 1986, pp. 222–38.

28 E. Millstone, E. Brunner and I. White, 'Plagiarism or protecting public health?', *Nature*, 1994, vol. 371, pp. 647–8.

29 F. Buttel, 'The recombinant BGH controversy in the United States: toward a new consumption politics of food?' Paper delivered to the joint annual meeting of the Agriculture, Food and Human Values Society/Association for the Study of Food in Society, Toronto, June 3–6, 1999.

30 W. Vandaele, 'BST & the EEC: Politics vs. Science', *Bio/technology*, 1992, vol. 10, pp. 701–2.

31 Anon., 'Why industry should take the "Fourth hurdle in its stride"', *Animal Pharm's EuroBriefing*, December 1989, p. 6–9.

32 Commission of the European Communities, *COM 94 (219) final*, Brussels, European Commission, 1994, p. 16.

33 D. Barling, 'The European Community and the Legislating of the Application and Products of Genetic Modification Technology', *Environmental Politics*, 1995, vol. 4, pp. 467–74.

34 OECD, *Safety Evaluation of Foods Derived by Modern Biotechnology: Concepts and Principles*, Paris, OECD, 1993, p. 16.

35 FDA, 'Statement of policy: foods derived from new plant varieties', *Federal Register*, 1992, vol. 57, pp. 22984–23005.

36 R. Hoyle, 'Eating biotechnology', *Bio/Technology*, 1992, vol. 10, p. 629.

37 Commission of the European Communities, *COM 91 (629) final*, Brussels, European Commission, 1991.

38 Commission of the European Communities, *Bulletin of the European Commission, Supplement 3/91*, Brussels, European Commission, 1991.

39 Commission of the European Communities, 1993, op. cit.

40 Commission of the European Communities, 1994, op. cit.

41 P. Wheale and R. McNally, 'Biotechnology policy in Europe: a critical evaluation', *Science and Public Policy*, 1993, vol. 20, pp. 261–79.

42 Cantley, 1995, op. cit., pp. 635–6.

43 Commission of the European Communities, 1994, op. cit., p. 1.

44 Ibid, p. 3.

45 *Official Journal of the European Communities*, 1997, L. 43, pp. 1–6.

46 D. Barling, 'Environmental sustainability or commercial viability? The evolution of the EC regulation on genetically modified foods', *European Environment*, 1996, vol. 6, pp. 48–54.

47 Gene Watch UK, 'GM crops and food: a review of developments in 1999', *Gene Watch UK Briefing*, no. 9, Tideswell, Gene Watch UK, 2000.

48 National Farmers Union, *Written Evidence of the NFU of England and Wales to the House of Lords' European Communities Committee Enquiry into EC Regulation of Genetic Modification in Agriculture*, London, NFU, 1998.

49 D. Barling, 'Regulatory conflict and the marketing of agricultural biotechnology in the European Community', in J. Stanyer and G. Stoker (eds), *Contemporary Political Studies 1997*, Nottingham, Political Studies Association of the UK, 1997, pp. 1040–8.

50 Friends of the Earth Europe, 'EU Environment Council adopts "de facto" moratorium on GMOs', *FoEE Biotech Mailout*, 1999, vol. 5, no. 5, p. 7.

51 D. Barling, 'GM crops, biodiversity and the European agri-environment: regulatory regime lacunae and revision', *European Environment*, 2000, vol. 10, pp. 157–67.

52 S. Nottingham, *Eat your Genes: How Genetically Modified Food is Entering our Diet*, London, Zed Books, 1998, p. 133.

53 For a more complete analysis of both quantitative and more qualitative survey evidence from Europe, see D. Barling, H. de Vriend, J. Cornelese, B. Ekstrand, E. Hecker, J. Howlett, J. Jensen, T. Lang, S. Mayer, K. Staer, R. Trop, 'The social aspects of Food

Biotechnology: a European view', *Environmental Toxicology and Pharmacology*, 1999, vol. 7, pp. 85–93.

54 Anon., ' Boycott begins against products containing US genetically engineered soybeans', *World Food Regulation Review*, vol. 6, no. 6, 1997, pp. 22–3.

55 D. Buffin, 'Genetic segregation: an interview with Malcolm Walker', *Pesticides News*, 1998, vol. 40, pp. 6–7.

56 Memorandum from J. Sainsbury plc to the House of Commons Select Committee on Agriculture, 15 November 1999; see http://www.publications.parliament.uk/pa/cm199900/cmselect/cmagric/71/7111.htm.

57 M. Smith, 'Novel foods create novel dilemmas for trade partners', *The Financial Times*, 22 June 1998, p. 7.

58 Anon., 'Commissioner Bangemann concedes criticism of Novel Foods Regulation', *EU Food Law*, June 1997, p. 6.

59 Barling, 2000, op. cit.

60 N. Avery, M. Drake and T. Lang, *Cracking the Codex: An analysis of Who Sets World Food Standards*, London, National Food Alliance, 1993.

61 Anon., 'EU–US beef dispute update', *Bridges Weekly Trade News Digest*, 2000, vol. 4, no. 11, pp. 12–14.

62 D. Hencke and R. Evans, 'How US put pressure on Blair over GM food', *The Guardian*, 28 February 2000, p. 8.

63 D. McCrea, 'Codex alimentarius – in the consumer interest?' *Consumer Policy Review*, 1997, vol. 7, pp. 132–8.

64 E. Allen, 'Greens and free-traders join to cheer GM crop deal', *The Financial Times*, 31 January 2000, p. 11.

65 M. Wong, 'Differences widen on use of modified foods', *The Financial Times*, 29 February 2000, p. 14.

# Index